Ethical
&
Aesthetic

ALSO BY JOSIAH THOMPSON

The Lonely Labyrinth:
Kierkegaard's Pseudonymous Works
(1967)

Six Seconds in Dallas:
A Micro-Study of the Kennedy Assassination
(1967)

EDITOR
Kierkegaard: A Collection of Critical Essays
(1972)

KIERKEGAARD

JOSIAH THOMPSON

KIERKEGAARD

19 73

ALFRED A. KNOPF   NEW YORK

THIS IS A BORZOI BOOK
PUBLISHED BY ALFRED A. KNOPF, INC.

Copyright © 1973 by Josiah Thompson
All rights reserved under International and Pan-American
Copyright Conventions. Published in the United States by
Alfred A. Knopf, Inc., New York, and simultaneously in
Canada by Random House of Canada Limited, Toronto. Dis-
tributed by Random House, Inc., New York.

Library of Congress Cataloging in Publication Data:

Thompson, Josiah, date.   Kierkegaard.

Bibliography: p.
1. Kierkegaard, Søren Aabye, 1813–1855.
B4376.T46   1973   198'.9   72–11043
ISBN 0–394–47092–3

Manufactured in the United States of America
First Edition

CONTENTS

III   CLOISTER

ILLUSTRATIONS

(following page 106)

A portrait of Kierkegaard, 1853–55; and his visiting card.
(Frederiksborg Museet, Hillerød)

Kierkegaard's father and mother.
(Bymuseum, Copenhagen)

Nytorv in 1839, and Kierkegaard's home.
(Øregaard Museet, Hellerup)

The Borgerdydskole in Klareboderne.
(Gyldendal Publishing Company, Copenhagen)

Two idealized portraits of Kierkegaard as a young man.
(The Royal Library, Copenhagen)

Regine Olsen at the time of her engagement to Kierkegaard.
(Bymuseum, Copenhagen)

Regine Olsen in 1855.
(The Royal Library, Copenhagen)

A letter, with sketch, from Kierkegaard
to Regine during their engagement.
(The Royal Library, Copenhagen)

The cover sheet of *Corsair* and caricatures of Kierkegaard.
*(*Corsaren, *1846)*

Sketches of Kierkegaard.
(The Royal Library, Copenhagen)

A CHRONOLOGY OF
SØREN AABYE KIERKEGAARD

1756   SK's father, Michael Pedersen Kierkegaard, born in Sæding, West Jutland.

1768   MPK goes to live with his uncle, a hosier, in Copenhagen.

1777   Sæding village priest releases MPK from serfdom.

1788   MPK receives royal patent "to deal in East Indian and Chinese wares, as well as goods coming from our West Indian islands . . . and to sell the same at wholesale and retail to all and sundry."

1794   MPK marries Kirstine Røyen.

1796   Kirstine Røyen Kierkegaard dies childless; MPK inherits his uncle's fortune.

1797   MPK retires from business in February. In April he marries Kirstine's maid, Ane Lund. A daughter, Maren Kirstine, is born in September.

1799   Nicoline Kristine born on October 25.

1801   Petrea Severine born on September 7.

1805   A first son, Peter Christian, born on July 6.

1807   Søren Michael born on March 23.

1809   Niels Andreas born on April 30.

1813   The year of the "crazy money"; financial crisis in Denmark. A last child, Søren Aabye, born on May 5.

1821   SK enrolls in Copenhagen's Borgerdydskole.

1828   SK confirmed by Pastor (later Bishop) J. P. Mynster.

1830   SK graduates from the Borgerdydskole and enters the university.

1834   SK makes his journalistic debut with a piece in the *Flying Post* entitled "Also a Defense of Woman's Superior Capacity."

1835   SK spends a summer holiday at Gilleleje in northern Sjælland. Writes down his resolve "to find the truth which is true for me."

1836   SK publishes two additional articles in the *Flying Post*.

1837   SK meets Regine Olsen for the first time while visiting the Rørdams in Frederiksberg. In September he begins teaching Latin at the Borgerdydskole and moves to his own apartment on Løvstræde.

1838   MPK dies on August 9. SK inherits over 30,000 rd. His first book, *From the Papers of One Still Living,* is published in September.

1840   SK completes his examination for the theological degree, visits his ancestral home in Jutland, and on September 10 becomes engaged to Regine Olsen. In November he enters the pastoral seminary for practical

training in the ministry. In April he moves from his
flat on Kultorvet to Nørregade 230A.

1841   In January SK preaches a sermon in Holmen's Church.
In the summer he defends and publishes his dissertation for the M.A. degree, *The Concept of Irony*. In
October he breaks his engagement to Regine and flees
to Berlin.

1842   SK attends Schelling's lectures in Berlin, but returns
to Copenhagen in March. Writes *Either/Or*. Begins,
but does not complete or publish, *De Omnibus Dubitandum Est*.

1843   *Either/Or* published in February. SK makes a short
visit to Berlin in May. *Two Edifying Discourses* is
published in May and *Four Edifying Discourses* in December. In October *Fear and Trembling, Repetition,*
and *Three Edifying Discourses* are published.

1844   *Three Edifying Discourses, Philosophical Fragments,
The Concept of Dread,* and *Prefaces* are all published
in June. *Two Edifying Discourses* is published in
March and *Four Edifying Discourses* in August. In
October SK moves from Nørregade 230A back to the
family town house at Nytorv 2.

1845   *Three Discourses on Imagined Occasions* and *Stages on
Life's Way* are both published in April. SK spends two
weeks in Berlin during May.

1846   *Corsair* attacks SK in January. *Concluding Unscientific
Postscript* is published in February, followed by *A
Literary Review* in March. In May SK once again
makes a two-week visit to Berlin. In October Meyer

Goldschmidt resigns as editor of *Corsair* and leaves Denmark.

1847   *Edifying Discourses in Various Spirits* is published in March and *Works of Love* in September. In November Regine marries Friedrich Schlegel. In December SK sells the family home at Nytorv 2.

1848   In early spring SK leases an apartment at the corner of Rosenborggade and Tornebuskgade. *Christian Discourses* is published in April, and in July the two-part article, "The Crisis and a Crisis in an Actress's Life." By November he has finished *The Point of View for My Work as an Author,* but this book will not be published until after his death.

1849   *The Lilies of the Field and the Birds of the Air* and *Two Minor Ethico-Religious Treatises* are both published in May. *The Sickness unto Death* is published in July and *Three Discourses at Communion on Fridays* in November.

1850   In April SK moves to another apartment at Nørregade 43. *Training in Christianity* is published in September and *An Edifying Discourse* in December.

1851   In January SK publishes in *Fatherland* "An Open Letter . . . Dr. Rudelbach." In April he moves outside the city's walls to Østerbrogade 108A. In August *Two Discourses at Communion on Fridays* and *On My Work as an Author* are published. In September *For Self-Examination* is published.

1852   In April or October SK moves back inside the city to a cramped two-room flat let out of a larger apartment at Klædeboderne 5-6. He continues writing in his journal and completes *Judge for Yourself* (published in 1876).

1853   On Easter Monday SK writes in his journal: "The Christian thing is not to produce but to exist." Six months later his journal falls silent.

1854   Bishop Mynster dies in January. Hans Martensen is named Bishop in April. In February SK writes an article attacking the established church, but does not publish it until December.

1855   *This Must Be Said, So Let It Now Be Said; Christ's Judgment on Official Christianity;* and *The Unchangeableness of God* are published in May, June, and September respectively. From January through May SK attacks the church in various articles published in *Fatherland.* In May he begins publishing his own broadside, *The Instant,* which goes through nine issues before he falls ill in September. On October 2 he enters Frederiks Hospital, and dies there on November 11, most likely of a staphylococcus infection of the lungs. His funeral a week later ends in a near-riot at the gravesite.

PREFACE

Søren Kierkegaard's life could be called cloistered, even for a philosopher. The son of a retired merchant, he lived as a gentleman student of theology in a provincial capital of Europe and died a bachelor at the age of forty-two, the author of a number of controversial philosophical and religious works. His significant relationships boil down to a conflict-filled love for a father old enough to be his grandfather, an engagement broken after little more than a year, a literary spat with a tabloid, and a vitriolic attack on the established church of Denmark just before his death. Except for this final desperate assault, Kierkegaard moved through Danish society without raising a ripple. There is little of history and not much of a story in all this. What, then, is the attraction?

The answer lies in the extraordinary timeliness, for us, of his thought. Born in 1813, the same year as Richard Wagner, he was virtually unheard of outside Scandinavia in the nineteenth century. Though his works were quickly translated into German, they aroused little interest and he was unknown even to Nietzsche as late as 1888. It was only after the First World War that his writing began to be translated into French and English, and not until the early 1940's, as the Second World War drew to its close, that he began to achieve international recognition.

It was then that a new political term, "totalitarianism," was soon joined by a new philosophical term, "existentialism." If totalitarianism was a twentieth-century repudiation of nineteenth-century democracy, existentialism was equally a critique of traditional metaphysics and Christianity. And it was Kierkegaard who not only first pricked the bubble of Hegelian metaphysics, but also exposed the mendacity of conventional "lip-service" Christianity. True Christianity was not dogma guarded by a bureaucracy, but a life passion—an intensely personal existence lived in imitation of Christ. So saying, as the final act of an otherwise private life, in a searing attack upon the second highest power of the realm after the King—the Lutheran state church—Søren Kierkegaard died.

He died like a man who has completed to his own satisfaction a set task which has exhausted him. Having used up virtually all his funds, he signed himself into the hospital and said to his visitors that he was quite willing to die. One could speak of a martyrdom for his ideas, but as an imitation of Christ it fell short, for Kierkegaard had attended so well to his own crucifixion that there was no need for anyone else to take a hand. As with Shakespeare's melancholy Dane, the rest was silence.

Until, nearly a century later, Søren Kierkegaard began to find his niche as the father of existentialism. His works have been translated, anthologized; his ideas discussed in a host of books and journals, general and scholarly; his influence is all-pervasive. His answer to nineteenth-century positivism, the philosophical expression of the hopefulness generated by scientific "progress," is that to the individual man, reality is not "objective" and scientifically determinable, but remains ever problematical, ambiguous. The focus of Kierkegaard's thought is the individual human consciousness, and his most persistent theme is the difficulty of locating any firm reference point in the quicksand of that terrain. Again and again he tells us what a desperately difficult thing it is to be a human being—difficult because we secrete illusion from our very pores; desperate because we can't stop yearning for the replacement of illusion by a reality so unknown it can only be called divine. To be human is to be of two minds (*Tvesyndethed*), insofar as it entails both being-as-such and consciousness of one's being. Man is accordingly a creature of duplicity and doubt, a dissipated being whose life inevitably boils off in theories he can never validate, hopes he can never realize, passions he can never satisfy. When Sartre remarks that "man is like a leak of gas, escaping into the imaginary," he is speaking Kierkegaard's language.

Howard Nemerov's perception that a poet's gift for prophecy "is not to invent the world that will be there in the future, but to bring into being the mind that will be there in the future," seems to describe Kierkegaard's career. An isolated "genius in a market town," he not only brought into being the mind of the future but mapped out that mind's problematic nature. In his life and work he reflected and measured the volatility of consciousness—then proceeded to demonstrate that it is nevertheless the most "solid" reality we possess, the ground of our being. To show how he arrived at this paradox is the purpose of this book.

The translations from Kierkegaard's works and papers are my own. Where an English translation exists I have checked it against the original, in most cases modifying it to assure accuracy and consistency of usage.

To the John Simon Guggenheim Memorial Foundation go my thanks for making possible a year's stay in Denmark, as well as to the Ford Grant Committee of Haverford College for providing the released time necessary to complete the book. In Copenhagen the staff of the Royal Library spared no effort to make Kierkegaard's manuscripts and journals available to me. My Danish friends Nora Dalgas, Hanne Willert, and H. P.

Rohde were equally kind in checking some of my translations and helping me reject some very bad ideas. Back in the United States my friends and colleagues Richard Bernstein, Louis Mackey, and James Ransom were of great help in sharpening the thesis of the book. Adeline Taraborelli typed the manuscript with accuracy and persistent good humor.

Two women have been crucial in giving the book its present shape. One is Sophie Wilkins, my editor at Alfred A. Knopf, Inc., whose mark can be found not only on every page of the manuscript, but also on the mind and heart of the author. The other is my wife, Nancy, who did not just endure this book but helped make it.

JOSIAH THOMPSON

Haverford, Pennsylvania
June 5, 1972

BEGINNERS

How they are provided for upon the earth, (appearing at
    intervals;)
How dear and dreadful they are to the earth;
How they inure to themselves as much as to any—what a
    paradox appears their age;
How people respond to them, yet know them not;
How there is something relentless in their fate, all times;
How all times mischoose the objects of their adulation and
    reward,
And how the same inexorable price must still be paid for the
    same great purchase.

—Walt Whitman, *Leaves of Grass* (1860)

I

CHILDHOOD

1

"THE STRANGE ONE...
THE PECULIAR ONE"

IN the autocratic, almost military atmosphere of Copenhagen's Borgerdydskole,* there was no such thing as an impudent student. All the more remarkable, then, what happened one morning in Professor Mathiesen's class.†

According to one of the students, the class had gotten quite out of hand. The boys had laid out their *Smørrebrød*, uncorked their beer, and begun to toast each other raucously. Suddenly Professor Mathiesen appeared in the doorway. "I'll report the whole thing to the principal," he warned. While the rest of the class gathered round Mathiesen's desk, hoping to cajole him with pleas and promises, one boy kept his seat. "Will you also tell the principal," he called from across the room, "that this is the way we always behave in your class?" Mathiesen sat down and made no report.

The boy who made the remark was hardly a troublemaker. To most of his teachers he seemed quite unremarkable. Always

---

* The name means School of Civic Virtue. It was a private school founded in 1787, the outgrowth of a society formed to encourage "modesty and thrift" among the citizens of Copenhagen.

† This anecdote is related in a letter from one of Kierkegaard's classmates, Franz Welding, to H. P. Barfod dated October 23, 1869, in the Kierkegaard Archives of the Royal Library, Copenhagen, D, Pk. 5, Læg 32. Succeeding notes and citations will be found only in the Notes section beginning on page 243, where they are keyed to the text by page and line number.

second or third in his class but never first, he showed a healthy respect for authority and for the value of good marks. One classmate recalled that "he appeared to be very conservative, to honor the King, to love the church, and to respect the police." His retort to Mathiesen suggests this. It is much more a waspish comment on Mathiesen's failure to keep order than an attempt to undermine it. But respect was not servility, and the boys knew things about Søren Kierkegaard that his teachers didn't. They knew, for example, that he frequently took advantage of his desk's position (just by the master's, and somewhat out of his sight) to crib from the book—especially in history and geography. They knew too that he and another boy would often switch essays, Søren writing the boy's Latin composition while the other composed Søren's Danish. A few of them probably knew that he had to borrow a few cents here and there from his friends because his father, although a rich man, kept him on a niggardly allowance. First and foremost, however, they knew him as "the strange one . . . the peculiar one."

His strangeness began with his appearance. It was primarily his dress that singled him out, for in contrast to the other boys' casual assortment of clothes, young Kierkegaard always wore the same formal costume. It consisted of jacket and knickers, oddly cut from a dark, coarse tweed, knee socks, and shoes, instead of boots like his classmates. This outfit won him the nickname "Choirboy," which the boys used interchangeably with "Søren Sock," an allusion to his father's start in business as a hosier. "As a child I was mistaken for an old man," he later complained in his journal, "and that showed itself even in my clothes."

Frail and oddly dressed, thin-faced with large light-blue eyes, his thick hair sticking up like a coxcomb, he had the pinched and riven air more often seen in the children of minor civil servants. An acquaintance, Hans Brøchner, recalled that Søren's clerklike presence seemed to demand a counter to stand behind. The term *Fremmed* keeps recurring in descriptions of him; it means both "strange" in the sense of having odd or peculiar traits, and "a stranger" in the sense of an alien, a foreigner. According to Franz Welding, a member of his class:

> There were certainly few of his classmates who understood SK or got close to him. . . . He went his own way, nearly always turned in on himself, never speaking of his home, never inviting anyone there, nor ever visiting anyone elsewhere. For the rest of us, who lived a more regular boy's life, SK was a stranger and an object of pity. . . . We looked on him as one who lived at home in a mystical half-darkness of strictness and eccentricity. In school he was still to all appearance joyless—working not from inclination but because he had been forced into it. As for friends, so far as I can remember, he had none. In spite of the fact that we often worked together and that he liked the pastries I could give him (my father was a baker), as boys we never became close. . . . The more contact the rest of us had with him, the more it became apparent how alien he was to our interests, and we quickly gave it up.

The one relationship the Choirboy managed to sustain with his fellows was polemical: he teased them. According to Frederik Meidell, even as a very young boy Kierkegaard was ill-tempered and unpopular with his cousins and other relatives; he never missed an opportunity to tease and bait the other children, sometimes driving them to tears. One of his classmates at the Borgerdydskole remembered how Søren's "wise mouth" cost him many bloody noses; another remembered the day when the Choirboy's classmates got their collective revenge— they put him up on a table and while two held his arms and two his legs, the rest gave his behind a going over with rulers and bookstraps. But more often than not the Choirboy used his wit to good advantage in the school that had become for him a battleground. One day one of the larger boys was crying in class. "What's the matter?" asked the teacher. "Søren's been teasing me," the boy answered, only to receive the uncomforting reply:

"How so? You could easily put him in your pocket." If it's difficult to grasp how a diminutive "choirboy" could so devastate one of his schoolmates, Welding's description offers some help:

> In spite of [the trouble] it often brought him, this frail and ever fugitive boy could give his spirits free play, and he teased most of his classmates with nicknames (not always of his own invention) and by laughing and making faces at them. I don't remember him to have been really witty and cutting with words; he was more a baiter, an egger-on, observing the effect even if it often boomeranged. . . . When I look back, it seems to me that on the whole SK primarily had an eye for the loose joints in personalities, for whatever didn't go with the rest, for whatever stood out. Hence he attacked the tall who had second-rate minds, the fat who were distinguished only by their size; he assailed all those who were ahead physically but lagged mentally.
>
> These outbreaks of an urge to tease seemed conspicuously unrelated to his otherwise noiseless and quiet path among us, his otherwise withdrawn and introverted character.

But where Welding notes a contradiction, we can see a relationship between these two facets of young Kierkegaard's personality. He was a boy whose slight build and oddity of dress made him an easy target for the taunts and blows of his peers. As he could not compete with his stronger schoolmates in their games and contests, he discovered the sneer and the icy put-down as a means of defense. If he could not make his schoolmates like or admire him, he could at least make them angry and afraid of his tongue; their anger was a victory of sorts: they noticed him! Words came to be more than tools; they became his weapons in the perpetual battle with other people. Even more important, he came to discover his own mentality as an instrument of defense. Thirty years later he would write in his journal:

> Tender, frail, and weak, in almost every way denied the physical qualities required to make me a whole human being

like the others; melancholy, soul-sick, in so many ways deeply and inwardly unfortunate: one thing was given to me—a mental superiority; probably so that I would not be completely defenseless.

It remains unclear to this day what Kierkegaard had in mind in saying he was "denied the physical qualities required to make me a whole human being." Were we not already acquainted with the exaggerated, faintly stylized character of the laments he scattered through his journal, we might think he was referring to some gross physical deformity. One Danish critic has interpreted the passage in this way, using it to buttress his view that Kierkegaard was in fact a hunchback. The critic points out that Kierkegaard at seventeen was discharged from the Royal Guards after only three days' service as "unfit for duty," that contemporary portraits show him somewhat stooped, his head protruding forward, and that all accounts say he walked with a crabbed, jerky gait. But the record itself does not sustain such an extravagant conclusion—none of Kierkegaard's friends or enemies ever used the term "hunchback" to describe him, and his hospital medical record makes no mention of it.

Although there is no conclusive evidence that Kierkegaard was a hunchback, it is perhaps more to the point that he felt and behaved as if he were. "As a sick man longs to cast off his bandages," he wrote in 1845, "so does my sound mind long to cast off the body's weakness, that sweaty, sodden poultice which is the body and its weakness." Throughout his journal, he mentions his body only to denigrate it. Aware of himself as "peculiar to look at," as having a "laughable exterior," he lived in his body as in a rented room. Sometimes it seemed to him to be a "heavy weight" which he must push away "as a drowning man might push away with all his might another drowning man clutching at his legs." Opposed to this weight of flesh was his healthy spirit that longed to break free: "Eminently armed with spirit, I raised myself ironically above everything that had to

do with the animal side of being human." Perhaps it was this
judgment on his own body that made him turn a sympathetic
gaze on cripples of every sort, on the "exceptions" who, try as
they might, could never "realize the universal." Many years later
in *Fear and Trembling* he quoted the Duke of Gloucester's
lament from *Richard III*:

> I, that am rudely stamped, and want love's majesty,
> To strut before a wanton ambling nymph;
> I, that am curtailed of this fair proportion,
> Cheated of feature by dissembling nature,
> Deformed, unfinished, sent before my time
> Into this breathing world, scarce half made up,
> And that so lamely and unfashionable
> That dogs bark at me as I halt by them—

And indeed after Kierkegaard's notorious spat with the scandal sheet *Corsair* in 1846 it was not dogs that barked at him,
but children and loafers who abused and jeered at him on the
streets. But he was not unprepared for this, since even as a
child he had been aware of himself as the butt of others' jokes,
as strange, "counterfeit" in some primordial sense. "I was born
in 1813," he later wrote in his journal, "in the year of the crazy
money, the year when so many counterfeit notes were put into
circulation. I can best be compared with one of them." Whether
or not he was actually deformed, he experienced his body as a
deformity, as a private shame which, at the end of his life, he
saw as originating in an old man's criminal concupiscence.
"Through a crime I came into existence," he jotted down on
September 25, 1855, "I came into existence against God's will."

In that year (1855) Kierkegaard was living in a shabby flat
only a few blocks from his old school. His wanderings through
the city often took him through Klareboderne, and we can
imagine him hesitating for a moment, looking up at the double

windows of the building where he once worked and played and first committed his personality to the world. We can juxtapose the two Kierkegaards: the Choirboy teasing his playmates by calling names and making faces in the schoolyard, and the "old" man of forty-two gazing up at his school, plotting his continuing attack on the Danish state church. So many of the child's traits seem to lie buried in the prematurely old adult. For a time some of them had apparently disappeared, only to emerge disguised but essentially intact; others had remained visible from first to last: his way with language, for instance.

Language performed many tasks for Kierkegaard, that philosopher, poet, and master of the sermon, but at the end it reclaimed its original function for him as weapon. Just as the ten-year-old schoolboy used words to tease his playmates, so would the forty-year-old thinker use words to tease his adult contemporaries. He teased them first in his newspaper articles, then in his doctoral dissertation, then in his pseudonymous works, next in the *Corsair* episode (where he received a "bloody nose"); finally, in 1855, he died teasing, searing church and society with wit and passion.

Regarding his body, his "exterior," as a source of vulnerability, Kierkegaard turned inward and became a master of disguises. A penchant for secrecy and deceptiveness runs as a constant thread through his life and work. It can be seen in the portentous mystery in which he wrapped the events of his youth, in his interest in romantic irony and in what he later called "indirect communication," in his deception of Regine, his fiancée, and in the curious hide-and-seek game of the pseudonyms that began shortly thereafter. Kierkegaard's whole life was wrapped in a veil of self-consciousness; as he put it, "I was always, always outside myself." It was predicated upon the possibility of maintaining always a distance between the thought and the face, the interior and the exterior. From be-

---

HO

THE Kierkegaard town house
square called Nytorv, a ten-mi
skole. As Copenhagen town ho
Less than fifty feet wide, its fa
gled close to the new city hall
On its left, the corner building
An earlier city hall in the cente
in 1795, and the present one
years after Kierkegaard's father
architect, Andreas Kirkerup. T
thirty years later the house was
$133,000.* It was a good hous
the pilaster mansions with tria
the square, but a solidly respect
retired hosier who himself had

* Since the currency reform of 1873, a
Danish currency. That reform made a r
of present buying power the equation
i det gamle København (1967), Jan M
1830's would be worth about 50 krone
equation 1 rd. = $7.00 would seem a
actual character of goods and services
century and a half. In Copenhagen o
restaurant cost ⅓ rd., a year's rent on
of the city came to 170 rd., and the
amounted to 200 rd.

ginning to end he rem
mysteries, and elaborate
between himself and the

Kierkegaard, the "eve
and quiet path" was int
became the hermetic ar
turbed only by the urge
Yet in this introductory
the roots of his personal
these roots we must mc
gerdydskole to the priva
and live "in a mystical
tricity." . . .

thirty years before. Søren Kierkegaard would live in this house for two-thirds of his life.

In late afternoons the square was a tranquil place as the sun slipped behind the city hall, long shadows creeping eastward. The staircases and doorways along the eastern side were warmed by the sun, and the muted yellows, greys, and blues of the façades glowed in the sharp northern light. A few cabs were parked near the center of the square in hopes of occasional customers from the city hall, and a small knot of peasants were still displaying their wares around the now shadowed fountain. Church bells pealed the hour, and occasionally came the call of a vendor or the strain of a familiar tune. "A wandering musician played the minuet from *Don Juan* on a sort of flute," Kierkegaard recalled in his journal a few years later, "and the apothecary pounded his medicines and the girl in the courtyard scoured the steps and the stableboy groomed his horse, knocking the currycomb against the stone, and from another part of town came the sound of the shrimp man's voice."

On Wednesday and Saturday mornings the square was transformed by the bustle of market day. Early in the morning, farmers from outlying regions would swarm in to display their wares on cases and tables. Here one could buy corn, grain, eggs, butter in great tubs, peas, pork products, poultry, and a host of things the farmers made in the long winter evenings. In the southern half of the square the meat wagons congregated in the early mornings, and their drivers made themselves a couple of marks by carrying sides of meat, geese, tubs of butter, and pork products from the farmers' stands and wagons to the shops and delicatessens in the surrounding streets. After their morning work was done they lay about in the sunlit doorways and staircases by the Nørregade corner and, as one old Copenhagener remembered, "could only be budged from there by the idea of going off for a fresh half-pint." Nytorv remained the city's principal meat market until 1910.

On holidays the square was transformed in other ways. On the King's birthday, January 28, a small boy could see golden apples dancing in the fountain only two hundred feet from his window, and on another annual occasion, the so-called *Herredagen*, a regular pageant was enacted before his eyes. First, on the day before, two heralds wearing velvet capes and riding magnificent horses arrived in front of the city hall and read a proclamation, while the Royal Horse Guards with their sabers and tufted helmets formed a semicircle behind him. Next day the King would appear with all his retinue to open the first session of the High Court. Crowds would gather in the square to watch the King alight from his golden coach and make his entrance into the city hall. Watching from the windows of the Kierkegaard town house immediately above, a visiting niece thought, "it was almost as if the whole city had come to do us honor."

In the summer of 1825 there were six Kierkegaards living in the house at No. 2 Nytorv. Besides old Michael Pedersen Kierkegaard, now nearly seventy, and his wife Ane, in her late fifties, four children were still at home. Søren Aabye was the Benjamin of the family, four years younger than his nearest sibling. He had turned twelve on May 5 and in June had completed his fourth year at the Borgerdydskole. Next in age were two brothers: Niels Andreas, sixteen and several classes ahead of Søren at the Borgerdydskole, and Peter Christian, later Bishop of Aalborg, now twenty and a theological student at Copenhagen University. Finally there were the two sisters, Nicoline and Petrea. Nicoline had left home the year before to marry the clothier Christian Lund, but she remained close to her family. Petrea, now twenty-three, was still at home (she would be married three years later to Christian's brother, Ferdinand Lund, who was a bank assistant). Two other children had died: the oldest of the family, Maren Kirstine, in 1822 of a kidney inflammation at the age of twenty-three, and a twelve-year-old boy, also named Søren, in 1819 of a brain hemorrhage after knocking heads with another boy in the school playground. It was a household dominated by men, a strict patriarchy.

The mother, Ane Lund Kierkegaard, born in Jutland of a peasant family, had come to Copenhagen in the closing years of the eighteenth century to earn her living as a domestic. For a while she worked for a hosier, Mads Røyen, who was a business acquaintance of Michael Pedersen Kierkegaard. In 1794 Kierkegaard married Røyen's sister Kirstine, and Ane Lund came along as the maid. She was there when Kirstine died two years later, and she quickly replaced her mistress in Kierkegaard's bed. Kierkegaard married her a year later, on April 26, 1797, less than five months before the birth of their first child. The marriage contract itself was an odd document which spelled out the sums she would receive in the event of death or divorce. Since it denied her the normal inheritance rights of a wife, it had to be altered before royal authority would approve it.

Apparently Ane retained much of the submissive status of a servant throughout her marriage. The single portrait we have shows her in middle age—a rather plump and contented figure, with round features and a double chin, staring out from under a lace bonnet. The picture agrees with a grandchild's description of her as "a nice little woman with an even and happy disposition." According to the grandchild, her sons' intellectual development was beyond Ane's comprehension, and it was only when some indisposition or other brought them back under her care that she was in her element. If she could get them into bed, "then she wielded her scepter with delight, and cared for them like a mother hen protecting her chicks." She herself was illiterate: her signature on official papers was written with a guided pen, and when her eldest son decided to give her some books toward the end of her life, he chose a songbook and a hymnal. We do not know what part she took in running the household, but it could not have been significant: for a while the house had a rather stiff housekeeper, one Miss Møller, and in any case, Michael Kierkegaard did much of the shopping. Long into the second marriage the old man continued to think of his first wife as his real one, and when the girls wanted to learn to sew or to hear something read aloud, they went not to their mother but to a family friend, Fru Boesen. Never once mentioned in the twenty volumes of Søren's *Papers,* the mother is referred to only occasionally in the papers and letters of her eldest son, Peter. Like a well-trained servant she remained always in the background, stirring scarcely a ripple in the lives of the seven children she bore and raised.

"Daughters were not the most favored creatures in that old-fashioned home," Henriette Lund recalled. "In Grandfather's opinion girl children did not need much learning. On the contrary, from an early age they should accustom themselves to waiting on their better-read brothers and helping with the housework." Although there were servant girls in the house, the two daughters had to brush their brothers' clothes and help with the cleaning—chores not usually done by girls of their class. Their father was so strict with them that on one occasion Councillor Boesen had to caution old Michael not to treat his daughters so harshly. Their marriages to the Lund brothers not only improved their lot but also brought the happy voices of grandchildren into the dour atmosphere of the house on the square. Henriette, a daughter of Petrea, became a great favorite with her Uncle Søren.

Of the three brothers Niels Andreas was probably the most attractive, but also the most unlucky. At this time he was still attending the Borgerdydskole and enjoying it immensely. Unhappily for him, his father soon decided that Niels would go into business, even though books were his life. After a brief but unsuccessful foray into the Copenhagen business world, he was sent off to make his fortune in America.

Of all the children, Peter and Søren were probably the most

alike. Peter had been graduated first in his class and was now acquiring a brilliant reputation at the university. He would go on to Göttingen to win his doctorate and also the nickname "The Debating Devil from up North." Still later he would enter the ministry of the Danish state church and eventually would become Bishop of Aalborg. Unlike Søren he was physically powerful and enjoyed the outdoors; he took several walking tours through Jutland and southern Sweden. But his life, like that of his youngest brother, was shadowed by a curious melancholy that finally overwhelmed him in his later years. After recovering from a serious typhus attack in 1826 he wrote in his diary: "God spared me for what I feared more than death: fantasy."

To the external observer, fantasy would have seemed out of place at 2 Nytorv. It was a home encased in a thick layer of rough Jutland wool, one whose atmosphere had more than a whiff of the small hosier's shop. Henriette Lund remembered that "hurry was unknown in the house," and that the prevailing tone was serious, almost austere. Yet it was precisely this austerity that made it a kind of cocoon, protecting and nurturing the youngest child's imagination. In the few glimpses we get of Kierkegaard's childhood, brief recollections scattered through his journal, he never relates incidents involving other children, or events he witnessed, but rather the somber reveries of a child alone with his thoughts.

The child sits by a window outside which "there grew about ten blades of grass." But that was enough to set his imagination in motion, and soon "these blades had become a huge forest, which had all the denseness and darkness that the grass had." When he was twenty-four the cry of a cock reminded him of the summer mornings of childhood. "The crowing of the cock announced a new happy day, told how I had everything again: the cool morning air, the dew on the grass that prevented me from tumbling about as I would have liked." Returning later that year to the site of these childhood mornings, the familiar scene gave him a poignant awareness of how it all had been: "When I stand and look out over the old Røyen estate . . . and the wood in its enormity broods in the background and makes the thicket dark and secret . . . I see myself so vividly as a little boy running around in my green jacket and grey trousers—but sadly I have become older, I cannot recapture myself." In all these recollections it is the particular sound or scene that sticks in his mind—not an event, not an adventure, not other people, but the precise texture of *that* sound or scene. "When one is a child and has no toys, one is well provided for," he later wrote, "for then imagination takes over. I still remember with wonder my childhood top, the only toy I had—what acquaintance was as interesting as this!" Alone in the drawing room of the house on the square, the child spent hours spinning his top across the wide, white-scoured planks as he gave himself to his widening reveries.

It is sometimes unclear how willingly young Søren accepted the iron-handed rule of Michael Pedersen Kierkegaard. Søren wrote: "From a child I was raised in obedience, absolute obedience," but Henriette Lund suggests that this obedience was not total. "His father usually called him 'The Fork,' " she recalls, "because of his early developed penchant for satirical remarks." But if there is doubt concerning young Søren's acceptance of his father's discipline, there is none at all about its severity. Søren remarked once that his father was so strict about money matters in particular that he must have been born on the *Terminen*—the due date for a promissory note. As Georg Brandes has related, Michael Kierkegaard rarely gave his sons money for little things even when they entered the university, and he demanded that his daughters do extra chores at home as well as shop in the marketplace "bareheaded, with knitted shawls over their shoulders." At certain times his severity was carried to absurd extremes. When Søren accidentally knocked over a saltcellar at table, his father berated him for being "a prodigal son." A business assistant recalled that the old man was extremely exacting about the polish on shoes and boots— "not a single spot or grain of sand must be found." Michael Kierkegaard maintained his strictness without resorting to strong words or emotional scenes, but simply by projecting his own mood of deep seriousness. Once when Nicoline dropped a valuable soup tureen he said nothing, believing that the gravity of her offense was so apparent that she needed no scolding. "Obedience was for him not merely a thing of great importance," Henriette Lund observed; "I think it was the main prop of his life."

With few exceptions, the people who came to the Kierkegaard home were either relatives or business associates of the father. There were, for example, the two hosier families, the Agerskovs and the Lunds. Christian Agerskov had married a relative of Michael Kierkegaard's first wife and then moved to Buddinge, a suburb of Copenhagen. The Kierkegaard and the Lund children often visited there; it was in Buddinge that young Søren gave everyone a scare by taking a nasty fall from a tree. Old Henrik Lund came from a neighboring county in Jutland and had a shop in Nygade, just off the Nytorv. His two sons married the Kierkegaard daughters and often visited the grandfather, children in tow. There was the wholesaler Johannes Hammerich, whose two sons Martin and Frederik were a few years older than Søren and remembered him as "a little wildcat." There was the office head in the Exchequer, Johannes Boesen, who had seven children and bore the minor title Judicial Councillor; Frederik Hammerich once said that old Kierkegaard respected his friend Boesen twice as much because of the title. Finally, there was the family of cousin Michael Andersen Kierkegaard, who with Agerskov took over the family business when Michael

Pedersen Kierkegaard retired in 1797. Although it ultimately went bankrupt under his management, the families remained close.

There was little sophistication in this group of family and friends. One of the Lunds later became a distinguished naturalist, but on the whole it was a homespun group, "sound" people, whom the father had met in church, in business, or at the meetinghouse of the Moravian Brotherhood on Stormgade. As in all things, the father's word was decisive. He selected the family's friends, just as he decided what goose to have for dinner and which child should go to the university.

But such a patriarchal household was not atypical. Michael Kierkegaard was not the only businessman in Copenhagen who had come from the Jutland heath, nor was he the only father to enforce obedience and see to it that all his household, in Brandes' words, "look up to the king, admire the clergy, and honor the police." This was a city of shopkeepers, a nineteenth-century bourgeois culture filled with deference for kings and chancellors, ministers, bishops, excellencies, and kings' councillors, a city whose watchword in a time of poverty was "Now we will all save." Extreme foresight, meticulousness in money matters, conspicuous piety, strict morality, ceremonious respect for authority—these were not so much peculiarities of the Kierkegaard home as aspects of its Copenhagen setting. Michael Kierkegaard only darkened and strained the characteristic elements of Copenhagen family life in giving 2 Nytorv its tone of Jutlandesque severity.

Why then did life in what Søren later called "the enigmatic family" so mark and cripple him? To answer this question we must look more closely at the familial embrace that bound together an old man and a young boy, that poisoned a child's innocence with an old man's melancholy.

3

FATHER

IN the square stands an old man talking to a peasant woman. She leans forward across a small portable counter, several sweaters under her black shawl, a patterned kerchief tied under her chin to keep out the early October chill. Before her on the counter lie some chickens, a few ducks, and on the end, a fat goose. They talk for a moment, she pointing out the excellence of the goose, he demurring. Their voices have a rough similarity, both lacking the mannered, clipped consonants of the educated classes. She does most of the talking. He remains taciturn, aloof, but when he does speak, his voice is powerful and resonant, not the voice of an old man. He mentions a price; they haggle for a moment and then strike a bargain; meticulously he counts out the change, takes the goose by the neck, and turns away.

The dignified figure now crossing the square, goose slung over his shoulder, is dressed in a long beige coat, a vest, and velvet trousers tucked into the tops of Hungarian boots that are freshly shined, each with a tassel in front. The little pigtail he wears at the back of his neck adds to his singular air. He has a powerful build with the heavy bones of a peasant, and his walk, head slightly bowed, expresses a kind of rough seriousness. His grey hair is smoothed back behind his ears, giving prominence to his firm but somewhat flat and heavy features. The chin is strong, the lips thin, and the striking eyes clear and open. "They had a distant expression," his granddaughter recalled, "as if they were still staring dreamily out over the Jutland heath." They were not the rheumy eyes of an old man but those of a daydreaming child, one whose "dreams now went much further, beyond this earth's narrow boundaries, to reach the goal of their longing—the eternal land." Behind their gaze was a kind of serenity, as if "he had become accustomed to look at life's sorrow and pain with other eyes than the worldly." When the young girl tried to sum up her grandfather in a single image, she thought of him as "a pilgrim wandering in a strange land."

The old man crossed the square, passed the horse cabs waiting before the city hall, and entered the house next door. He deposited the goose in the kitchen with Frøken Møller and made his way to the front room that opened on the square. The windows were shut now to keep out the cold, but the morning light slanted across the room, warming the wooden chair and little white-painted table by the window. A few books lay on the table: a Bible, a volume of Pastor Thisted's recently published edifying discourses, and several works by the German philosopher Christian Wolff. The old man sat down in the chair, and as he did so his eye was caught by a shrimp man crossing the square behind the cabs. "Ak, I should have remembered to tell Petrea to stop by Højbroplads to get some of the new shrimp. They're in season now." Continuing this train of thought, he guessed that there were probably other things he had forgotten this morning. His mind really wasn't working as it used to. Last week he had nearly forgotten to cash one of the royal notes he held! Perhaps he ought to resign as superintendent of the Sunday school. He had so many things to think about, and these days he had such trouble keeping his thoughts on the present. They were always slipping off into the past.

He picked up Wolff's *Reflections on God, the World, the Soul of Man, and Things in General*, which he was reading in

the original German—he regarded Danish as a hopelessly provincial language and was proud that he, an unlettered peasant
boy, had managed to teach himself a major European language.
He read:

> § 1089 This highest Bliss produces in GOD a constant
> Pleasure, indeed to the highest degree: because it is produced
> by the apprehension of Perfection (§ 404). The latter also
> brings with it complete Contentment; for since GOD possesses
> everything in the highest degree, nothing is left over for Him
> to wish beyond this Pleasure. And accordingly His Wish is
> fulfilled in All Things: which again may not be said of His
> Creatures. . . .

As on so many occasions recently, he couldn't keep his mind on
the text. Perhaps it was just that he was getting older. No. It
was something else, something more foreboding, as if the past
held some secret which, if he could just remember it properly,
would explain everything. But try as he might, he couldn't make
it out.

There had been that odd fire the spring before. Late one
April night the chemical laboratory around the corner on Frederiksberggade had caught fire. For a while it had seemed as if 2
Nytorv would also go up, and he remembered how cheerful he
had been as he made his way out to the pavement with the rest
of the family. Strange. A man's house and much of his fortune
is about to go up in flames, and he's cheerful. He was thinking
that night of the Biblical verse: "The Lord giveth and the Lord
taketh away. Blessed be the name of the Lord." But the Lord
did not take away. Just when he resigned himself to losing
everything, the fire was brought under control. His own home
was scarcely damaged—it was as if the Lord had made up His
mind to punish him, and then at the last moment had decided
on something else. And this had happened so often in the past.
Sometimes he wondered if long life and prosperity had not been

given him as a reproach for his sins. Is that what the Lord wanted him to see—that he, a miserable sinner, did not deserve the blessings heaped upon him? Or were the blessings only given him so that later he, like Job, would feel their loss all the more keenly?

As so often in the past, his mind drifted back to the beginning. He remembered himself at eleven tending his flocks alone on the Jutland heath: the oppressive grey sky, the wind, the damp heather under his feet. And worst of all, the loneliness—always the same, day after day. Once when he was hungry, cold, and wet through, he had climbed up on a hillock, raised his eyes to that silent grey sky, and cursed the God that would make an innocent child suffer so. And this day had stuck in his memory . . . principally because of what happened only a few months later.

There were eight children in the family and not nearly enough money to feed and clothe them all. Suddenly he was told that he was being sent off to work for his hosier uncle in Copenhagen. It seemed to him then, as it did now, a miraculous event. God had interceded in his life, saved him from abject poverty, and removed him to the relative luxury of the capital. And it all happened just *after* he had cursed this God. Why?

Only lately—with the death of two of his children within three years—had he begun to suspect the true meaning behind the prosperity which began with that miraculous removal. But that was another story.

For a long time the prosperity itself had absorbed all his attention, coming as it did slowly, in bits and pieces. The beginning in Copenhagen, although idyllic in comparison with Jutland, was not easy. In the early years he lived in a cellar in Østergade, getting what schooling he could when he wasn't working for his uncle, first as an errand boy and then as an assistant in the shop. In 1777 the village priest in Sæding sent his release from serfdom. His family worked one of the priest's fields (hence their surname: Ki[e]rkegaard, or churchyard), and legally the priest owned them. Old Michael still had the paper: "I, the undersigned, Nicolai Satterup, priest for Bølling and Sæding, manorial owner of Annexgaard in Sæding, give Michael Pedersen Kierkegaard of said Annexgaard . . . free pass, to be and to live where he will without begging my permission in the future."

Three years later Michael obtained his citizenship, and with that a market pass which permitted him to take to the highways —to Hillerød, to Helsingør—selling Jutland woolen goods, lisle stockings, Randers gloves, and woven caps. This was the happiest time of his life, tramping the old roads, feeling the wind in his face, smelling the wild flowers in June and the wet leaves in September, and all the while laying away dollar after dollar. In 1785 he used a few of these dollars to join Mads Røyen, another hosier, in buying a fine building on Købmagergade. Røyen lived and kept his shop there, while Michael had his own shop a bit farther up the street. Day in and day out he stood behind his counter, and day in and day out the pile of dollars grew. At first there was a nasty legal battle with the silk and clothing merchants, but his uncle and old Henrik Lund carried the fight to the High Court, finally winning for all hosiers the right to sell every kind of homemade wool and linen goods as well as Danish-produced felt and swanskin.

By the time the decision was handed down, Michael had won an even more important concession from the King. He still had the official paper. Dated September 19, 1788, it gave him royal patent "to deal in East Indian and Chinese wares, as well as goods coming from our West Indian islands such as sugar (refined and unrefined), syrup, and coffee beans, and to sell the same at wholesale and retail to all and sundry." This meant that he could now legally deal in silk goods, a precedent that threatened the clothiers and prompted them to bring another

losing suit. He was proud to remember that he had not forgotten the King's generosity: In 1808 he, Mads Røyen, a cousin,
and three other hosiers had put up the money to build a small
gunboat for the Danish navy which they christened *De Seks
Venner* (The Six Friends).

He remembered those years immediately after he had received the royal patent with a certain ambivalence. They were
profitable years. He was making money, more money in fact
than he had believed it possible to make. Then, on top of his
own profits, came the news that his uncle had designated him
residual legatee: when the uncle died Michael would inherit all
his wealth! But the money seemed to mean less and less. He was
careful about money, then as now. But it was a carefulness bred
of habit; his heart wasn't in it. Money was so easy to make that
it often seemed as if he had nothing to do with it: dollar fell
on dollar in a kind of natural process beyond his control. And
on top of this, he was lonely. Not homesick—that would be too
strong a word. But he was in his late thirties, and he had spent
the last twenty-five years among strangers. He needed a family.

Kirstine Røyen seemed like a good choice. She was Mads
Røyen's sister, she had a dowry of 568 rd., and she was only a
year younger than Michael. They were married in 1794, and
now—thirty years later—he found it difficult to remember just
what she had been like. He was certain he still loved her, but it
was like loving a ghost, like loving the Kirstine that could have
been but never was. He had trouble now remembering how she
wore her hair, how she dressed. But after all, they had only been
married two years before she became ill. She and his uncle both
died in 1796; in a single year he became both a widower and a
rich man.

The next year had been terrible. The money kept flowing in,
but now it seemed more like a reproach than a piece of luck.
The fire of 1795 burned through 55 streets, destroying 941

buildings in the center of Copenhagen, but he was miraculously spared. Spared was too weak a word; the general destruction around him actually enhanced the value of his own property. He was rich—but for what? His wife had died and he had no children. He had not even seen his family since he left the heath. At least some of the money could be used to make his mother's life a bit less harsh. And so he built for his family in Sæding a solid home—not of mud, like the other houses there, but of red brick, with wide timbers under a thatched roof. Yet this seemed so insignificant and so far away, while here in Copenhagen his life had turned sour. He had a premonition that he too, like Kirstine, might be marked for an early death, and in a way he longed for it. If the God he had cursed had made him prosperous only to make him, like Job, suffer the destruction of his prosperity, then he hoped it would come soon. As for his business—the daily routine, the constant hassles, the endless decisions—it bored him utterly; he would give it up. Hence just when many of his friends were fully entering the world of commerce and society, he was refusing that world, was withdrawing from it. He remembered that it was February 3, 1797—less than three months after his fortieth birthday—when he signed over his business to M. A. Kierkegaard and Christian Agerskov.

Was it the same year or the next that he married Ane? Probably the same, for he remembered seeing the lawyer incessantly that winter. Ane had been Kirstine's maid and had stayed on with him after her mistress's death. There had been no seduction; she was simply there and he was lonely. They came together and immediately she was pregnant, something that Kirstine had never managed over two years' time. He found the whole thing oppressive, principally because he loathed being forced to do anything. He would marry her, of course, but at least he could see to it that she didn't have a wife's usual inheritance rights, but only household effects and 200 rd. a year.

Furthermore, as the contract put it, "should the unexpected happen, that the temperaments cannot be united, it must be permitted us to live separate from table and bed, in which case my future wife will take her body linens and clothes, in addition to which I will give her once and for all 300 rigsdaler for the purchase of necessary household effects, and 100 rigsdaler yearly as long as she lives." He had to admit now that his precautions had proved superfluous. They *had* gotten along. It was comfortable having a wife like Ane, and she had given him seven children. Five years later, he recalled, he had drawn up a will leaving her one-third of his fortune.

The children came along with clocklike regularity. First, Maren Kirstine in September 1797, less than five months after their marriage. Then two more daughters, Nicoline Kristine and Petrea Severine, in 1799 and 1801. In the spring of 1803 he and Mads Røyen bought houses in Hillerød, 25 miles north of Copenhagen. There a first son, Peter Christian, was born a few months before they moved back to Copenhagen in the fall of 1805. Two more sons, Søren Michael and Niels Andreas, followed in 1807 and 1809, and it became clear that their home on Østergade was too small. He recalled how pleased Ane and the children were when he told them he had bought one of the new houses on the Nytorv.

These had been pleasant if not happy years. The voices of young children filled the house, and he had left himself enough to do—keeping his finances in order, running the household, and now and then helping with some civic project. More important, he had enough time to read and think. During those years the family usually went to hear Pastor Bull of Helliggeist. Not only did Bull have a good mind, but he wanted only to preach the gospel in a simple and direct way. Moreover, he lived his Christian principles as well as preaching them. Michael sent all the girls to Bull for their confirmation. But the Congregation

of Moravian Brothers on Stormgade was less cold and forbidding. Here there was a seriousness and piety that reminded
him of the religion he knew as a boy in Sæding. Unlike the
other churches, this one had no high pulpit with pews ranged
below, but only a low dais facing rows of benches. Here people
knew each other well—had it not been for the Brothers he would
never have met Johannes Boesen—and here there was no attempt
to adopt the gospels to the latest theological fad. The time he
gave to the Congregation—even all the hours of planning and
raising money for the new meetinghouse—was time well spent.

And through all these years both his health and his fortune
prospered. His premonition of an early death in 1797 had
clearly been mistaken; instead of getting weaker with the gathering years, he grew stronger. And while others were wiped out
by the war with England or the bombardment of Copenhagen
in 1807, his own wealth multiplied. It seemed as if Divine
Providence were watching over both his health and his fortune,
assuring strength to the one and prosperity to the other. But
to what end? To what end?

For a while in 1813 it seemed to him that he knew the answer.
Wouldn't it be appropriate for that God he had cursed many
years ago to let his fortune increase so that the whole could
be taken from him at a stroke? Especially at a time when he
had six young mouths to feed and another soon to arrive. He
remembered reading the papers during the winter of 1813 with
growing apprehension; they were filled with war news and
pessimistic reports about the economy. The currency was in dire
straits, as he had known for some time. Inflation was rampant
and Finance Minister Schimmelmann was taking God knows
what liberties with the Mint. Michael had put most of his money
into royal bonds—but even these were not secure. On January 5,
1813, the news broke like a thunderclap: Schimmelmann was
out, and with him the old Kurantbank monetary system. A new

Rigsbank was being set up whose daler notes would be worth six of the old dalers. In effect the government was devaluing its currency to one-sixth its former value. And he remembered too the care with which he had read the final part of the royal decree: in deference to foreign creditors royal bonds could be exchanged at face value for new Rigsbank bonds of the same denominations. Once again he was saved! While many rich men saw their wealth shrink overnight to one-sixth its value, his own property was scarcely affected. Relatively, he had become much, much richer. But why? Why?

He remembered asking himself that question as the winter turned to spring and he awaited the birth of Ane's child. This child was certainly what one might call an "unexpected blessing"—he was now fifty-six and Ane forty-five. On May 5 of that puzzling year the child was born. Another boy. Still thinking of his wife Kirstine (as he often did in those days), he decided to name the child after her recently deceased brother-in-law. At the christening Ane did not hesitate when Pastor Bull asked her: "And what shall this child be named?" "Søren Aabye Kierkegaard," she replied.

4

SON

THE boy knocks. From within a voice answers. As the boy enters the drawing room the old man puts down his book, shifts his spectacles, and turns to see what it is he wants. "Father, may I go out?" The shadows are already creeping up the walls of the houses across the square; it must be getting on toward six. "No, it's too late," the old man answers. "Dinner will be ready soon . . . But if you like we can take one of our walks in here." He rises from the chair, lays his spectacles across the open book, and gently takes the child's hand. Together they begin to walk up and down the drawing room.

The boy is given his choice of where they shall go—west out of the city to Frederiksberg Castle, north along Strandvejen to the beach, or simply through back streets and thoroughfares inside the city walls. Today the boy decides to go out Vesterport to the castle. "While they walked up and down the room the father described everything they saw. They greeted passersby; the carriages rattled past and drowned the father's voice; the cake-woman's wares were even more attractive than usual." After half an hour's walking with his father, the boy "was as exhausted as if he had been out for a whole day." He "soon learned from his father how he, too, could exercise this magic power. What before had been an epic became now a drama. Dialogues were held on the journey. If they walked over familiar ways, they each kept a sharp watch over the other to see that

nothing was overlooked. If the way were unfamiliar . . . [the boy]
would add suggestions, while his father's almighty imagination
was able to construct anything, using every childish fancy as an
ingredient in the drama. It was as if the world were being
created as they talked; as if his father were God, and he God's
favorite." Twenty years later Kierkegaard noted that these
magic walks had the effect of "teaching him to enjoy the taste
of ambrosia," that they "developed in him an almost vegetative
tendency to drowse in imagination." As for the father, the boy
remembered him always as a man with a powerful yet morbid
imagination—"The truly strange thing about Father was that he
had most of what one would have thought least: imagination—
a really melancholic imagination."

Another scene: The eldest brother has brought one of his
friends home from the university. The stranger sits facing the
father, who occupies his customary chair, saying little. On the
floor the youngest brother sits cross-legged, listening. The discussion turns to a theological point and proceeds "with an almost
solemn decorum." The stranger is asked to state his whole argument, and then the father replies. Sitting on the floor, the little
boy is engrossed. He hears the father's reply, "and in a moment
everything was turned upside down. How this happened remained a puzzle, but he was entranced by the drama. The
opponent would speak again . . . and [the boy] could almost
hear his heart beat, so impatiently did he await what would
happen. It did happen! In an eye blink everything was turned
upside down. The clear became unclear, the certain doubtful,
contradictions became obvious. . . . This was the kind of reversal
the boy used to witness when he listened to his father argue. He
quickly forgot what was said, both by his father and by the
opponent, but the thrill in his soul he didn't forget." Remembering all this, the eldest brother later remarked, "My father was
the most gifted man I have ever known."

Another scene: The child has been given a set of pictures of

great men. He sits at his father's feet idly turning them, one by
one. Here is Napoleon, the emperor. He sits on "a snorting
steed, with the tossing feather, a regal expression on his face,
riding at the head of the thousands and thousands you cannot
see, with hand outstretched in the command: 'Forward!' " The
next figure "is dressed as a hunter; he stands leaning upon his
bow and gazes straight ahead with a glance so piercing, so
confident, and yet so anxious. This is William Tell." The father
explains "something about the man and his remarkable glance,
saying that Tell has one eye on his beloved son, that he may not
hit him, and one on the apple on the boy's head, that he may not
miss it." In this way the child is led from picture to picture until
he "comes to one which had been deliberately laid among the
others. It shows a man crucified." At first the child does not
understand why the man is hanging on the tree. But the father
explains "that this is a cross, and that to hang on it means to be
crucified, and that crucifixion in that land was not only the most
painful death but also an ignominious mode of execution employed only for the worst criminals." The child has "a very
strange feeling," and wonders what could have prompted the
father to lay this ugly picture with all the beautiful ones. "Who
is he? What did he do?" the child asks. The father replies that
"this crucified man is the Savior of the world," that "the
Crucified One was the most loving man that ever lived." The
boy will recall thirty years later: "Already as a little child I was
told as solemnly as possible that the 'many' spat upon Christ who
yet was the truth. . . . This thought is my life . . . and though I
were to forget everything, yet I would never forget how I was
told this as a child, and the impression it made upon me."

A final scene: One of the father's oldest and most trusted
friends has come to visit. The two old men sit chatting while
the youngest son plays on the floor. The boy hears a sigh and
looks up in time to see the dejection on his father's face as he

tells his friend: "I'm good for nothing. I can do nothing. My only wish is to find a place in some charitable institution."

Sometime later the father looked in on his son and saw that he was greatly disturbed. Then he stood quietly before the boy and said: " 'Poor child, you are walking about in a silent despair.' (But he never questioned more closely. For how could he? He himself was in silent despair.) Otherwise there was never a word exchanged on the subject. But the father and son were perhaps two of the most melancholy men who ever lived."

Taken together, these scenes (drawn with more or less confidence from Søren Kierkegaard's boyhood) show some of the charm and also some of the desperation of his relationship with his father. It was this relationship which, above all, made him the man he later became; the shadow of Michael Pedersen Kierkegaard was cast across the whole path of his life.

Kierkegaard's journal is filled with complaints about his early life, about his lack of a real childhood. "My life began without any immediate experience, with a terrible melancholy," he wrote in 1848, "in earliest childhood deranged in its deepest foundations." And the following year: "I never knew the joy of being a child. The frightful torments I suffered disturbed the calm which is the prerequisite for being a child . . . because of the unrest within me I was always, always outside myself." In the posthumously published *The Point of View for My Work as an Author* he put it this way:

> In the proper sense of the word I had not lived, except in the character of spirit; a man I had never been, and a child or youth even less. . . . For my misfortune (almost, I might say, from birth, completed by my upbringing) was . . . not to be a man. But when one is a child—and the other children play or joke or whatever else they do; oh! and when one is a youth—and the other young people make love and dance or whatever else they

do—and then in spite of the fact that one is a child or youth,
to be spirit! What torment! I've never had any immediate experience and so, in the ordinary human sense of the word, I've
never lived. I began at once with reflection . . . I am reflection,
from first to last.

There is something disingenuous about these complaints, as with
all Kierkegaard's lamentations concerning his melancholy and
introversion. They convey a suggestion of the masochist's love
for his own suffering, a suspicion that he cries out precisely in
order to bring on his anguish. At the same time they carry more
than a germ of truth, for everyone who describes Kierkegaard
as a child agrees that there *was* something extraordinarily "old"
about him. And it was not simply a matter of his dress or
manner; his whole psyche seemed to be that of an old man, bent
under the weight of a nameless burden:

> It's really awful when a man's consciousness has borne such
> a weight from childhood that neither the soul's elasticity nor
> its freedom can throw it off. Sorrow in life can certainly op-
> press consciousness, but if the sorrow first comes at a mature
> age it doesn't have time to take that form; it becomes a histori-
> cal factor, not something that lies, as it were, beyond con-
> sciousness itself. He who has borne such a weight from child-
> hood on is like a child who has been taken from its mother
> with forceps and who always bears a physical trace of the
> mother's pain.

For Kierkegaard, the source of this burden is found not in a
mother's pain, but in a father's melancholy. "An old man," he
later wrote, "who himself was enormously melancholy . . . had a
son of his old age upon whom the whole of that melancholy fell
in inheritance."

The term "melancholy" recurs in descriptions of Michael
Kierkegaard. Business associates and family acquaintances re-

ferred to him regularly as "old" Kierkegaard (old Kierkegaard did this, old Kierkegaard said that), but within the family, in the descriptions furnished by his two sons and his granddaughter, it is the word melancholy that predominates. The Danish is *Tungsind*, meaning heaviness (*Tung*) of spirit (*Sind*); in a modern idiom we might say that Michael Kierkegaard suffered from chronic depression. Although considerable scholarly effort has gone into a search for the origins of this depression (Was it guilt generated by his cursing God on the Jutland heath? Or was it guilt prompted by his taking Ane to bed so soon after Kirstine's death?), no firm conclusion has emerged. There are hints in Søren's journal that his father's depression grew worse with age, and that toward the end of his life it verged on the psychotic. Once in his boyhood Søren mentioned to his father his enthusiasm for a literary character he had encountered in his reading—a master thief, a kind of Robin Hood. Søren pointed out that such a character had only used his powers in the wrong way and might still be saved. Very solemnly the old man replied: "There are offenses one can only fight against with God's continued help," and admitted that he himself longed for "a venerable confessor to whom one could open one's heart." At other times he hinted to Søren that the family lay under a divine curse because of some inexpiable sin he had committed. Because of him there was "a guilt upon the whole family"; it would "disappear, wiped out by the powerful hand of God." As the years passed his outlook darkened until, at the end, the whole world stood revealed to him as a tissue of corruption; it was "a sinful world," he wrote to his sister just weeks before his death; he wanted only "a blessed leaving of it."

There is clearly an edge of morbidity to Michael Kierkegaard's depression: a psychiatrist might judge that he was suffering from a common malady of the old called involutional melancholy. But the little boy playing at his feet knew only that the world

his father lived in, the world that bounded the child's horizon
and shadowed his play, was a world of greys and blacks, a barren
landscape of brooding mystery. Just as Michael Kierkegaard had
come to live with one woman while remaining loyal to the ghost
of another, so too had he chosen to linger in life while loathing
it. Hence refusal became his life's secret, the "inheritance" he
bequeathed to his youngest son. The world of men—its affairs,
its delights, its entanglements—must ultimately be refused;
somehow, one must get *beyond* it. This was the lesson the child
was learning from his father in many ways, some subtle, some
more direct.

The child learned it, for example, from the severity of the old
man's manner, from his somber dress, his bent carriage, his slow
and deliberate gait, the sad and wistful expression in his eyes.
He learned it from the uniform of drab, rough woolens in which
he himself was regularly sent off to school, and from the way
his father summarily discouraged any spontaneous excitement,
any joy in what the senses could provide. He learned it most
directly, however, from the Christianity his father taught him.

For Michael Kierkegaard's Christianity was not that of the
Wedding of Cana or the invitation to little children, but that of
Christ suffering on the cross, of Gethsemane and Calvary, of
"my Lord and Master whom they spat upon." The martyrdom
of Christ was only a symbol for the fundamental corruption of
the world. In *The Point of View* Kierkegaard tells us how he
was "strictly brought up as a child in the notion that the truth
must suffer, be mocked, spat upon," and of the "inner resentment that had been in me from childhood, because I learned
(long before I could in any way have seen it) that lies and baseness and injustice ruled the world." The Christianity of the
father was a religion of the Beyond, a doctrine that relativized
and finally negated the earthly life.

From first to last, Kierkegaard's relation to this teaching was ambivalent. He said in 1848 that his "life's difficulty," the reason why his life was so "dreadfully confused," was that he had been "brought up by an old man extremely strict in Christianity." Six years later he complained, "I know only too well how my life has been botched by my being raised in Christianity from childhood on." Yet this doctrine also attracted him:

> It's terrible when I think, even for a single moment, over the dark background which from earliest time was part of my life. The dread with which my father filled my soul, his own awful melancholy, the many things in this respect I can't write down. I got such a dread of Christianity, and yet felt myself so strongly drawn to it.

Christianity was presented to him as a brooding mystery. His father was a devout and pious man, yet this did not save him from the rack of guilt and self-reproach. "The greatest danger for a child with respect to the religious," Kierkegaard later wrote, "is not that his father or tutor should be a freethinker, or even a hypocrite. No. The danger lies in his being an obviously pious, God-fearing man, so that the child is all the more disturbed by the recognition that deep in the father's soul lies an unrest which is untouched even by the pious fear of God."

Kierkegaard's lifelong ambivalence toward Christianity cannot be disentangled from his ambivalence toward his father. He hated this old man who had so branded and crippled him: "As a child I was strictly brought up in Christianity; humanly speaking, crazily brought up. A child travestied as a melancholy old man. Terrible!" He also loved the father "who made me unhappy, but out of the best of convictions. . . . I love such a man." He complains: "Merciful God, how terribly unjust to me was my father in his melancholy—an old man who put the whole weight of his melancholy upon a poor child," and then in the next line he exclaims: "And yet for all that, he was the best

of fathers." For although the old man was solemn and strict, he
opened himself and his world to the child. He was (as Søren
later pointed out) the boy's sole playmate, and there grew between them a share of that strange intimacy which often links
the very young and the very old.

The year his father died, Søren jotted down on a gilt-edged
sheet of paper Lear's affectionate farewell to Cordelia:

> So we'll live,
> And pray, and sing, and tell old tales, and laugh
> At gilded butterflies, and hear poor rogues
> Talk of court news, and we'll talk with them too,
> Who loses, and who wins, who's in, who's out;
> . . . In a walled prison, packs and sects of great ones,
> That ebb and flow by th' moon.

Cordelia and Lear would only be "God's spies," but when Søren
and his father strode up and down the drawing room together
it was "as if the world were being created as they talked; as if
his father were God, and he God's favorite." This identification
of the father with God is no slip, but reveals the nerve of much
of Kierkegaard's later theology. God the Father loves his creatures, yet must be cruel to them: "In Christianity God is spirit—
hence His immense severity that stems from love." Just as his
father destroyed Søren's childhood out of love, so out of love
God makes man suffer that he might become spirit: "I learned
from him [Michael Kierkegaard] what father love is, thereby
getting an idea of the divine father love." In Kierkegaard's
theology, his childhood becomes a paradigm for the relation of
God to man. After complaining that "the frightful agonies I
suffered" made it impossible for him ever to have experienced
"the joy of being a child," he continues:

> Yet at times it seems to me as if my childhood had returned
> again, for unhappy though my father made me, it seems to me

that I am now experiencing what it means to be a child in relation to God. It was as if all my first childhood was so terribly wasted, in order that I could more truly experience it a second time in relation to God.

For Søren, Michael Kierkegaard was both God and God's victim, both lover-torturer and the tortured. Try as he might, Søren could not simply hate or simply love this man who towered over his life. His father's shape was embedded in his psyche, the old man's secret inscribed indelibly in his heart: The world was irredeemably corrupt; one could hope only for "a blessed leaving of it." This secret was the boy's inheritance. When a few years later he wrote in his journal, "The whole of existence is infected for me," and when still later he curtained his room heavily to keep out the sunlight, he was only living out his "inheritance."

The lonely child, his birdlike body clothed in rough grey woolens, could neither reject nor understand the weight that was laid upon him. Laughed at by his schoolmates and ignored by his brothers, sisters, and cousins, his one playmate a father old enough to be his grandfather, he could only sense his isolation from other children, his oddity of dress, his feeling of being "old" and burdened. It became natural for him to identify with the physically deformed, the weak, the outcasts of existence. With respect to the human race he was a "counterfeit," or as he put it much later in his journal, he was "bound in agonizing misery, like a bird whose wings have been clipped." "Once, long ago, I was in the deepest sense wing-shot," he wrote, "I am first and always an unfortunate one set outside the universally human."

Doomed to remain a pariah in the world of men, Kierkegaard chose to live his life symbolically, finding what sustenance he could in the interstices of imagination. He rejected the world, but he rejected it only to reapprehend and embrace it as the product of imagination. Hence as we shall see, his dream is of an experience that has been transmuted into allegory. As a child Kierkegaard had already decided (or had had it decided for him) that his life would be a refusal, that his rasping, high-pitched voice would find its strongest resonance in saying "No!" Later he would come to discover in that refusal the lineaments and also the difficulties of his identity as a writer.

When Kierkegaard and his father pace up and down their Nytorv drawing room, what they are rehearsing is precisely this refusal. They imagine turning a corner into Frederiksberggade and hearing the bark of a neighbor's dog. Yet this imaginary bark has no surprise to it; it is wholly familiar. It does not startle because it has been, so to speak, "expected"—it is part of the story. Now a carriage rumbles past. But this carriage has none of the strangeness, the imperviousness of an actual carriage. It too is "part of the story" and as such is totally under their power; it is theirs as a real carriage could never be. Now they will buy a *Wienerbrød* at a corner bakery. The little pastry exudes pure deliciousness: on top the icing glistens; the odor of the freshly baked dough rises to the nostrils; the feather-light texture can be felt. Everything is "just right"—the light on the sidewalk, the fresh wind with its hint of the sea, the sounds of people laughing, carriages rumbling, dogs barking—just right because all of it is nourished and formed by nothing but imagination. Slowly, inevitably, a singular thought has taken root in the young boy's mind. It is not necessary to live in the world. On the contrary, the world—its resistance, its burdens, its conflicting demands—can be transformed. One need only dream. Narcissus has found his solitary pool, and Kierkegaard his future: he will be a dreamer.

II

YOUTH

5

GILLELEJE 1835

"KIERKEGAARD has lost his last daughter," wrote a friend of the family in 1835. "Now the old man has only two sons left out of seven children."

The first to die had been Nicoline, the second eldest daughter, wife of Christian Lund and mother of four small children. She was delivered of a stillborn child on August 30, 1832, and worsened steadily over the following week. Although some of her family wanted to shield her from the knowledge of her approaching death, Michael Kierkegaard would have none of it. "No," he said, "my children are not brought up like that," and immediately went to her bed and told her the truth. She died on September 10.

Next to go had been Niels, carried off a year later by a fever in Paterson, New Jersey, while trying to make his fortune in America. According to P. Munthe-Brun, who knew both Niels and his family, the boy left Denmark "really because he couldn't take it any longer with his family. . . . The father forced him to stay in a shop, although he wished to study like his brothers; he must not have any enjoyment, or contact with anyone. He was treated as the Cinderella of the family and died just when he seemed to have made for himself a comfortable life. Now his family regrets it, but too late."

The mother, Ane Kierkegaard, had become ill the following

June. One of the doctors thought it might be typhus. She lingered
with a fever for over a month, and died finally on July 31, 1834.
Bishop Mynster officiated at her burial and ten carriages followed the casket to the cemetery. Peter Christian was worried
because this was more than the law allowed, but old Michael
could not be dissuaded.

The last daughter, Petrea, had been closest in age and temperament to Søren. Even after her marriage to Ferdinand Lund, her
brother would often visit her in the late afternoon. Lund would
come home from the bank to find his wife and Søren "playing
and gesticulating like two children." Petrea gave birth to a
healthy baby boy on December 13, 1834, and died two weeks
later. Like her sister, she left four small children.

Four deaths in less than two and a half years—no wonder
Søren would write: "then it was that . . . I felt the silence of
death gathering around me." The three of them—Michael
Pedersen, melancholy and crochety; Peter Christian, stolid and
self-righteous; Søren, acerbic and inwardly preoccupied—huddled together in the many rooms of the house that now was too
large for them. From his rooms on the first floor the father could
hear Peter's students climbing the stairs when they came for
their tutorials. The two sons had rooms side by side on the
second floor. In Peter's there was a desk by the window where
the students sat while "the Doctor" (so called because of his
Göttingen degree) corrected their Latin compositions or discussed a point of theology. And off to the side lay Søren, reading.
One of the students later recalled that only once had Søren ever
ventured to interject an opinion.

His uncharacteristic reticence may have been caused by in-
security in the presence of a brother who was already well
respected in the intellectual circles of Copenhagen. Not only
had Peter Christian earned a doctorate from Göttingen, but he
had brilliantly passed the official theology exam at the university

after three and a half years of study. When Poul Møller came to Copenhagen in 1830, Peter Christian (then only twenty-five) had been considered as a possible replacement for him in the chair of philosophy at Christiania (Oslo). In 1834 Peter Christian began lecturing at the university in addition to teaching his regular classes in Latin, Greek, and religion at the Borgerdydskole. His expertise in Latin disputation and theology won him a following among the younger university students who came to him for tutoring. More important, his dialectical talents brought him notice in Grundtvig's circle of renegade theologians, who in the early 1830's were questioning the assumptions of the established church. These men—Grundtvig himself, Lindberg, Lars Boisen, Engelbreth, and Oldenburg—were guests in the Kierkegaard home, and Peter read both Engelbreth's and Oldenburg's manuscripts before they were printed. By belonging to their circle and sharing their confidence, he in no way diminished his stature in the eyes of Copenhagen's establishment: these were renegade theologians, not political theorists. He was a conservative in politics and rather a prig in some ways, but he was also a young theologian with superb credentials and great promise.

Søren resented him. He was too good, too brilliant in a conventional way. His achievements seemed always to be so orthodox, so bourgeois, and as the oldest son his opinions seemed to carry a weight in the family that was undeserved. Much later Søren complained in his journal of Peter's "pusillanimity" and his "uprightness": "Fundamentally, Peter has always looked on himself as better than me, and so put me down as the false brother. And there he's right, for he has always been more upright than I. His relation to Father was that of an upright son, while mine was often blameworthy—yet Peter has never loved Father as I loved him." Peter for his part saw his brother, younger by eight years, as the prodigal son who sooner or later would find his way back to the narrow path. In March 1835, for example, he wrote in his diary: "Søren doesn't seem now to be reading for his exam *at all*. God help him out of all this inner unrest in a good way and to his soul's salvation." The year before, Peter had been unable to go to Communion because he was still at odds with Søren, and much later, after *Either/Or* was published, he could not forgive his brother for writing "The Diary of the Seducer," a work he felt contributed to the corruption of the younger generation. Despite their temperamental differences, both brothers attended the same schools and received essentially the same education as future theologians—but the establishment within which Peter flourished was to Søren so constricting that ultimately he had to break its bonds altogether.

At the beginning of his university career Søren had worked hard enough, passing both parts of the Second Examination on schedule with excellent marks—*magna cum laude* in Latin, Greek, Hebrew, and history, and *summa cum laude* in mathematics, practical and theoretical philosophy, and physics. During the first year his name can be found on attendance lists for the usual lectures in the liberal arts. But by passing the two parts of the Second Examination in the spring and fall of 1831, he put the liberal arts behind him and moved into the systematic study of his chosen discipline—theology. Here his progress is more difficult to follow, since over half the theology lecture lists for the next four years have been lost. From those which survive, it is possible to see that he attended the usual lectures on dogmatics, Christian philosophy, and New Testament hermeneutics. His exercise books are filled with exegetic discussions, translations of the Gospels into Latin, and references to various Biblical commentaries. This material might not have been so forbidding had it been taught with brilliance and humanity. Unfortunately, the theological faculty of Copenhagen University in the early 1830's was, in the words of Valdemar Ammundsen (later a professor on that faculty), "respectable, taken as a whole, but not especially brilliant."

So the years passed, the Biblical commentaries piled up, and Søren fell further and further behind. Had he followed Peter Christian's schedule, he would have received his degree in 1834. As it was, in June 1835 he wrote to P. W. Lund: "I am supposed to study for a theological degree, an occupation that does not interest me at all and so does not advance particularly quickly. I have always preferred a free and perhaps somewhat indefinite study rather than the *table d'hôte* where one knows in advance the guests and the menu for each day of the week."

In actuality, Søren was becoming quite familiar with the menus of the many Swiss cafés that were just then springing up in Copenhagen: Fellini's and A Porta on Kongens Nytorv, Pleisch's on Amagertorv, and a new tea shop that had opened across from the Kierkegaard home on the Nytorv. He was behaving like the rich man's son he was. He smoked four cigars a day, attended lectures irregularly, read only what he pleased, and could usually be found in the Student Union, in a café, or walking around town in animated conversation with one of his acquaintances. He showed up at home only for meals, and if his tea shop bills are any indication, even this was not too often.

His appearance itself had changed. The Choirboy had finally shed his odd costume and donned the fashions of the time, which he wore with nonchalance. By 1837 he had run up tailor bills of 492 rd. (about $3,400), and in June 1835 he described himself as a "man in modern dress, glasses on his nose and a cigar in his mouth." The author Henrik Hertz made his acquaintance at about this time in the Student Union. "He was lying on the sofa in a comfortable position," Hertz recalled, "and addressed me in familiar tones like an old acquaintance." They met often after that, and Hertz was quite taken by Kierkegaard's "sprightly, intelligent conversation." Above all, Hertz remembered "his characteristically muted, often somewhat castrated-sounding voice, and his sudden transition from a very cheerful to a deeply serious expression."

It was in this period that Kierkegaard decided to try his hand at journalism. A friend and fellow student, P. E. Lind, had written a satiric piece for the December 4, 1834, *Flying Post* entitled, "Woman's Superior Origin Defended." Kierkegaard wrote a sequel to this entitled, "Also a Defense of Woman's Superior Capacity," that was published on December 17. Witty yet vapid, filled with circumlocutions, it gives the impression of a young man trying hard to be funny and failing more often than not. After a number of wry comments on women in history, for example, Kierkegaard begins his last paragraph by observing that "recently a woman was the only one to have proved the immortality of the soul—a book that, together with Kristiane Rosen's *Cookbook*, has served to keep life in many."

We can only guess what Michael Pedersen Kierkegaard thought of all this. Most likely he saw it as highly unbecoming in a serious young man preparing for a post in the church or the university. Søren's classmates were getting their degrees and moving out into the world. Anger, Bahneberg, Borries, Bruun, Møller, Ryge—six of his nine former schoolmates—were graduating in 1835, while Søren was frittering his time away at Pleisch's and falling further and further behind. His tutor of the year before, H. L. Martensen, could see that he had talent, but was annoyed by his "irresistible urge to sophistry, to hair-splitting, that came out on all occasions," and Professor Müller had said on several occasions, "What in the world are we going to do about Søren?" Possibly with an eye to separating Søren from the bad influence of his friends and the distractions of Copenhagen, in June 1835 Michael Kierkegaard provided his son with ample funds for a two-month holiday in the country.

In late June Søren left Copenhagen and traveled north by

coach the forty miles to the fishing village of Gilleleje at the
northern tip of the island of Sjælland. He lodged at the local inn
adjacent to the harbor, and there the innkeeper, Christopher
Mentz, and his wife Birgitta saw to his needs. On one of his
excursions into the surrounding countryside he took along the
Mentzes' son, twelve-year-old Rudolph, and they were caught in
a violent thunderstorm in the middle of Grib's Forest. For the
city youth of twenty-two this holiday was a first encounter with
nature—with the marshes, the pebbled beaches, the great forests
of northern Sjælland. Sometimes he took a coach to visit historical monuments in the vicinity—Gurre Castle and Esrom—or to
journey south through Grib's Forest to Nødebo. Often he went
on foot, striding over the gently rolling hills around Gilleleje
or strolling along the beaches to the east and west. He took a
two-day trip to Kullen in Sweden, and on July 24 climbed to the
top of the Gilbjerg, the highest point in the vicinity. Yet in his
descriptions of these excursions—of driving through the shadows
of Grib's Forest, or sitting by a still northern lake, or listening
to the gulls and the roll of the sea from the Gilbjerg—there is a
curious remoteness. He seemed attentive not to the details of a
scene, but to its imaginative possibilities.

Sitting by Gurre Lake, for example, he felt he was living
hundreds of years ago in King Valdemar's time. "While the
rustling of the trees lets us hear King Valdemar's hunt," he
wrote, "the rushes seem to breathe applause—the blond maidens
admiring the rider's horsemanship and bearing." On another
occasion, watching the rise and fall of the waves from the
Gilbjerg, he was almost carried away by the scene's beauty:

> And as I stood there in the still evening, the sea with a deep
> but quiet seriousness struck up its song; my eyes met not a
> single sail upon the vast surface, and the sea set limits to the
> sky and the sky to the sea . . . the few that are dear to me
> came forth from their graves. . . . I felt myself so content in

their midst, I rested in their embrace, and it was as if I were out of the body, and in a higher aether was wafted to and fro with them. Then the hoarse screech of the gulls reminded me that I stood alone, and everything vanished before my eyes, and I turned back with a sad heart to mix myself in the swarm of the world, though I will not forget this blissful moment.

The mood in the journal entries made during Kierkegaard's Gilleleje holiday is subdued, reflective, and a little sad. It suggests that the experiences Søren describes occupy only the fore-stage of consciousness, and that behind them more personal concerns are being examined, compared, adjudicated; it gives the impression that his stay in Gilleleje was proving to be a period of intense self-examination and reflection.

And indeed on August 1 Kierkegaard wrote up a long summary of his meditations. The entry, nearly eight pages in the Danish edition, full of youthful enthusiasm and exaggeration, reveals Kierkegaard's self-searchings at the age of twenty-two. The central theme is his failure to know himself. "One must learn to know oneself before knowing anything else (γνωθι σεαυτον)," he wrote. "It is only after a man has thus understood himself inwardly, and has thus seen his way, that life acquires peace and significance; only then is he done with that tiresome, unlucky fellow traveler, his life-irony, that shows itself in the sphere of the understanding." As for himself, he has had plenty of the "sphere of understanding." In fact, it seemed to him that he "had not drunk from the cup of wisdom, but had fallen into it." For a time he had thought his problem was one of finding the right course of study or the right profession, and he had played with the idea of abandoning theology for law. He had even considered the idea of becoming an actor, "so that by putting myself in another's role I could, as it were, find a surrogate for my own life, and find distraction in outward change." But soon he recognized that this was the wrong approach: "What did I find? Not my Self, which was what I was looking for (thinking of my soul, if I may say so, as shut in a box with a springlock which external circumstances, by pressing upon the lock, were to open)." If he were truly to come to know himself, he would have to turn in another direction, away from external circumstances:

> What I really lack is to be clear about what *I am to do*, not what I am to know, except insofar as some understanding must go before every action. The thing is to understand what I am cut out for, to see what the Divinity really wants *me* to do, it is a question of finding a truth which is true *for me*, of finding *the idea for which I can live and die*. What good would it do me to discover a so-called objective truth, to work through the philosophers' systems and then be able, if required, to review them all and point out the inconsistencies within each? What good would it do me to be able to develop a theory of the state and combine all the details into a single whole, and so construct a world in which I did not live, but only held up to the view of others? What good would it do me to be able to explain the meaning of Christianity and many other particular phenomena, if all this had *no* deeper meaning for *me and for my life?* . . . What good would it do me if truth stood before me cold and naked, indifferent as to whether I recognized her or not, and producing in me a shudder of fear rather than a trusting devotion? I surely do not deny that I still recognize an *imperative of understanding* and that through it one can work upon men, *but it must be taken up into my life,* and that is what I now recognize as the most important thing. That is what my soul longs after, as the African desert thirsts for water. . . . That was what I lacked in order *to lead a complete human life* and not merely one of the understanding, so that thereby I should not come to base the development of my thought—well, upon something one might call objective—something that in any case is not my own, but rather upon something that grows together with the deepest roots of my existence.

Although this passage has been cited by students of Kierkegaard more often than any other journal entry, what has never been remarked is the oddity of Kierkegaard's alleged project of self-knowledge. For he proposes to "understand" himself really by looking away from himself. He will come to know himself not by testing that self in action or by trying to comprehend its situation in all its complexity, but rather by *finding* an idea for which he can live and die. Often in these entries from August 1835, Kierkegaard seems to be searching for a scenario that he can live. Earlier, he had worked on the assumption that he possessed a self which could be released by outward circumstances "pressing upon the lock." Now he knows only too well that outward circumstances may press as they will; there is nothing hidden behind the lock. Suffering in real life from the absence of any "plot," finding within himself only a disturbing question mark, he hopes to discover in that singular truth which will be *true for him* the lineaments of a substantial identity.

To the last sentence of the passage cited above, Kierkegaard added a puzzling yet revealing marginal comment:

> In spite of all his knowledge, how near man lies to madness! What is truth but to live for an idea? In the end everything must be based upon a postulate; yet in the moment when it no longer stands outside him, but he lives in it, then it ceases for the first time to be a mere postulate for him.

The very idea of a postulate that can be "lived in" is a puzzling, even contradictory, notion. For we ourselves *postulate* our postulates; we "sponsor" them, so to speak, and they never lose the taste of that original sponsorship. What would it mean to "live in" a postulate? Might it not be very much like what we all experience in falling into dream?

Think first of the dream's presentation to us as story, for, as Sartre has suggested, it is as a story that we first confront our dreams-to-be. At the outset, for example, there is only the bare notion of pursuit, of someone being chased, and we begin to follow the story as if we were reading a novel. But as we sink under the spell of the dream, the story compels our belief in it. It is not just "someone" being chased; it is *us*, and we are running . . . a crowd is chasing . . . we are frightened. In an instant the imagined world of the dream has totally absorbed us. We are *in* the dream in a way we are never in a story. For a story can be put down, but a dream must be dreamed to its end. The events of the dream thus have an extraordinary finality; they occur as if they were not able *not* to happen. More important, we are both in the dream and outside it at the same time. We are not acting out the role of flight; *we are fleeing*. Yet at the same time we are spectators to the flight, watching ourselves flee, knowing it is us, yet still outside . . . watching. In the dream our consciousness doubles back on itself, annihilating, yet also preserving, the distance between dream and dreamer. Entering a dream as if it were a story, we quickly recognize we have entered a story *that we live*.

The ideal of such a state, where the individual lives fully within some particular postulate or "plot," haunts much of Kierkegaard's later work, from his early discussions of the "life view" (*Livs-Anskuelse*) to his later portrait of the "knight of faith" and the struggles incident to religious conversion. Perhaps more to the point is the fact that on several occasions in the years which followed he experienced moments—not unlike the daydream on the Gilbjerg—when it seemed to him that experience itself had been transmuted into dream. In July 1837, for example, he wrote in his journal:

> Sometimes one experiences a phenomenon which, although it occurs in the realm of spirit, might be compared to a kind of vegetative, digestive slumber—to a comfortable feeling of convalescence. Consciousness here appears as a moon, over-

shadowing the stage from proscenium to background; one
slumbers on in the whole . . . , in the Oriental ondreaming in
the infinite, where all is experienced as if it were fiction—and
one gets the same mood as from a grandiose poem: the world's
existence, God's existence, my existence is poetry, wherein all
the multiplicity, the frightful irregularities, the things which
are indigestible for human thought, are smoothed out in a
misty, dreaming kind of existence.

This "dreaming kind of existence," where experience itself has
been transformed into "fiction," he described again two years
later:

Just as in nervous cases, moments occur when the eye's nerves
have become so microscopically sharpened that one can *see
the air* . . . so too in spiritual matters ecstatic moments occur
wherein the whole of existence appears so poetic, so distended
and transparent for contemplation, that even the most insignificant of the "bad infinity's" mass products seems at the least
to suggest allegorically the most profound truth—indeed,
seems only to have reality and existence insofar as it is an
allegory.

These passages mark the direction of Kierkegaard's quest.
For as we shall see, in the years following his Gilleleje summer
holiday Kierkegaard seemed to flee the world in the direction of
an experience of life transformed into dream. We say that we
"lose ourselves" in our dreams, and it was precisely this en-
chantment of consciousness that Kierkegaard sought. Most of
the time he was pursued by that "tiresome fellow traveler, his
life-irony"; there was no "plot" to his life but only a disturbing
vacuity. Yet at certain moments irony and vacuity were left behind, and he experienced what can only be described as a kind
of apotheosis. He stands on the Gilbjerg four hundred feet
above the sea listening to the gulls and the roar of the surf
below. He looks at the sea, smells it, hears its rumbles, yet the

whole scene comes to him as if he had entered an image, as if he were no longer perceiving but imagining. In moments like this the world took on a finality and brilliance denied it at other times. The "frightful irregularities" were smoothed out and became parts of a giant allegory. This was the vision that guided his pen as he sat in his rented room at Gilleleje and scribbled his pledge to find "the truth which is true for me . . . the idea for which I can live and die."

6

A HOST OF SHADOWS

KIERKEGAARD's resolve to find a personal truth went hand in hand with a growing rejection of conventional Christendom—an awkward position for an aspiring theologian. On June 1, 1835, he wrote to P. W. Lund that in Christianity the contradictions were so great as to "prevent a clear view." After pointing out that he "grew up, so to speak, in orthodoxy," he went on to remark that "as soon as I began to think for myself, the huge colossus started to totter." By October he had moved even further away from Christendom:

> With all his life and faith, the Christian may yet easily be taken for a person with a definite fixed idea. . . .
> When I look at a number of particular examples of the Christian life, it seems to me that Christendom . . . actually robs such individuals of their manhood and makes them geldings.

In an undated journal entry from the same time he sounded almost Nietzschean in his condemnation of Christianity's "sickly air":

> In Christianity we come upon this strange, sickly air. . . . Almost always when Christians have occupied themselves with the future, there one finds punishment, destruction, ruin, eternal suffering, and torment. Luxuriant and dissolute as

their fantasy is in this respect, it becomes feeble in dealing with the happiness of the chosen faithful, which is described as a blissful staring out of large, fixed pupils, or a moist, swimming gaze that prevents any clear seeing. . . .

Now why all this? Certainly not to blame the Christians, but rather to show the acknowledged *de facto* contradiction in the Christian life, in order to warn anyone whose breast is not yet tied up in such spiritual corsetry not to let himself in for it carelessly; that is, in order to protect him from such narrow-chested, asthmatic notions.

But in the autumn of 1835 Kierkegaard was not so much offended with Christianity as simply bored with it; beginning on November 4 all mention of religious topics vanishes from his journal for the next half year.

A petition Kierkegaard made later to the theology faculty claiming that he had temporarily given up theology in favor of philosophy might suggest that he tried to find in philosophy the "truth" he failed to discover in religion. But his journal entries and reading notes of the next four years do not bear this out. They show a run-of-the-mill understanding of some of the great philosophical systems, but no firsthand study of any particular philosopher, with the possible exception of Fichte. Although Kierkegaard used Hegelian concepts and techniques at certain points, his knowledge of Hegel remained superficial. He read some of Hegel's Danish and German disciples and was familiar with a series of second-rank speculative theists, but he seemed to lack interest enough to immerse himself in the work of any single thinker. His attitude toward philosophy is perhaps summarized in his remark of 1837: "Philosophy is life's dry nurse; · it can stay with us but not give milk."

If we are to judge from his reading notes and the receipts of booksellers, Kierkegaard's principal study during this period was along aesthetic lines, with an emphasis on folk literature.

He sought his "truth," it would seem, neither in philosophy nor in religion, but in literature. More important, his whole outlook on life was drawn from the literary sphere. Lacking a better word to describe it, we might call it "magical."

Kierkegaard's love of fairy tales and magic is well known. He owned many volumes of fairy tales—the auction catalogue of his library lists sixty-four—and reading them always gave him great enjoyment. "Why does the soul rest itself," he asked in 1837, "and find such strength in reading fairy tales? When I am tired of everything and 'filled with the days,' a fairy tale is always the renewing bath that does me good." Sometime later he spoke of overhearing one little girl telling another a folk tale. "Then a long way off he saw an old castle," the child said. "I don't believe," Kierkegaard remarked, "that even the greatest poet could produce such an effect as these stirring memories of fairy tales: of 'the castle a long way off,' and the 'then' or 'they went on a long way until,' etc." It was not simple amusement or diversion, however, that Kierkegaard drew from folk literature and tales of magic. For in actual fact, his fundamental project— the idea of finding his own particular truth—was itself a magical notion.

As he put it in the Gilleleje entry: "It is a question of *finding* a truth that is true for me, of *finding* the idea for which I can live and die" (italics added). The idea of finding so personal a "truth" is reminiscent of those folk tales where the hero must find the magic talisman—the key which opens the secret door or the phrase which solves the terrible riddle. This impression is strengthened by Kierkegaard's admission in the same entry of his admiration for "those great men who have found the precious stone for the stake of which they sell all, even their lives." In an entry written three days earlier, he remarked: "Lucky is the man [who] . . . has found what that great philosopher . . . wished but could not find: that Archimedean point from which he could lift the whole world, that point which precisely for that reason must lie outside the world, outside the limitations of time and space."

At just this time Kierkegaard began speaking of life as a riddle. "Life has always interested me most in virtue of reason and freedom," he noted in a June 1, 1835, letter to Lund, "and to clarify and solve the riddle of life has been my constant wish." In a journal entry written a year and a half later he used the same phrase, remarking, "I want to go into a madhouse to see if the profundity of madness will not disclose the solution to life's riddle." Still another aspect of this magical outlook on life is illustrated by a journal entry a few years later in which Kierkegaard quoted Herodotus and noted: "When a person has one thought, but an infinite one, he can be borne through the whole of life, light and flying, like the hyperborean Arabis who, borne by an arrow, traveled round the whole world." '

Young Kierkegaard seems to stand before life as before a secret door whose key is missing. Life is a riddle whose solution must be found. There is a "precious stone" which gives one the peace of mind to risk everything, an "Archimedean point" outside the bounds of time and space, from which one can metaphorically lift the whole world. Behind all these statements lies the presumption that something can be found which will transform life. It is against the background of this essentially magical presumption that Kierkegaard develops the crucial notion of the *Livs-Anskuelse*.

The Danish *Livs-Anskuelse* (like the better-known German *Lebensanschauung*) means an outlook on life, a philosophy of life, a life view. When later in *Either/Or* Kierkegaard chose to define the term as "a conception of life's significance and purpose," it is this more ordinary meaning he had in mind. But such a brief definition gives no inkling that his use of the term originated in his magical thinking. To see this genesis, we must turn to his first published work, a minor essay in literary criticism entitled *From the Papers of One Still Living*.

Published in 1838, it is a sustained assault on Hans Christian Andersen as a novelist. For our purposes, its main interest lies in Kierkegaard's complaint that Andersen lacked a life view to give his work depth and direction:

> A life view is more than an essence or a sum of propositions, held fast in its abstract impersonality; it is more than experience, which as such is always atomized; it is, to wit, the transubstantiation of experience, it is a conquest over all empirical standpoints, an unshakable certainty in oneself. . . . If we are now asked how such a life view can be acquired, then we reply that for him who does not let his life be frittered away, but so far as possible seeks to trace all its particular manifestations back to a source in himself, to such a man there must come the moment in which a curious light suffuses life. This does not in the least demand that one has understood all the possible details (to whose successive understanding, however, one has the key). Yet may I reiterate that there does come this moment when, as Daub remarks, life is understood backwards through the idea.

Kierkegaard's mention here of "the moment in which a curious light suffuses life" is reminiscent of those other magical "moments" described in the last chapter. Achievement of a life view would appear to signal a transformation of consciousness—as Kierkegaard puts it, a "transubstantiation of experience"—and this transformation is nothing less than the reconstitution of life as dream. Having found the life view, one lives in *it*, not in the world. Pursuing this line of thought, Kierkegaard points out in his journal in 1839 that the life view may also serve a protective function:

> There is a life view which is acquired through tears but which is stronger than iron, like the shirt in the fairy tale: "When

with tears she spins the flax, with tears bleaches it, with tears sews the linen into a shirt for me, this shirt will guard me better than any shirt of mail; it is impermeable." But this life view protects only the person who himself has forged it, not, like that other shirt, anyone at all.

Such a notion of a life view which "protects" its owner like a magic shirt of mail, or Siegfried's horny skin of dragon's blood, has its rightful home in the world of magic. It is only the last in a series of names for the "infinite idea" on which one flies through the whole of life; it is the solution to "life's riddle," the "truth which is true for me."

By the summer of 1836, Kierkegaard was referring to Christianity as only one life view among many. In a pregnant remark he compared Christianity with philosophy: "Philosophy's central idea is Mediation—Christianity's, the Paradox." A bit later he contrasted Christianity with paganism, and even compared "religion" (meaning Christianity) with the life views symbolized by Don Juan, Faust, and Ahasuerus: "The three great figures Don Juan, Faust, and the Eternal Jew represent, so to speak, life outside religion in its threefold direction." Here Kierkegaard evidently means by Christianity not a fixed dogma, but rather what he calls the "Christian life view." It is the Christian life as lived from within, as a viable scenario for himself, that comes to interest him.

In other studies from this period he often compared irony and humor. "Humor," he wrote, "is also the joy which has won a victory over the world," and "the humorist, like the wild animal, always walks alone." Irony is "aristocratic," while "humor is reconciled with the whole of existence." It is evident that Kierkegaard was not thinking of irony and humor as different literary rubrics, but rather as exemplifying alternative ways of life. Likewise the "three great figures" mentioned above are not curiosities of folk literature, but representatives of definite life

views. Don Juan personifies the immediate life of sensual experience, Faust the life of doubt, and Ahasuerus the life of
despair. As such it is the life view they represent—or rather, as
Kierkegaard points out elsewhere, the fact that they do represent
a life view—which makes them interesting.

Kierkegaard's consideration of these alternatives, like his toy-
ing with the idea of becoming an actor, is part of a tormented
quest for "surrogates" for his own life, a quest which perhaps
began in September 1834. In a book published that year, the
first volume of a series called *A Collection of Danish and Nor-
wegian Tales of Criminals*, he read a long account of "Peter
Mikkelsen, the so-called master thief." The idea of such a master thief fired his imagination, and on September 17, 1834, he
observed:

> Such a master thief will also boldly and freely admit his crime
> and suffer punishment for it as a man who has become con-
> scious of living for an idea, and precisely because of this he
> acknowledges the reality of the State and does not repudiate
> it. . . . He opposes only abuses. We may well think of him
> as one who might irritate a court of justice, but in this we
> see only a kind of mockery, a declaration in action of a vanity
> that goes with his idea.

In January 1835 he expanded on the notion of the master thief:

> Naturally he may be thought of as equipped with a high degree
> of humor (as much as can be reconciled with his discontent),
> and this will make him satirical. . . .
>
> He is not a man who seeks to lead others astray; on the
> contrary he discourages them from leading such a life. He
> has tasted its bitterness, and only because he lives for an idea
> does he hold out in it. . . . He feels himself tragically mis-
> understood.

In February Kierkegaard described various imaginary scenes involving the master thief—a forest meadow in the moonlight, a

country inn. In March a final note on the master thief contrasted this figure with that of the Italian robber:

> When one compares the master thief with the Italian robber, one can see an essential difference in that the social element predominates in the latter. We cannot think of him except in the center of a robber band, in whose midst he gives himself up to pleasure when the dangers and difficulties of the robbery are overcome. Yet for the master thief something far deeper manifests itself, a certain melancholy trait, an introversion, a dark view of life's circumstances, an inner dissatisfaction.

Although it is by no means clear just what idea the master thief lived for, it is obvious that his personality was modeled on Kierkegaard's. The thief's ambivalent attitude toward established order; his readiness to endure suffering "for an idea"; his awareness of being outside the common run of mankind; his satiric bent and his mockery of everything that might "irritate a court"; above all, his melancholy and introversion—these elements in Kierkegaard's own character were ascribed to the master thief. It is almost as if in writing a script for the thief, Kierkegaard were tailoring a role for himself.

In another entry at this time Kierkegaard suggested that geniuses are unable to read a book properly because "while reading, they develop themselves more than they understand the author." Whether or not Kierkegaard considered himself a genius, in his notes of this period he did seem more often than not to become the character he had been reading about. "The misfortune really is that no sooner has one developed something than one becomes it oneself," he wrote in a draft letter from 1836. "I told you the other day about an idea for a Faust. Now for the first time I feel *it was myself* I was describing. I hardly read or hear about an illness before I have it."

Later in *Repetition* he wrote, "The individual has a host of shadows, all of which resemble him and for the moment have

an equal claim to authenticity." In the literary studies that fill
the pages of his youthful journal he was exploring some of these
shadows, trying out various daydreams as substitutes for his own
life. Yet as we shall see, there was a dark side to this literary
quest. For by continually trying to find "surrogates" for his own
life, by spending so much of his energies in pursuing shadows,
Kierkegaard became, as he himself recognized, "ghostly," an
inhabitant of a "spirit world." His attempt to find the life view
which "protects" ended in failure. As he acknowledged as early
as 1838, it was his reflective self which kept him awake and uneasy, denying him the composure he required in order to accept
and live any of the life views he came across. But precisely in
that failure—in his inability (so to speak) ever to fall asleep—
lay the seeds of his later work.

7

SO I FARED FORTH INTO LIFE

ON August 21, 1835, Kierkegaard received 80 rd. from home to pay his bill at the Gilleleje Inn, and on the 24th he returned to Copenhagen. The best summary of the next three years comes from his own pen:

> So I fared forth into life—initiated into all possible enjoyment ·
> yet never really enjoying, but rather (this was my single
> pleasure with respect to the pain of melancholy) working to
> produce the appearance that I enjoyed. I was acquainted with
> all sorts of people, yet it never crossed my mind that in any of
> them I had a confidant, and it most certainly never occurred
> to any of them that he was my confidant. That is to say, I was
> constrained to be and remained an observer. As observer and
> spirit I was extraordinarily enriched by experience; I was able
> to view close at hand the sum total of pleasures, passions,
> moods, feelings, etc.; I got training in seeing a man through
> and through as well as in imitating him. My imagination and
> dialectic always had material to work with, and also had time
> enough, free from all bustle, to be idle. For long periods I was
> busy with nothing but dialectical exercises with an addition of
> fantasy, trying out my mind as one tunes an instrument—but
> I was not really living. I was tumbled about in life, tempted
> by the most various things, even by delusions, and alas! also
> by the path of perdition. So I was in my twenty-fifth year [SK
> turned twenty-five on May 5, 1838], to myself an enigmatically
> developed and extraordinary possibility whose significance

and purpose I did not understand, in spite of the most eminent
reflection which, if possible, understood everything. . . . In
the proper sense of the word I had not lived, except in the
character of spirit; a man I had never been, and child or
youth even less.

Of the enjoyments that were not really enjoyed, scarcely a
trace survives in Kierkegaard's journal. What did survive were
the bills:

12 Oct. 1837	235 rd.	Tea Shop
17 Oct. 1837	44 rd.	Madame Frey's Tobacco Shop
14 Nov. 1837	280 rd.	Tailor Kunitzer
7 Dec. 1837	350 rd.	Reitzel's Bookshop
27 Dec. 1837	31 rd.	Salomon's Bookshop

Credit was no problem, since it was well known that the Kierkegaard family had money and that ultimately the father would
make good any debts. And so he did. In the father's account
book is a receipt in Søren's handwriting from January 14, 1838,
for the last payment of a sum of 1,262 rd. ($8,800 in present
buying power). It is accompanied by a note: "In this way my
father has helped me out of financial embarrassment, for which
I give him my thanks."

Until September 1, 1837, Kierkegaard lived at home, and it
is unclear just what funds his father gave him. We do know
that he had to borrow small sums from various people: 50 rd.
from a fellow student named Agerskov; 60 rd. from Herr Sager
in 1836; 50 rd. from Reitzel's Bookshop in the same year. Peter
Christian's account book shows that in October 1836 Søren borrowed a single rigsdaler from him; true to form, Peter Christian
did not keep the loan a secret, but on the same day asked for
reimbursement from their father. This constant shortage of cash
must have been embarrassing and occasionally inconvenient—in
November 1836, for example, the Student Union informed Søren
that if he didn't pay his debts he would be denied entrance.

His daily four cigars made frequent trips to Madame Frey's necessary, and his voracious reading kept the books flowing in from Reitzel's. As a rich man's son, he was expected to do more than his share of picking up the check at cafés around town. One of his acquaintances was the chief police clerk Jørgen Jørgensen who, according to a contemporary, "went out every morning without a cent in his pocket, without knowing how he would eat or drink, but came home every evening well-fed and well-drunk. He lived on other people's checks, smoked their cigars, and drank their wine." Jørgensen was at least ten years older than Kierkegaard, a ruddy-complexioned man with a sauntering gait, whose years of drinking showed in his bloodshot eyes. He was a well-known Copenhagen character, noted as a wit and raconteur, and Kierkegaard's acquaintance with him lasted many years. In 1840 he lent Jørgensen 50 rd. (which was never repaid), and he mentioned the police clerk in his journal as late as 1847. On the night of April 18, 1836, he described Jørgensen's drunken conversation:

> By watching the corners of his mouth one could see that he was drunk. He thought that poetry was really something secondary, an excrescence, and praised philosophy. He praised memory, envied me my youth, and talked of the falling leaves and the whistling, howling wind. "Half of life is spent living it, the other half repenting it, and I am fast entering upon the latter."

Another acquaintance was the philosopher Poul Møller, now in his early forties, who had taught Kierkegaard moral philosophy at the university. From 1836 to 1838 Møller lived at Nytorv 17 on the south side of the square, separated from the Kierkegaard home only by the city hall and courts building; and professor and student met often on the way to and from the university (just a block to the north) and at various university functions. In 1836 both were present at the dissertation defense

of Frederik Lange—Kierkegaard as a spectator and Møller as an
ex officio opponent. Møller had jotted his questions on small
pieces of paper and slipped them into his copy of the dissertation. At one point the notes fell out and the audience was much
amused to see a professor of philosophy crawling around on the
floor to retrieve them. Møller introduced each of his questions
with the phrase *"Graviter vituperandum est"* (it must seriously
be objected), and as soon as Lange answered, he said very
pleasantly *"Concedo"* (I concede) and went on to the next note.
After an unusually short period of questioning, Møller excused
himself, saying that the press of time did not permit him to
continue the interesting discussion. On his way out he passed
Kierkegaard among the spectators and said in a half whisper:
"Shall we go down to Pleisch's?"

The combination of living at home with Peter Christian and
his father and never having enough cash finally forced Søren to
a showdown in July 1837. He entered a receipt for 20 rd. in his
father's account book with the notation: "Since from the coming
first of September 1837 I will leave my father's house and cease
to be a participant in his household, he has promised me 500
rd./year for my subsistence." This was not an enormous sum,
but Søren had also accepted Michael Nielsen's offer of a job
teaching Latin at the Borgerdydskole. These two sources of income, together with his father's payment of his debts, con-
siderably eased Søren's financial predicament.

He moved only three blocks away, to a small flat at Løvstræde
128. Just across the street lived his friend P. E. Lind, and on the
adjoining tree-shaded square his recent tutor, H. L. Martensen.
On the next street over, Købmagergade, were Christian Lund,
Søren's brother-in-law, and the large household of Michael
Andersen Kierkegaard.

Called "young Michael" to distinguish him from Søren's
father, this cousin was now over sixty years old and a wealthy

man. When he died in 1867 at the age of ninety-one he left an
estate valued at 295,000 rd. (about 2 million dollars). His dis-
tinguishing characteristic was a penchant for composing terrible
occasional verse, which he recited with gusto. He had two children—Julie (married in 1835) and Hans Peter (a cripple, lame
in one side, but otherwise healthy)—and a household which included the widow and children of another kinsman, A. A. Kierkegaard. Among these children was Niels Christian Kierkegaard, who in 1838 drew a well-known but highly idealized
portrait of Søren.

Søren often visited in this jolly home. Peter Christian sometimes accompanied him, but the elder brother was not comfortable with the card games that were the regular entertainment
there. Søren, on the other hand, enjoyed them enormously and
played them with all the seriousness customary in that household. They played "Boston" and often used the variation where
three people are dealt seventeen cards and the fourth person
only one. Although the fourth person's position was considered
disadvantageous, Søren maintained that it "was quite the best
imaginable, and that he wished always to be the fourth man."
He liked to startle the family with such paradoxes and once declared "with the most serious face in the world, that he considered the old primer we used in our childhood to be one of the
most interesting books in the world. He said he still read it
often and got much profit from it."

It was in this home that Hans Brøchner first met Søren in the
fall of 1836:

> I saw Søren Kierkegaard without knowing who he was; I was
> told only that he was Dr. Kierkegaard's brother. He spoke very
> little that evening, but obviously was observing everything
> closely. The only definite impression I got was of his outward
> appearance, and this rather amused me. He was twenty-three
> then, and there was something unruly in his whole appearance.

He had a remarkable coiffure; his hair was brushed up into a tufted coxcomb almost six inches above his forehead, and he looked disheveled in consequence. I got the impression, without quite knowing why, that he was a shop assistant—perhaps because the family were tradespeople—and from his odd appearance I immediately jumped to the conclusion that he must be a draper's assistant.

During the following year Brøchner saw him several times in the evening at restaurants. "I can remember," Brøchner later wrote, "being surprised at the luxury of the meals Søren Kierkegaard ordered, with half a bottle of wine and the like, while I myself occasionally had a 'half beef.' " Kierkegaard was very friendly to Brøchner, who was seven years his junior, and lent him a book on the German romantics, Eichendorff's *Poets and Their Companions*. Brøchner wrote:

> I remember taking it back to him two weeks later, excusing myself for keeping it so long (I was a passionate student of theology at the time). To my surprise he countered by asking me if I had finished it *already*. He evidently could see with his sharp glance that "No" hovered on my tongue, and he enjoyed embarrassing me so roundly—which on this occasion was all too easy. I blushed a little, and that sight always attracted him in "the young man" [a reference to a character in Kierkegaard's *Stages on Life's Way*].
>
> Two things stand out in my memory from the visit to his home when he lent me the book. One is my astonishment at his library, which was impressively large. The other was an eccentricity of Kierkegaard's: He was going out again after lending me the book, and when he blew out a candle as we were leaving, he explained that he always did this with care and standing well away from it, because candle smoke was dangerous to inhale and might injure his chest.

Though hypochondriacal in itself, this foible seems to have arisen from a legitimate concern for a chest that was weak and especially vulnerable to infection. His brother-in-law Ferdinand Lund mentioned in a letter of April 2, 1841, that Kierkegaard's "chest has been attacked, and he has *again* begun to spit blood" (italics added). Earlier, Kierkegaard wrote in his journal in the spring of 1838: "For me everything is 'wandering': wandering thoughts—wandering rheumatism." Although "wandering rheumatism" is also a symptom of tuberculosis, the evidence is much too slim to sustain the conclusion that Kierkegaard suffered from this disease. The only certainty is that his health, as always, was delicate, and that he was aware of it.

The amusement which Kierkegaard seemed to enjoy above all others in these years was the theater. Then as now, the Royal Theater was the center of Copenhagen's musical and dramatic life. During the season, which lasted from September to June, it was the gathering place not only for businessmen and their wives, army officers, and the royal family, but also for a small clique of intellectuals and music and drama enthusiasts. Students, critics, newspapermen, officials, teachers, writers, actors, and musicians took their seats nightly in the part of the theater adjacent to the royal box called the "ordinary royal parterre." They chose this section because it was relatively inexpensive and barred to women, and they were certain to meet here other like-minded souls with whom they could discuss the performance in the intermissions. It was in this sophisticated group—which included such men as Hans Christian Andersen, J. H. Lorck, Henrik Hertz, H. P. Holst, Peter Rørdam, F. C. Sibbern, I. A. Damkjer, and F. J. Hansen—that Kierkegaard could usually be found. When after a performance of Weyse's *The Banquet at Kenilworth* in March 1836 this group decided to set up the Music Union, Kierkegaard was invited to take part in writing the bylaws. According to Angul Hammerich's history of the Music Union, Kierkegaard accepted a glass of punch and began writing the first draft. Unfortunately, with his dialectical turn of mind he saw so many difficulties in every concrete proposal that the entire group left the meeting shaking their heads and thoroughly confused.

Kierkegaard loved the theater because beyond the footlights he found dramatizations of the very roles which he was imaginatively exploring on his own. In 1836 he saw *Don Giovanni* for the first time. Later he wrote in his journal: "In a way I can say of *Don Giovanni* what Donna Elvira says to him: 'Thou murderer of my happiness.' For in truth this play has so diabolically grasped me that I can never forget it; this piece drove me, like Elvira, out of the still night of the Cloister." In another entry dated Thursday afternoon, January 26, 1837, he noted: "This evening for the first time I shall see *The Magic Flute*, which seems to me to bear a significant relation to Don Juan and to supply the link between him and the Page in *Figaro*." The Royal Theater was not only the place where Kierkegaard could see some of the characters that most interested him brought to life, but in itself was a set piece offering glamour, rustling silks, and occasional flirtations: "The 30th of November [1836] when they gave *The Two Days*, the encounter with an unknown but beautiful woman (she spoke German) who was alone in the parquette with a little brother—she understood the music."

Kierkegaard's statement that although he was acquainted with all sorts of people, he never had a confidant is borne out by his contemporaries. Vilhelm Birkedal said that when they met on the street, Kierkegaard would take his arm (as was his custom with everyone) and walk along companionably. "But I had the feeling," Birkedal went on, "that he wanted to pump me and experiment with me psychologically . . . I was afraid of having any deeper dealings with SK than were necessary when I met him. I did not want to be pumped." Holger Rørdam, an eight-year-old boy when Kierkegaard used to visit in the Rørdam home, recalled "his animated and noisy arguments, his sharply upthrust hair, . . . and the fact that he made fun of my Jutland dialect." J. A. Ostermann said that Kierkegaard at this time "was usually in the company of someone or other, but most of these people stood equally close and equally far from him."

In November 1835, Ostermann and Kierkegaard carried on a debate of sorts at the Student Union. Ostermann gave an address on "Our Newest Journalistic Literature," and two weeks later Kierkegaard replied with a speech entitled, "Our Journalistic Literature." This rebuttal was sharp in tone and well documented in its polemic against the liberal press, which had claimed responsibility for the recent political reforms culminating in the establishment of provincial advisory councils. Kierkegaard showed convincingly that this claim was empty, that the reforms had been made on the initiative of the government, and that up until 1833 the press had been singularly apolitical, occupying itself with aesthetic and literary questions. Ostermann was in the audience during Kierkegaard's speech but chose not to reply. He wrote later that he knew his opponent was not actually concerned with politics or the question at issue, but had only used the occasion to show off "his glittering dialectic and wit." "As one truly interested in politics," Ostermann continued petulantly, "I had no wish to involve myself with an opponent whom I knew was only slightly interested in the reality of the topic."

Kierkegaard continued his attack the following spring in three articles for J. L. Heiberg's *Flying Post*. Just as he ended his literary career twenty years later as a polemicist, so now he began it as one, teasing wittily *Copenhagen Post, Fatherland*, and Orla Lehmann, the leader of the liberal clique at the Student Union. These pieces—especially the first—established Kierkegaard's reputation among the literati of Copenhagen. The first two appeared under the anonym "B," and many thought the first article so brilliant that it must have been written by Heiberg himself; Poul Møller even ran after Heiberg in the

street to congratulate him. Peter Rørdam wrote: "In the Student
Union there has been a change: their chief and leader, Lehmann, totally beaten, and with him the paper for which he used
to write—*Copenhagen Post.* The victor is the young Kierkegaard, who writes in the *Flying Post* under the mark 'B.' " Rørdam's own prejudices influenced his judgment, however, for he
exaggerated the degree of Kierkegaard's victory. These are
biting, witty articles but they lack the thorough documentation
of Kierkegaard's Student Union speech the previous fall. More
important, they lack a single focus and central issue. Orla Lehmann subsequently asked Kierkegaard in print what the articles
were about; Kierkegaard's reply glittered with sarcastic sallies
but shed no more light on their central point.

It was their wit which attracted attention and brought Kierkegaard notice in the small circle of intellectuals and literary
people who frequented the home of J. L. Heiberg and his pretty
actress wife, Johanne Luise. Heiberg wrote him on March 16
sending extra copies of the second article and thanking him
enthusiastically for his work. Within a month or two Kierkegaard became a regular guest at their home in the evenings. On
June 4 he attended a special *soirée*, at which Poul Møller and
Henrik Hertz were also present. The wine flowed, witty conversation bubbled from every corner, and at the center of the merri-
ment was Kierkegaard—sparkling, acerbic, enormously witty.
After the party he returned to the Nytorv town house, where he
was still living, climbed the darkened steps to his room, and
wrote in his journal:

> I have just now come from a party where I was its life and
> soul; witticisms streamed from my lips, everyone laughed and
> admired me, but I went away—yes, the dash should be as long
> as the radius of the earth's orbit ————————————
>
> ——————————and wanted to shoot myself.

8

SOMETHING GHOSTLY
ABOUT ME

THE most important part of the story of these three years is not conveyed by the bills Kierkegaard ran up, the parties and plays he attended, the acquaintances he made. He has already told us that these things occupied only the foreground of his life and that this foreground hardly touched him—"in the proper sense of the word I had not lived." It is this feeling of a life unlived, of an experience muted by reflection and volatilized in imagination, that lay at the center of Kierkegaard's life both during these years and afterward.

When Kierkegaard began turning out books at a great rate in the early 1840's he employed a copyist to prepare his manuscripts for the printer. This man, Israel Levin, often spent several days at a time in Kierkegaard's quarters copying manuscripts, talking with his employer, and even eating with him. Their periods of intimacy gave Levin the chance to observe Kierkegaard in the privacy of his home, a place where many of the public masks fell off. What struck Levin most was the almost demonic power of Kierkegaard's imagination:

> The conception was enough for him. He could poeticize himself into any existence; thus for a week he lived only to think and feel like a miser and did so with utmost consistency, although he spent money as usual. Once he admitted that he had

an enormous desire to commit a real theft, then live with his bad conscience, in fear of being found out. Thus he unburdened himself in dreams and poetic pictures and with his articulateness and his almost demonic imagination, it was surprising the effects he could produce. . . .

We talked about Andersen one evening in Frederiksberg Gardens: "Andersen has no idea what fairy tales are." And then he produced in an instant six or seven fairy tales, so that I became almost uncomfortable. So vivid was his imagination, it was as if the pictures were before his eyes. It was as if he lived in a spirit world.

Later Kierkegaard used the term spirit world (*Aande-Verden*) to describe himself:

> There is . . . something ghostly about me, something which makes it impossible for anyone to put up with me who has to be with me day in and day out and so sustain a real relation to me. Of course in the light *surtout* in which I usually show myself, it's all quite different. But at home, it should be noted, fundamentally I live in a spirit world.

The metaphor of the ghost who inhabits a spirit world is particularly apt to characterize the personality we come to know in the early *Papers*, for like a ghost Kierkegaard often seems so free-floating as to lack a body. In reading his journal we get no impression of a man rooted in the world through his body—involved in desire, or fearful of pain and death. "I was always, always outside myself," he remarked in 1849, and by this meant he was always outside his body. His body was for him only an object among objects, something "out there" which now and then caused him discomfort or inconvenience. Much later he would come to view his weak body as the necessary condition for what he called "a true spiritual life," but now he could only look on it as an impediment: "Just as the conquering general whose horse has been shot out from under him calls for a new horse, oh! that my conquering spirit might call—a new horse, a new body!" His thin legs and birdlike torso gave him an appearance of angularity, and this was accentuated by his manner of walking. Brøchner describes his crabbed gait, his zigzag progression down the street that forced his companion first into the gutter and next into the window wells of the adjacent buildings. All in all Kierkegaard, as he himself knew, had no vestige of bodily grace or beauty: "What I properly lack is the body and all the presuppositions that go with it."

Since the "spirit world" was not coextensive with Copenhagen of the 1830's, it was necessary for Kierkegaard to construct a persona to carry on transactions with that outward sphere, to entertain acquaintances with witty ripostes, write similarly witty articles, attend lectures, sit in cafés, and have commonplace conversations at the dinner table with his father and brother. But he was only playing a part; it was all a mask, a pretense. "I am a two-faced Janus," he said in 1837; "with the one face I laugh, with the other I weep." In the same year he spoke of this playacting as a kind of revenge: "Everyone takes his revenge on the world. Mine consists of bearing my care and sorrow shut deep within me, while my laughter entertains the crowd." He seemed to seek out company, although he never opened himself to anyone. He equivocated, dodged, never said quite what he meant. As Levin pointed out, "He talked a lot about double reflection; all his own speech was more than seven-doubled reflection." And so when Kierkegaard complained in February 1836, "People understand me so little, that they do not even once understand my complaints, that they do not understand me," we do not take him seriously—the last thing in the world he wanted was to be really understood. He was, he tells us, "always clad in the costume of my deceit." "Incognito is my element . . . the incommensurable sphere . . . wherein I can move freely."

In withdrawing behind his "incognito" he made sure that every act and every perception would be the act or perception of a false self. His real self—his "spirit"—did not inhabit either his acts or his perceptions; his acts were strained and unspontaneous and his perceptions equally distant, at a second remove.

An acquaintance once remarked that the studied character of Kierkegaard's conversation gave the impression that the words were all prepared in advance. And Meyer Goldschmidt described an incident in the summer of 1838 while he and Kierkegaard were walking back from Frederiksberg engrossed in literary talk. "There was a long pause," Goldschmidt said, "and then all at once he gave a little jump and tapped himself on the leg with his Spanish walking stick." As Goldschmidt recalled, there was something forced and artificial about this seemingly spontaneous gesture:

> There was something sprightly about it, but it was altogether different from the sprightliness one sees elsewhere in the world. The movement was peculiar and almost painful to me. . . . It was as if this learned, slender man wanted to enter into the joy of life, but either could not or must not.

In the shadows of Goldschmidt's description we can almost hear Kierkegaard whisper to himself: "Now he takes a little jump, tapping his leg debonairly." He cannot enter into Goldschmidt's world (the so-called joy of life) because he has interposed a screen of consciousness between his real self and the persona which acts in that world. The persona does something; he criticizes what it does. The persona talks; he observes what it says and what others say to it. Like the Baudelaire of Sartre's description: "He was the man who never forgot himself. He watched himself see; he watched in order to see himself watch; it was his own consciousness . . . that he contemplated. He saw things only through this consciousness; they were paler, smaller, and less touching, as though seen through an eyeglass." "Death and hell," Kierkegaard wrote in 1836, "I can abstract from every-thing but *not from* myself; I cannot forget myself even when I'm asleep."

Nor is it just his actions which were forced, doubly reflected; his perception itself seemed to lack spontaneity. He often ap-peared to be mixing perception and recollection as when, riding in a coach through the countryside, he saw a young farm girl and scribbled in his travel diary: "Greetings to you, village beauty! . . . Do but look straight at me, so that I do not entirely forget you." Earlier in the diary he exclaimed: "Greetings to you, mighty Nature, with your fleeting beauty. It is not you I desire, it is the memory of you." Hans Brøchner recalled how Kierkegaard would customarily stop at the entrance to Freder-iksberg Gardens to "inhale the scent of the flowers for a few moments, and then take away the memory of this 'moment' with him." When they later met in Berlin, Brøchner noticed that Kierkegaard did the same thing, substituting a flower-bordered nook in the *Tiergarten* for the entrance to Frederiksberg Gar-dens. It often seems as if Kierkegaard were trying to live the present as if it were the past, trying to perceive the world as if he were remembering it. Standing before these flowers which are present to his senses, their scent becomes for an instant a re-membered scent. For a time too brief to measure they lose their otherness as one of the "bad infinity's mass products" and for an instant absorb the nuance of image. In various ways Kierke-gaard thus attempted to experience the world *as if it were an image*. This intention, in a sense the axial one of his life, can only be understood against the background of his awareness of existence as "infected."

Throughout his life Kierkegaard denigrated as petty and com-monplace everything that made the world worldly. "It is those little things which embitter life so," he wrote in 1837. "I can

gladly push on against a storm until the blood is ready to burst
out of me, but the wind that blows a bit of dust into my eye
can make me so angry that I stamp my feet. Those little things
—just as a person would carry out a great work, and then a fly
settles on his nose." Ten years later he complained, "How un-
suited I am to practical affairs. . . . My ideality suffers indescribably under the confusion, inaccuracy, and nonsense which is the
secret of practical life." Yet it is not simply that the world is
filled with petty annoyances. For at the most primitive level of
Kierkegaard's awareness of the world, there is a fundamental
estrangement, a primordial sense that it is alien, infected: "The
whole of existence makes me anxious, from the smallest fly to
the mystery of the Incarnation: everything is unintelligible to
me, most of all myself; the whole of existence is infected for
me."

Driven by his uneasiness in this infected world, Kierkegaard
set out to explore the inner being that suffered so acutely in its
alien surroundings. To him the terrain of subjectivity was no
less infinite, no less powerful or self-contradictory, than the
outer world that tormented him. In his later work he sought to
explore this terrrain exhaustively. But everything has its price,
and for Kierkegaard the price was a progressively attenuated
relation to his surroundings.

By living in the world only through a persona, he risked the
deadening of spontaneity and vitality at its root; both action
and perception were deflected into forced and artificial modes.
More than this, the very artificiality of the persona came to
haunt him. It was as if he himself had become a cliché, as if his
speech were made up solely of quotations. In 1837 he wrote:

> At times I see myself encircled by a dreadful cliché-like figure
> —I would describe it as the compendium of a man—a kind
> of sum of feelings and concepts—a long thin man whom

nature (as it were) has stopped at every turn. He should have
long arms; but look, from shoulder to elbow he is immensely
long and from elbow to hand so very short; the same is true
of his fingers, of his face—and every speech begins with such
a promise that, full of hope, one sets up a terrific standard;
and see, it ends in nothing.

Yet this compendium of a man was surely himself, the image he
had borne and nurtured. As he admitted: "While I declaim
against others for not studying sources but compendia, I live
myself as a compendium. While I can win every argument, I
have on my back a ghost of my own imagination that I can't
argue away." There is in this journal entry the hint of a theme
that sounds through other entries from these years—the intimate combination of great power and impotence, of unlimited
freedom and slavery. By choosing to accept the world only
insofar as it has become image, Kierkegaard has assured himself omnipotence and unconditional freedom—in imagination.
If he so chooses, he can be anyone, do anything, possess everything. But all on one condition—that he do it in imagination;
hence the content of his being, doing, and having remain imaginary:

> I have the courage to doubt, I believe everything; I have the
> courage to fight, I repudiate everything; but I have not the
> courage to know something, not the courage to possess, to own
> something. Most people complain that the world is so prosaic,
> that things don't happen in life as they do in novels, where
> the lovers are so lucky. I complain that it is not in life as in a
> novel, where one has hardhearted fathers to struggle against,
> maiden's bowers to storm, and convent walls to scale. I have
> only the pale, bloodless, hard-lived midnight shapes to strug-
> gle with, shapes to which I myself give life and existence.

He is free and omnipotent—in the abstract. Like his creation
Johannes the Seducer: "He was not unequal to the pressure of

reality; he was not too weak to bear it, not at all, he was too strong; but this strength was really a sickness."

One aspect of this "sickness" was his growing disinclination to distinguish between himself and some of his imaginary creations. Not only the self-portrait embodied in his picture of the master thief but also his identification with Faust point in this direction. His remark, "The misfortune really is that no sooner has one developed something than one becomes it oneself," suggests that his own personality has become so chameleon-like as to take on the coloring of any idea he entertained. There is also evidence in the journal entries of this period of something resembling the disintegration of personality. In the spring of 1836 Kierkegaard's consciousness seemed to be ripping itself apart:

> The one thought succeeds the other; just as it is thought and I will write it down, there is a new one—hold it, grasp it— Madness—Insanity! . . .

> When I notice that my head is beginning to act up—the poet ought to have what the Northmen expected in heaven, a wild boar from which one could always carve a slice and which always grew back again.
> Shoot a bullet in his head, snip, snap, snout, so my tale is out; tip, tap, tin and another can begin.

> A man walked along thinking about suicide; at that very moment a slate fell and killed him and he died with the words: God be praised.

Yet perhaps the most important clue to what was happening to Kierkegaard's awareness of self is found in an entry of a very different type from the same period: "Strange vibrations soon round off the past for me in a poetic intuition, and then it seems most interesting to me—but soon I am disillusioned, precisely because (to use a line from *The Gold Cross*) the idea comes from no one but myself." His self has become ubiquitous;

wherever he turns he finds it. But he also discovers the horror of the solipsist at being able no longer to distinguish between true and false emotions, actual memories and imaginative reconstructions. His anguished cries about his "terrible" suffering—his "melancholy" and "introversion"—testify to the hardships and dangers of his chosen course. Not the least of these is that a life of infinite self-reflection and refraction comes not only to seem wholly artificial but even to have an air of duplicity about it, and to arrive at the phantasmal in the end.

Equally ironic and perhaps even more pathetic is a second consequence of his choice. Kierkegaard had turned inward into what he once called his "secret closet" in order to find there what was lacking in the world. Life out "there" was petty and commonplace; in "here" it would become rich and full. Flawed by none of the minor annoyances, the importunate demands, the mundane resistances that populated the world out there, this world would refresh and excite. It would be incomparably rich, incomparably full—its air would carry the seductive scent of ambrosia.

Instead of becoming rich and full, however, his interior life became poor and empty. At this time he began speaking of his consciousness as "far too roomy," as "so large that it hangs loose about me." A bit later he remarked, "My head is as dead and empty as a theater after the performance is over." With this growing impoverishment there came too a sense of ennui, even of paralysis. "Sadly my life is all too much in the subjunctive mood," he wrote on October 7, 1837. "Would to God that I had some indicative power," and on a loose sheet of paper from the same year: "I don't feel like doing anything; I don't feel like walking—it tires me out; I don't feel like lying down; for either I should lie down for a long time (and I don't feel like doing that), or I should get up again right away, and I don't feel at all like doing that." This at the age of twenty-four.

Boredom, emptiness, and enervation became his daily companions. He came to feel at the heart of his existence a gradual deadening, the fruit of his inability to ever really *be* in any given moment. Bonded only to the creatures of his imagination, his life lost its sense of personal duration. Time for him slowed and stopped; it backed up and became stagnant, as a stream does behind a dam.

> And when one has lived a half-score years in that dreadful still life, so miserable and thin a life, that only so much cream has risen to its top as can be swallowed in a single moment without appearing gluttonous. The beat of that life is too slow for me to march to.
>
> It is frightful the way I have to purchase every day, every hour—and the price is so variable.
>
> At the present time I live like a chess piece of which the opponent says: that piece cannot be moved—as an idle on-looker, for my time is not yet come.

With the cessation of time there came too a congealing of the life flow, the onset of winter and of death. At the age of twenty-five Kierkegaard said he wished to write for a reader "who like me is dead," and later during his engagement he remarked that Regine was "as young as a child" while he was "as old as a very old man." The frost of a Scandinavian winter had entered his soul. "All the flowers of my heart," he wrote, "turn to ice flowers."

As in Ronald Laing's description of the schizoid individual, Kierkegaard begins by feeling "outside the life going on *there,* which he affects to despise as petty and commonplace, compared to the richness he has *here,* inside himself." But then, ironically, the inversion is made, the autistic, intraindividual world that was to be so rich is revealed as essentially impoverished. Again as if following Laing's scenario, Kierkegaard next "longed to get *inside* life again, or to put it another way, to get life inside him."

Kierkegaard's life, in fact, was not a mere succession of ironies, but rather a profoundly dialectical progression. He began by attempting to re-create himself in a character of his own making, thereby hoping to encounter himself. But as we have seen, this attempt to create substance out of the stuff of literature failed utterly, and he was left with a ghostly self inhabiting a spirit world. He rehearsed a similar movement in his relation to the world. Finding it infected, flawed by the little things, he rejected it—only to attempt its reapprehension as image. There were times when the world for him was lit up with value, when perception had become a kind of recollection, when one got "the same mood as from a grandiose poem." It was this transformation of experience that he sought and never stopped seeking. Yet what he finally achieved was something far different—not the richness of the world of imagination, but its essential poverty. Thus he ends, not by singing the praises of the world he has constructed, but by lamenting "the pale, bloodless, hard-lived midnight shapes . . . to which I myself give life and existence."

Rudolph Friedmann caught something of this dry and fatal air, something of the dark beauty of Kierkegaard's life, when he wrote:

> With Kierkegaard there was an indivisible union between name ["churchyard" or "cemetery" in Danish] and personality. The black drapery of introversion, the fatal perfume of white funeral roses, and the loneliness of the heaths of Jutland, clung to him. Only those who have been chosen for loneliness can understand loneliness, the autistic wandering through the streets, the flowering of the personality that takes place amidst dark avenues of the night alone and without friends, the caressing of the cold windows of life with passionate and hopeless, withdrawn lips.

Friedmann has caught something startlingly true about Kierkegaard, a brief glint off the dark side of the Kierkegaardian moon. For Kierkegaard himself admitted in 1848: "I have in my melancholy yet loved the world, for I have loved my melancholy," and later the same year, in recollecting an earlier love affair: "I was unhappy in my love; but I cannot think of myself as happy unless I were to become another person. But I was blissful in my unhappiness. . . . There is a melancholy in everything in my life, but also again indescribable bliss." He complained perpetually of his melancholy and his introversion, yet in actual fact he loved his melancholy and willed his introversion.

9

THE LONGEST
PARENTHESIS

PETER Christian did his courting correctly and with deliberation —first asking his father for an increased allowance, then speaking to the girl's mother, and only last asking the girl. Her name was Marie Boisen, and her father, before his death, had been Bishop of Lolland. She was not a pretty girl (but not plain either), and she had a pleasant disposition and a lovely singing voice. They married in October 1836, and immediately moved into Nytorv No. 2 with old Michael and Søren. Much later, Peter Christian remembered how Marie's entry into the old house had brought "a mild sunlight up over our old father." On Marie's side, it would seem there were more shadows than sunlight; she spoke in a letter to her mother on New Year's Eve 1836 of how "still and lonely" Christmas had been. Even for old Michael the period of sunlight was short-lived. For the girl was delicate and vulnerable to every cold and infection that came in range. On July 1 of the following year, just as summer was blossoming in northern Europe, she took to her bed.

At first it seemed no more serious than any of the other fevers that had plagued her during the winter and spring. But within a few days it took a more serious turn, and the doctor diagnosed it as a kind of gastric fever that might be typhus. Without consulting Peter Christian his father had the family lawyer draw up wills, which both Marie and Peter Christian signed on July 5. Her fever and chills grew worse, and she was sometimes lucid, more often delirious. Toward the end her young voice, clear and strong, could be heard singing old hymns through the walls and darkened passageways of the house. She died on the morning of July 18, 1837, and was buried four days later. Just as he had arranged her will, Michael Pedersen Kierkegaard arranged and paid for her ample, if not ostentatious, funeral.

Just what effect her death had on Søren is unknown. During these years he was convinced that the many deaths in the Kierkegaard family were the product of a curse that would doom all the children to die before the patriarch, old Michael. Marie's demise, less than nine months after her wedding, must have strengthened this conviction. But his journal mentions neither her nor her death, whereas it does take somber note of the death next spring of his friend and teacher, Poul Møller.

Møller had a very special relationship with Kierkegaard. Not only had he taught the young man moral philosophy in his first year at the university, but he also seemed to have a fundamental understanding of Kierkegaard's personality and predicament. Like his young friend, Møller combined a witty exterior with an inner melancholy. As a contemporary recalled, "It always struck me that Poul Møller was never happy, that his gaiety was really the effect of repressed pain." The teacher and former pupil traveled in the same literary circles, and at one party (possibly the Heiberg *soirée* of June 1836) Møller said sharply to Kierkegaard: "You are so polemical through and through that it's just terrible!" Kierkegaard remembered the remark, mentioning it twice in his journal, and in 1844 he dedicated *The Concept of Dread* to Møller, who had died in 1838. In a draft of the dedication he referred to him as "my youth's enthusiasm, my beginning's *confidant,* mighty trumpet of my awakening, my departed friend."

Two weeks after Møller's death, Kierkegaard wrote in his journal:

April
> Such a long period has gone by in which I have not been able to concentrate upon the slightest thing—I'll now try to get going again.
> Poul Møller is dead.

That evening, a Sunday, he went to the Royal Theater to hear Nicolai Peter Nielsen recite Møller's long poem, *Rejoice over Denmark*. The next morning he wrote: "I . . . was especially moved by the words 'remember the traveler far away.' Yes, now he is far away—but I at least shall still remember him."

In that spring and summer of 1838 Kierkegaard was writing a long review of Hans Christian Andersen's latest novel, *Only a Fiddler*. Meeting Andersen on the street, he led him to believe that the review would be favorable. But when it finally appeared it turned out to be a spirited attack on the novelist's lack of a life view and on his conception of the poetic genius as a delicate flower. "The genius is not a candle that the wind blows out," Kierkegaard wrote, "but a fire that the storm only makes burn brighter."

Kierkegaard's antipathy to Andersen is difficult to understand, and this review provides no real clue to its basis. Most likely he was put off by Andersen's sentimentality, his easy acceptance of a bourgeois world that Kierkegaard was already finding abrasive. The two men occasionally nodded to each other in the street, but each (perhaps recognizing the chasm that separated their sensibilities) kept his distance. Like independent planets these two luminaries of Danish literature followed their own orbits, unmindful of each other.

Kierkegaard had hoped to follow up his small critical success of the year before by having Heiberg publish the Andersen review in his journal, *Perseus*. But Heiberg had serious reserva-

tions about its highly complicated, Latinized style, and Kierkegaard finally had to publish it at his own expense as a slim
book bearing the title *From the Papers of One Still Living.*
According to Andersen's memoirs, the book was so confusing
and difficult to read that Copenhagen wits claimed only two
people had read it—Andersen and Kierkegaard himself.

During these months Kierkegaard's health was uncertain at
best. On May 19 in an uncharacteristic state of euphoria, he
wrote in his journal: "There is an *indescribable* joy which glows
through us as unaccountably as the apostle's outburst is unexpected . . . a gust of the tradewind which blows from the Groves
of Mamre to the eternal habitations." Commentators have seen
in this entry everything from a religious experience to the manic
phase of a manic-depressive psychosis. Jørgensen suggests that
for a short time Kierkegaard's chronically bad chest had made
him febrile. Already in 1835 Søren had remarked on the odd
euphoria associated with what was then called "consumption"—
"the consumptive feels best, just when it is worst." More to the
point, Peter Christian noted in his diary at this time that his
brother had suffered a relapse and was quite weak. Whatever
the cause, Kierkegaard's exalted state did not last and his journal
resumed its leaden pace and melancholic tone.

Still ostensibly reading for his exam in theology, he was
living in his flat on Løvstræde. He saw his father and brother
only occasionally and under somewhat strained circumstances.
Peter Christian was off on a trip during most of July, and Søren
went to Hillerød for a short holiday at the end of the month.
But on Monday evening, August 6, all three dined together, and
Søren and his father were in especially good spirits. Peter
Christian's diary says that even though earlier in the day the old
man "had scolded Søren and refused him something, nevertheless [at dinner] he was satisfied and united with him." The next
morning Michael Pedersen called as usual for his morning coffee.

When the girl brought it up, he downed it according to his custom, but called her back in a few moments to say that everything was spinning before his eyes. He became nauseated and was put to bed. The doctor ordered an emetic but this only made things worse, and soon he lapsed into a coma. He died two days later, on Thursday, August 9, at the age of eighty-one.

For a son who had been arguing with his father until three days before his death, Søren's reaction was extravagant. To judge from his journal entry on August 11, 1838, he had been devoted to Michael Pedersen from first to last:

> My father died during Wednesday night (the 8th) at 2 a.m. I had so very much wished that he might live a few years longer, and I look upon his death as the last sacrifice which he made to his love for me; for he did not die from me but *died for me* in order that if possible I might turn into something. Of all that I have inherited from him, the recollection of him, his transfigured portrait, not transfigured [*forklaret*] by the poetry of my imagination (for it did not require that) but explained [*forklaret*] by many individual traits that I now can take account of—is dearest to me, and I will be careful to preserve it safely hidden from the world. . . . He was a "faithful friend."

Kierkegaard's disclaimer here betrays some understanding of the changes his imagination was already bringing about in his conception of his father. Alive, the old man had been a source of growing frustration—refusing his requests, disapproving his friends and activities, and throwing a pall of melancholy and piety over Søren's home life. Dead, he was transfigured into a "faithful friend" whose death at eighty-one (hawking sputum and slipping off into unconsciousness) is now seen as a kind of sacrifice: "he did not die from me, but *died for me*." This change betrays a pattern that runs through all Kierkegaard's personal relationships. It is not flesh-and-blood individuals that affect him, but rather their imagoes—phantom creatures which populate the inner world of his imagination. Thus it is that a father who was rather annoying in life is transformed in death into an ideal of father love, ultimately a reflection of divine paternity. Later on, a seventeen-year-old girl whom he could not bring himself to marry is transformed into his muse and beloved—"the unnamed whose name one day shall be named."

But such a reconstitution of living individuals into "meanings" has its perils, for now and then events invalidate the meaning. Something of the sort happened with respect to Kierkegaard's understanding of his father, as we can see by examining the famous "earthquake" entry made earlier in 1838:

> Then it was that the great earthquake occurred, that great upheaval which suddenly forced upon me a new and infallible rule of interpretation for many things. Then I suspected that my father's great age was not a divine blessing, but rather a curse; that our family's remarkable intellectual gifts were only given us so that we might tear each other to pieces. Then I felt death's stillness growing about me. Then I came to see in my father an unhappy man who would outlive us all, a cross on the tomb of all his hopes. A guilt must lie upon the whole family, the punishment of God must be on it. It was to disappear, erased by God's powerful hand, wiped out like any other mistake. And only now and then did I find some relief in the thought that my father had been given the hard duty of comforting us with the consolation of religion, of ministering to us all so that a better world might be open to us, even though we lost everything in this one, even though we were struck with the punishment that the Jews always called down upon their enemies: that all memory of us should be completely wiped out, that we should no longer be found upon the earth.

Here we see one of Kierkegaard's first attempts at creating a personal myth, and it is interesting to note that his father occupied the central role. In the portrait of this "unhappy man who would outlive us all, a cross on the tomb of all his hopes" there is a significant reflection of Ahasuerus, the Wandering Jew—a folk-literary character with whom Kierkegaard was preoccupied in these years. The origin of the curse on the Kierkegaard family was left unidentified. But it was "God's punishment" for this nameless sin which accounted for all the recent deaths, and it was that punishment which would shortly destroy both Peter Christian and Søren before their father's aged eyes. Implicated in the curse, Søren saw himself as a sacrifice.

In the event, however, it was neither Peter Christian nor Søren who died, but the father. And so the tokens on the board were given new meanings. Old Michael shed his identity as Ahasuerus and became the sacrifice—dying so that "if possible I might turn into something." It was as if the father's death had released the youngest son from a kind of spell. Søren had been in a state of suspended animation, a victim awaiting his turn, "a chess piece of which the opponent says: that piece cannot be moved . . . an idle onlooker, [whose] time is not yet come." The father's death freed him to become "something."

At that time Søren had done no serious work toward his theological exam for several years. With the announcement that his quarter share of the estate amounted to 33,594 rd. ($235,-000), all practical need for getting his degree vanished. He was a rich man; if he chose, he need not work for the rest of his life. A friend said to him: "Now you can get out of the exam, since you no longer have your father at you all the time." Kierkegaard replied: "No, my friend. Now I can't fob the old man off any longer with talk." At the same time he told Hans Brøchner: "So long as Father lived, I was able to defend my thesis that I ought not to take [the exam], but when he died, I was forced to assume his part in the argument as well as my own. Then I couldn't hold out any longer, but had to decide to read for the exam."

So he began to study in earnest. While Peter Christian moved downstairs into the father's apartment and made plans to rent the two upper floors, Søren took new rooms on Kultorvet and engaged a tutor. Like his earlier apartment on Løvstræde, this one was centrally located. P. E. Lind lived two blocks away on Store Kannikestræde, Jørgen Jørgensen nearby in Skidentorvet. Søren was four blocks from the university, where he once again began attending lectures, and only a little further from his tutor's residence on Studiestræde. With this tutor (an older cousin of Brøchner's, also named Hans) he worked through the driest theology, learned excerpts from church history, and taught himself by rote the names of the Popes and their dates. At least in the beginning, his studies made no radical change in his usual manner of life. "He frequented coffee houses," his niece recalled, "and went for walks just as eagerly in the streets. But from 7 to 11 p.m. he refused visitors . . . [and] studied diligently." Even this sacrifice of his evenings Kierkegaard felt sharply:

> Cornelius Nepos tells of a commander who was shut up in a fortress with a considerable force of cavalry, and who ordered the horses to be whipped every day so that they might not become sick through too much standing still. So I live in my room like one besieged. I don't want to see anyone, and every moment I fear that one of the enemy will try an attack—that someone will come and visit me. I don't want to go out. And hence not to be injured by so much sitting still—I cry myself tired.
>
> *10 May 1839*

But the pace of his work had to be quickened if he was ever to pass the hated exam. In July 1839 he wrote: "Now for a year's time, a mile's distance in time, I'll dive below ground like the Guadalquivir; but I shall come up again." In the early autumn he took the plunge, burying himself under copybooks, church histories, canon law texts, and Biblical commentaries. He marked the day by bringing his journal to an abrupt halt:

> I must give up you too, my *lucida intervalla*, and you, my thoughts who sit imprisoned in my head. I can no longer permit you your stroll in the cool of the evening. But don't lose courage, get to know each other better, mix with each other, and now and then I'll still creep in and steal a glance at you— *au revoir!*
>
> S.K.
formerly Dr. Ecstaticus

With the suspension of his journal comes an interruption in our knowledge of his activities and thoughts. He later wrote that "reading for my exam is the longest parenthesis I have ever experienced," and we can only speculate on what filled that nine-month parenthesis—lectures, rote learning, and scholarship, no doubt. On June 2, 1840, he submitted his request for examination to the theological faculty, and on July 3 he was examined by Professors Scharling, Engelstoft, and Hohlenberg.

The records give only the examiners' questions; a pity, for some of Kierkegaard's answers would be well worth knowing. Scharling began by asking: "What argument for Christianity is from first to last of greatest significance?" In light of the candidate's later conviction that Christianity was not rationally defensible, it would be most interesting to know how he replied. Taking up the questioning on the Old Testament, Engelstoft asked the candidate to translate Genesis IX, 16–29, from the Hebrew, and followed this up with questions on Abraham and Noah. Next the examination turned to moral theology, with the question of how a moral principle can be grounded, and then to

Kant, with the question of how the categorical imperative leads
to religion. The examination closed with questions from Hohlenberg about Kierkegaard's interpretation of certain passages in
the New Testament.

He passed easily but not brilliantly. Of the sixty-three candi-
dates, twenty-seven (Kierkegaard included) received *laudabilis*.
But theological studies then as now did not attract the sharpest
minds, and Kierkegaard stood only fourth among the honor
students. The examiners judged that although his written work
"showed much greater maturity and development of thought
than the others, still these contained a richer measure of positive
theological material." Of the three men who outdid him, two
went on to become priests in obscure parishes and the third became a schoolteacher and author of pedagogic tracts.

His degree behind him, for diversion Kierkegaard decided
to make a three-week pilgrimage to the family homestead in
Sæding on the west coast of Jutland. A good many of the notes
from his trip survive, scribbled in pencil in a small red-leather
notebook, the handwriting sometimes jerky as the coach lurched
over potholes or rocks, and on one occasion, written in Latin to
frustrate the prying eye of a fellow passenger. Taken together,
they hold some intriguing clues to Kierkegaard's mind and
temperament in the weeks just prior to the most momentous
decision of his life.

The trip was made in the comfort befitting a young man who
two years before had inherited a sizable fortune. During the
later stages he hired a private coach, and for the whole journey
he was accompanied by a servant, Anders Westergaard. This
man worked for Kierkegaard's brother and was only borrowed
for the trip, but later when Peter Christian moved out of No. 2
Nytorv, Anders went into Søren's service and his master came
to depend on him completely. It was Anders, for example, who
saw to it in later years that Kierkegaard's rooms were always

kept at exactly 57 degrees Fahrenheit. When his master changed flats Anders supervised the move, even to seeing that the many books in the library were replaced on the shelves in proper order. In time, Kierkegaard came to call Anders "my body."

The two of them left Copenhagen for Kalundborg on the mail stage at 7 in the morning of July 18. It was a summer Saturday and Kierkegaard's spirits were high; his first note in the small octavo notebook begins:

> Farewell my home.
> Farewell, take my greetings.
> Greetings to you, mighty Nature, with your fleeting beauty.
> It is not you I desire, it is the memory of you . . .

This entry sounds a *leitmotiv* of the travel diary: Kierkegaard's concern not with the details of his world but with their effect on him—his ever-changing moods. As we have seen, he relishes not so much his actual perception of nature as the memory of that perception. It was later the same morning as the post stage rolled westward across Sjælland, the red-clad postillion cracking his whip and hooting his horn, that Kierkegaard saw a young girl peering from a cottage window:

> Greetings to you, village beauty! You young girl, I mean, putting your head inquisitively out the window! Fear not. I shan't disturb your peace. Do but look straight at me, so that I do not entirely forget you.

The next morning they made the ferry crossing from Kalundborg to Aarhus. He had planned to take the fast and well-appointed steamship *Christian VIII*, but her sailing was canceled at the last minute and they had to settle for nine hours on a smack, probably the ancient *Diana*. Kierkegaard was bored silly by the conversation of four priests; at one point he even looked forward to the diversion of becoming seasick. But infirmity was not granted him, and he arrived that night in Aarhus bored but well.

After a few days in this major city of Jutland, the two travelers proceeded to Randers, where Kierkegaard took a boat trip on the river Gudenå. From Randers they made their way to Viborg, and here Kierkegaard hiked through some of the local scenery: Hald, Non Mill, Koldbæk stream, and the heath stretching beyond. Near Hald he met a vagabond lying on his back in the heather with only his stick beside him.

> We went together to Non Mill. We came past running water called Koldbæk. He assured me it was the most delicious water in the whole district, whereupon he went down to it, lay full-length on his stomach, and drank. . . . Happy life! So unconcerned as he lay there in the heather and slept! So content to refresh himself with the cold water! . . . Is not the simple life the one which most of all reminds us of our origins in Paradise?

Kierkegaard's thoughts, however, were not on paradise, or on the simple joy of the vagabond's life, but rather on his own lack of joy, his distance from paradise: "I am so dull and so lacking in joy, that I not only have nothing which fills my soul, but cannot conceive what *could* satisfy it."

As the journey led him toward the rugged west coast of Jutland and the land became more desolate, his diary took on a sadder, more autumnal tone. Approaching Sæding, he thought of his father who left this windswept coast so long ago, never to return:

> I sit here quite alone (I have often been just as much alone, but have never felt so conscious of it) counting the hours till I see Sæding. I can never remember any change in my father, and now I shall see the places where, as a poor boy, he tended sheep; the places for which, on account of his descriptions,

I have felt such homesickness. What if I were to fall ill and be buried in Sæding churchyard! Strange thought! His last wish for me would be fulfilled. Is all my earthly destiny to be found in that? God's will be done!

But as the diary makes clear, Kierkegaard is really haunted by a sense of his own unreality: "The terrible thing about the total spiritual incapacity from which I suffer is precisely that it is coupled with a consuming longing, a spiritual passion. And yet it is so formless, that I do not even know what it is I lack."

Lodging with his aunt in surroundings so primitive they reminded him of Odysseus' sojourn with Circe, his interest is whetted by the most morbid of the local peasant legends. He repeats in his diary the story of the Sæding man in a time of plague who outlived all his neighbors: "He dug deep trenches in the heather and buried the corpses in long rows." Looking out over the heath he is attracted by its very starkness: "Here everything lies naked and uncovered before God. . . . Here on the heath one can indeed say, 'Whither shall I flee from Thy presence?'" On this barren stretch of heath where his father once raised his hand to curse God, Kierkegaard seems to long for a conclusion to his own life, for an end to his torment of spirit, his sufferer's progress. "Just as one is accustomed to say *nulla dies sine linea*," Kierkegaard wrote, "so can I say of this journey *nulla dies sine lacryma*."

He stayed with his aunt in Sæding for three days—Sunday, Monday, and Tuesday, August 2 to 4. He had planned to preach his first sermon in Sæding church that Sunday (the record does not show whether he actually did), and he was surprised to find that the text for the day was Mark VIII, 1–10, the feeding of the four thousand in the wilderness—appropriate enough for this poorest parish on the Jutland heath.

In Sæding he played a rather cruel trick on the village schoolmaster, an awkward person named Jens Jensen Kirkebye. Because

Michael Pedersen Kierkegaard had set up a sizable fund for the
village school, Søren was received with obsequiousness by the
children and Kirkebye. "I was really afraid they'd erect a
triumphal arch for me," he later told Hans Brøchner. On the day
of his departure the children were drawn up in front of the
school to sing him a song composed by the schoolmaster in
Kierkegaard's honor. Kirkebye, who was to lead, stood in front
with his manuscript in hand, ready to give the sign to begin. Kierkegaard's carriage drew up. With his friendliest smile and a deep
bow, Kierkegaard took the manuscript as if to read it. At the
same time he signaled the coachman to drive off. Everything was
thrown into confusion since the schoolmaster, not knowing the
song by heart, could not get the tune started. "The children
stood silent and astonished," Brøchner later wrote, "and Kierkegaard rolled off to the main highway, nodding and bowing as he
went."

Kierkegaard and Anders stayed the night of August 4th
at the inn at Them. "It was crowded with counts and barons,"
Kierkegaard wrote, and he made the acquaintance of Count
Ahlefeldt, who invited him to the family estate in Langeland.
From Them they proceeded by the most direct route to Aarhus,
where on Thursday morning they boarded the *Christian VIII*
for a pleasant six-hour crossing to Kalundborg. A day later
they were back in Copenhagen. Anders returned to No. 2
Nytorv and Kierkegaard took up the free life of a man of letters
he had put aside the year before. All was unchanged—all, that
is, with one notable exception, for in early September he asked
State Councillor Terkel Olsen for the hand of his daughter, the
seventeen-year-old Regine.

10

SOVEREIGN OF
MY HEART, REGINE

WHEN they first met she had been Juliet's age—fourteen. She had gone to the Rørdams' in Frederiksberg for a morning party; Thrine Dahl had come visiting from Roskilde, and to make her feel at home Mrs. Rørdam had invited a few girls for coffee and cake. It was early May 1837 and the weather was too chilly to enjoy the garden, so the girls gathered in the parlor, chattering away while the coffee steamed. There was a knock on the door and Kierkegaard entered; unexpectedly, as was his custom, he had come to pay a call.

"He talked incessantly," Regine remembered many years later, "and his speech just gushed out and was intensely captivating." She recalled too that "he had made a very strong impression" on her, but was unable to remember any of the things he actually said. For his part, it is difficult to tell just what impression she made upon him. He noted in his journal that he had been out to the Rørdams', and then wrote: "Oh, how I feel that I'm alone —Oh, curses on that arrogant satisfaction in standing alone." He did not mention Regine in his journal for many months, and it is only from his first book *Either/Or* that we get some idea of what that first meeting was like. The protagonist, Johannes, has decided on the spur of the moment to visit a family he knows. He finds himself in the middle of a young girls' party:

I went in and noticed quickly that they were a bit surprised. . . .

It was very early in spring. The sun sent a few scattered rays as harbingers of its coming. Inside everything was still wintry, and this made the sunbeams so welcome. The coffee on the table gave off a rich aroma—and the young girls were happy. . . . I succeeded in turning their attention and talk to the question of the conditions under which an engagement ought to be broken. While my eye amused itself by flitting from one flower to another in the garland of girls . . . my inner ear listened to their observations on the question. A single word often enabled me to get an insight into a girl's heart and its history. How seductive is the way of love, and how interesting to investigate how far along this way the individual has come. I constantly stimulated them; cleverness, wit, aesthetic objectivity combined to make the relationship freer, yet everything was kept within the bounds of strictest decorum. . . .

Sometimes I carried the conversation to the verge of sadness; sometimes I let wantonness run wild; sometimes I tried them in a dialectical game. And what other subject contains so many possibilities in itself, however one looks at it?

Much of the tone of Kierkegaard's relationship with Regine is contained in this description drawn from their first meeting. His icy glance—always the observer, the manipulator; the young girls' innocence; the attenuated eroticism absorbed into wit and language; all these elements played a part in their courtship.

As this description might imply, it was not so much a courtship as a game or experiment, and he began it by spying on her. On Mondays and Thursdays Regine went to music lessons between 4 and 5 p.m., and each time she returned home by the same route—down Vestervold Gade, left on Vestergade, across Nytorv, and up Klædeboderne. Kierkegaard took to frequenting a pastry shop along her route, where he drank as little as possible

of the wretched coffee they served while he watched her passing.
He described it in *Stages on Life's Way*:

> For well onto a year . . . I have abandoned myself secretly
> and clandestinely to this love. I have seen her in society, seen
> her in her room, I have followed her path unobserved. This
> last was in a way the dearest to me, partly because it satisfied
> the secrecy of love, partly because it saved me the worry that
> someone would find out. . . .
>
> She went once a week to her singing lesson; that I knew.
> I knew where the singing teacher lived. Far from doing any-
> thing to thrust myself into these circles, I wished merely to
> watch her secretly. Now it luckily happened that there was in
> the same street a pastrycook whose shop she passed in going
> to and from her lesson. Here I had my hideout. Here I sat
> and waited; here I saw her, myself unseen; here love's secret
> growth waxed and developed before my eyes, to my great
> contentment. It was a second-rate pastry shop. I could be
> pretty sure of not being surprised . . . I drank the coffee
> without paying much attention to it, but here it was I waited,
> here it was I fed love with longing and refreshed it with the
> vision, and from thence when the vision had vanished I had
> much to take home with me. I never dared sit by the window,
> but when I took a table in the middle of the room my eye com-
> manded the street and the opposite sidewalk where she went,
> yet the passersby could not see me. Oh, beautiful time; Oh,
> lovely recollection; Oh, sweet disquietude; Oh, happy vision,
> when I dressed up my hidden existence with the enchantment
> of love!

She was so young that there was not much else he could do,
even had he felt free to do it. And she was lovely. A contemporary portrait by Bærentzen shows her in a scoop-necked
dress of the time, her shoulders white and well-formed, her curls
falling across high cheekbones and framing a generous mouth
and striking eyes—very clear, very direct. The critic Edvard

Brandes met her when she was middle-aged and he a boy of seventeen, yet remembered sixty years later that "she was radiantly beautiful—with clear, roguish eyes and a svelte figure." But this was not all. For she also came from a moderately wealthy family and her father, as an *Etatsraad* (State Councillor) and high official in the Ministry of Finance, had excellent connections. She was an extraordinarily good catch, and if Kierkegaard did not stir himself, his "vision" would very soon turn out to be someone else's wife.

Years later, in his journal for the year 1849, he declared, "Already before my father died I had decided upon her. He died. I read for the examination. During all this time I let her existence wrap itself around mine." He first mentioned her name in an entry in 1839, playfully changing the spelling to the Latin Regina:

> Sovereign of my heart, "Regina," kept safe and secret in the deepest corner of my breast, in the fullness of my life's thought, where it is equally far to heaven and to hell—unknown divinity! Oh, can I really believe what the poets say, that when for the first time one sees the object of one's love, one imagines that one has seen her long ago, that all love like all knowledge is remembrance, that love in the individual also has its prophecies, its types, its myths, its Old Testament. Everywhere, in the face of every girl, I see traces of your beauty, but it seems to me that I should have to possess the beauty of all girls in order to distill a beauty equal to yours; that I should have to circumnavigate the whole world to find the missing place, the place toward which the deepest mystery of my being points—and in the next moment you are so near to me, so present, filling my spirit so strongly that I feel transfigured, and feel that it is good to be here.
>
> Blind god of love! Will you reveal to me your secret vision? Shall I find what I am seeking here in this world, shall I experience the conclusion of all my life's eccentric premises, shall I fold you in my arms—or

ARE MY ORDERS TO GO BEYOND THIS?

Have you gone before me, my *yearning*, are you beckoning
to me, transformed, from another world? Oh, I will cast
everything from me in order to be light enough to follow
you.

2nd Feb. 39

Yet even in this entry, written apparently in the full flush of
infatuation, he seemed to be looking through and beyond Regine.
Would she be "the conclusion of all my life's eccentric premises,"
or did his yearning point toward a higher end and a more difficult salvation? This concern with Regine's meaning for him
(and conversely with the ambiguity of his love for her) can be
found in an entry from the Jutland pilgrimage, written only
weeks before his engagement to her. After complaining, "My
misfortune is that at the time when I went about pregnant with
ideas, I fell in love with the ideal . . . and therefore reality did
not answer to my burning desires," his thoughts turn to Regine
and to the proposal he is considering:

> Oh God, grant that this should not also be the case in love;
> for there too I am seized by a mysterious dread of having
> confused an ideal with a reality. God forbid! Until now that
> is not the case.
> But my dread makes me long to know the future and yet
> fear it!

Fearing the future, dreading that he has confused a flesh-and-
blood Regine with an ideal image, he nevertheless acted. "The
period from August 9 [the Sunday after his return from Jutland]
until the beginning of September," he wrote, "I used in the
strictest sense to approach her." Even before his trip to Jutland
he had visited the Olsen family, sometimes bringing the daughters small gifts of nuts or candy, now and then lending them a
book to read. In the closing weeks of August 1840 he came more

frequently, sometimes with sheet music for the girls to play on the piano. Finally he made his move:

> On September 8 I left my apartment with the firm purpose of deciding the whole thing. We met in the street outside their house. She said there was no one at home: I was foolhardy enough to take this as an invitation—just what I wanted! I went in with her. We stood alone in the living room. She was a little uneasy. I asked her to play me something, as she usually did. She began, but that did not help me. Then suddenly I took the music away and closed it—not without a certain violence—threw it down on the piano, and said, "Oh what do I care about music now! It is you I am searching for, you whom I have sought after for two years." She remained silent. I did nothing else to beguile her; I even warned her against myself, against my melancholy. . . .
>
> She remained silent. At last I left, for I was anxious lest someone should come and find both of us, and her so disturbed. I went immediately to the *Etatsraad*. I know I was terribly concerned that I had made too strong an impression on her, and I also feared that my visit might lead to a misunderstanding and even damage her reputation.
>
> Her father said neither yes nor no, but I could see that he was willing enough. I asked for a meeting: it was granted to me for the afternoon of the 10th. I did not say a single word to persuade her. She said yes.
>
> Immediately, I assumed a relationship to the whole family. My virtuosity was turned especially upon her father, whom, moreover, I had always liked a lot.
>
> But inwardly, the next day I saw I had made a blunder. A penitent such as I was, my *vita ante acta*, my melancholy: that was enough.
>
> I suffered indescribably at that time.

In a way the whole story is told in this journal entry written nine years after the event: the hysterical scenes, the pretense, the

An excellent portrait of Kierkegaard,
drawn from life by the Danish artist H. P.
Hansen during the period 1853–55.
Above the portrait: a reproduction of
Kierkegaard's visiting card.

Kierkegaard's father, Michael Pedersen Kierkegaard (1756–1838), and mother, Ane Lund Kierkegaard (1768–1834).

Nytorv in 1839. To the right of the columned Courts Building is Kierkegaard's home.

The Borgerdydskole in Klareboderne.

Two idealized portraits of Kierkegaard as a young man, drawn by his cousin Christian Kierkegaard.

Regine Olsen at the time
of her engagement to
Kierkegaard, an oil portrait
by E. D. Bærentzen.

Regine Olsen in 1855.

A letter from Kierkegaard to Regine during the period
of their engagement. The sketch shows Kierkegaard on
Knippels Bridge peering through a spyglass.

A cover sheet of *Corsair*. To the right and on facing page: caricatures of Kierkegaard from the pages of *Corsair*—(a) Kierkegaard (note the uneven length of his trousers in this and other caricatures); (b) Kierkegaard training a girl; (c) P. L. Møller and Kierkegaard on the street; (d) Kierkegaard reviews his troops; (e) Frater Taciturnus, one of Kierkegaard's pseudonyms, passes a prostitute on the street; (f) Kierkegaard encounters *Corsair's* editor on the street; (g) Kierkegaard giving away one of his books to a reader; (h) the whole world revolves around Kierkegaard (including familiar landmarks of Copenhagen such as the Frue Kirke and the Round Tower).

(c)

(d)

(e)

(f)

(g)

(h)

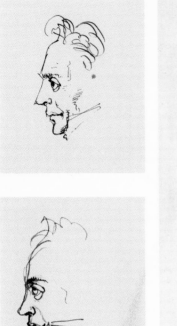

Sketches of Kierkegaard, drawn from memory by the Danish artist Wilhelm Marstrand.

recriminations and extravagant excuses—all the sad history of the year of his engagement. He had acted decisively, only to recognize the next day that it was a "blunder."

Yet what never emerges in this reconstruction is a plausible answer to the question of why he made the blunder in the first place. In an entry the following year (1841) he claimed that he "had never really thought of being married"; but this cannot be taken literally—after all, he had deliberately courted the girl and then, over a three-day period, made and renewed a proposal. Unfortunately, his journal of the time is not much help; the few entries are highly stylized and "literary," and their proper dating is in doubt. The best approach to an answer can be found in passages from Kierkegaard's later pseudonymous writings where the question of marriage assumes central importance.

The second half of his first and possibly greatest work, *Either/Or*, is devoted to a spirited defense of marriage by Judge William, himself a paradigm of the married man. As the story unfolds Kierkegaard is clearly presenting marriage as the ideal of a fully temporal, fully realized life. "The married man," he writes, "has not killed time but has saved it and preserved it in eternity. . . . He solves the great riddle of living in eternity and yet hearing the hall clock strike, and hearing it in such a way that the stroke of the hour does not shorten but prolongs his eternity." This life of rich, full duration is contrasted with the timeless prison of the aesthete bachelor, whose lack of temporality is expressed in the very sentences Kierkegaard used earlier in his journal to characterize "that dreadful still life" he knew so well.

In this battle for temporality, woman plays a special role. "A woman comprehends finitude," Judge William argues; "she understands it from the bottom up. . . . Therefore one may say her life is happier than that of man." Sometimes even the Judge begins to "subside into himself," overcome by "melancholy." But swiftly the presence of his wife brings him back to life:

> When I am sitting thus lost and abandoned and then look at my wife walking about the room lightly and youthfully, always occupied, always with something to attend to, my eye voluntarily follows her movement. I take part in everything she undertakes, and it ends with my being again reconciled with time, finding that time acquires significance for me, that the instant moves swiftly.

The idealization of the conjugal state apparent in the Judge's description is a familiar theme of Kierkegaard's later work—the "knight of faith" in *Fear and Trembling* is also a married man. Throughout Kierkegaard's life he never failed to identify "happiness" with the somewhat cloying domestic bliss of a Copenhagen burgher, and entwined with this image of happiness were his dead hopes for happiness with Regine. "Most men's ideals are usually the great, the extraordinary, which they never realize," he wrote later. "I'm all too melancholy to have such ideals. . . . It's clear to me that [earlier] my ideal was simply to be married and to live only for that marriage." Seven years after having rejected this ideal, he was still tantalized by the thought of Regine: "On those days—few and far between—when I was really humanly happy, I always longed for her indescribably."

But a full year ran its course before the final break was made. During that time Søren and Regine performed the intricate ritual of the engagement dance much like any other bourgeois couple. Taking his arm, she would accompany him on strolls up Bredgade or on the Esplanade, where on a Sunday afternoon hundreds of engaged couples were similarly occupied. It was not customary for engaged couples to go to church together, but he made up for this by bringing her Mynster's sermons, which he sometimes read aloud. They paid calls on the relatives of both families and busied themselves in becoming acquainted with all the tiresome family connections. Kierkegaard now had a flat on Nørregade, but she could visit him there only in the presence of a chaperone. Since Peter Christian had more important things to do, they most often saw each other at Regine's home on Børsgade.

The Olsen family lived in one of the lovely old houses just adjacent to the stock exchange that were called "The Six Sisters." Across the canal lay the old island of Gammelholm, and beyond lay Kongens Nytorv and the botanical gardens. From their windows they could look down and see the *Finlapperne*—long, three-masted vessels that brought cargoes of timber from Finland—lying against the wharf, their bowsprits extending across Børsgade almost into the windows of The Six Sisters. Across the canal and to the left lay Holmen's Church, whose bells tolled the quarter hour, their sound floating in through the double windows and rich drapes and making an indelible impression on Kierkegaard—"When the hour had come the signal rang in the midst of our drawing room chatter, and the evening whispers now began." Regine was the youngest of three children and the family pet. Later in a letter to Kierkegaard, her elder brother Jonas said that Kierkegaard's conduct had taught him to hate as no one before had ever hated, and it would seem they disliked each other from the start. But Kierkegaard got along famously with Cornelia, Regine's elder sister, and with her father. Even after the engagement was broken, Cornelia remarked, "Although I can't understand Magister Kierkegaard, I believe all the same that he's a good man."

Outwardly, Kierkegaard showed no sign of inner conflict during the year of his engagement. As a serious young man soon to be married, he set about preparing himself for a responsible post in the church or university. He had, of course, passed his theological exam, but to be eligible for a post in the Danish state church he also had to complete a course of practical training at the pastoral seminary. He enrolled in November 1840 and the following January preached his first sermon in Holmen's Church. The scripture was Philippians I, 19–25: "For to me to live is Christ, and to die is gain," and the sermon's content was vintage Kierkegaard: Death is a gain only for the true Christian, he for whom the hidden eternal life has dawned. The judges praised its "thoughtfulness and sharp logic" but complained that it was "quite difficult, and for the common man, on certainly too high a plane." "The tone was Biblical and the form not without popular appeal," they reported, "but the author has described the soul's struggles much too severely to attract the man in the pew, to whom such struggles are unknown." How the Kierkegaard of *Training in Christianity* would have relished that judgment!

As for the university, Poul Møller's chair in philosophy still lay vacant, and it was probably with an academic career in mind that he began work in the autumn of 1840 on his dissertation, *The Concept of Irony with Constant Reference to Socrates.* It is a long and tortuous work (350 pages in the original Danish edition), which the faculty readers passed only after registering unhappiness with its style. The university's rector, H. C. Ørsted, spoke for all of them when he said: "It makes an overwhelmingly unpleasant impression on me, particularly by two things I abhor: prolixity and artificiality." It is true that this work has none of the intimate warmth and sharp clarity of many of Kierkegaard's later writings. Yet the learned readers' offense at the style may in large measure spring from the fact that they missed the joke—it is essentially an ironic work on irony, and Kierkegaard's use of a heavy Hegelian language and structure is intended to mock that language and structure. But the prolixity and artificiality mentioned by Ørsted may also have a more private origin, for the book was really Kierkegaard's escape from a disintegrating relationship with Regine.

And so for a year he wrote his dissertation, did the required work at the pastoral seminary, and behaved as a young engaged man should behave. "Behave" is the operative word, for a central strain of pretense and dramatic artifice runs through Kierkegaard's engagement to Regine. One senses the absence of carnality, the lack of any sexual fire between this nymph of seventeen and her older fiancé. Emil Boesen once remarked that sexually speaking, "SK was the purest person he had known," and that "seldom has a love affair been so completely spiritually determined as SK's." Everything in the affair was stylized, literary. Regine herself later said that their love was "a spiritual affection," and this fact becomes obvious in their correspondence. Regine burned her letters to him, but most of his to her survive. Here is one that, although undated, most likely comes from the late autumn of 1840:

My Regine,

This letter has no date and certainly ought not to have one, for its essential content is the consciousness of a feeling which is indeed mine every moment, even if it sounds in all the different keys which love gives to it. That is precisely why it is not present at any particular moment, in contradistinction to the others (not present at exactly 10 o'clock and not at 11; not on November 10th in contradistinction to the 11th or the 12th). That feeling constantly renews itself; it is forever young, like the books that have come down to us from the Middle Ages. They, though they are hundreds of years old, are constantly—"printed this year." Today I was on Knippelsbro; this day has no date because there never is a day on which I don't undertake that expedition.

On Martinmas Eve, when I didn't appear until 8 p.m., I was in Fredensborg. I cannot say that was "yesterday" or "the day before yesterday" because I have no "today" to reckon from as a starting point. People were surprised that I drove alone. Formerly, as you know, I never rode alone, for care and sorrow were my faithful companions. Now my fellow travelers are less numerous. When I ride forth, they are the memory, the recollection of you; when I ride home the long-ing for you. And in Fredensborg these companions of mine meet, fall on each other's necks, and kiss. That is the instant I like so much, because you know that I love Fredensborg indescribably for an instant—an instant, but only an instant, which to me is priceless.

Now as this letter is undated, and therefore might have been written at any time whatever, therefore it follows that it can be read at anytime; even if some doubt should overtake you in the night, you can still read it at night. For truly, if I have ever for a single instant doubted whether I dared call you "mine" (you know how much I connect with that word; you who yourself have written that your life would be *con-cluded* with me, if I should be separated from you, so let it then be *included* in me, so long as we are united, because first then are we truly *united*) yet there is no instant when I have doubted—no (I write it with my soul's inmost conviction) not even in the darkest corner of the world shall I doubt that I am yours.

Yours forever,

S.K.

The playful, complicated, self-consciously literary tone of this letter was maintained in all his correspondence with her. Now and then he sent her little drawings—a sketch of an old woman, or of himself looking for her with a spyglass from Knippelsbro —and his final note (returning her ring) was so satisfactory from a literary point of view that he included it verbatim in one of his later novels.

Regine knew from the beginning that something was wrong. Only eight days after their engagement, she met him on the street and found him so distraught that she scarcely recognized him. Now and then when he came to visit, he would sit in a chair weeping instead of reading to her or listening to her play the piano. "Kierkegaard suffered frightfully from his melancholy," she remembered. "He was tortured by the thought that he had not been good enough to his father, whom he loved enormously." Later in his own journal Kierkegaard took up this theme of guilt as an explanation for his break with Regine, but even he seems unconvinced by it. The real reason, as he stressed on numerous occasions, was that she was too young and he too old. "There was a young girl I loved, charming was she, and so young . . . so attractive, so engaging: Oh, dreadful sorrow: I was an eternity too old for her." He was in fact ten years older, but this was not the age difference he had in mind. Rather it had to do with the "ghostly" quality of his personality:

> Suppose I got married to her. What then? In the course of half a year, in less time than that, she would have torn herself apart. There is—and this is both the good and the bad about me—something ghostly about me, something which accounts for the fact that no one can put up with me who has to see me day by day and thus have a real relation to me. . . . Fundamentally I live in a spirit world.

There was no way this nymph "with roguish eyes" could enter that spirit world; what could and did enter was his private vision of her. Later he wrote, "In order to love, I have to put the object at a distance," and it was thus he loved Regine—not as a flesh-and-blood seventeen-year-old, but as a "vision," a "lovely recollection." As vision he can take her home to "dress up my hidden existence" without introducing a disturbing alien element into that existence. His flight from Regine was nothing less than an especially poignant expression of his lifelong flight from the world. Kierkegaard escaped from Regine as flesh only to recapture her as muse. And it is as muse that she continued to live with him, inhabiting the shrinelike rosewood pedestal he ordered built for her:

> I had a rosewood pedestal made. It was constructed after my own design, and after the occasion of a word of hers. . . .

She said that she would thank me all her life if I would let her stay with me, that she would even live in a little cupboard. With this in mind it was constructed without shelves. In it everything is carefully preserved; everything that reminds me of her and everything that could remind her of me. Here also can be found a copy of each of the pseudonymous works for her; always there were reserved only two vellum copies—one for her and one for me.

But in the summer of 1841 Regine had not yet taken up residence in her rosewood pedestal. Henriette Lund saw her that summer, and although Regine was as affectionate as ever, her younger friend "could not help feeling that there was a cloud on the horizon, where before everything had been so bright." When it was time for the girls to part they walked together through the courtyard leading to Slotsholmgade. Henriette remembered "how the sun played on the water and on the façades of the buildings nearby," and she remembered too her last glimpse of Regine: "As I walked away I saw her in the clear sunlight with her hand over her eyes, standing in the same spot in order to wave me a last goodbye. . . . I went home with the feeling that something sad was hanging in the air." In midsummer the storm broke. As long as Kierkegaard had been busy with his dissertation he could postpone a final decision on Regine. But on July 16 the work was formally accepted by the university as "worthy of defense." On August 11 he sent back her ring, with the following note:

> In order not to put more often to the test a thing which after all must be done, and which being done will supply the needed strength—let it then be done. Above all, forget him who writes this, forgive a man who, though he may be capable of something, is not capable of making a girl happy.
>
> To send a silken cord is in the East capital punishment for the receiver; to send a ring is here capital punishment for him who sends it.

But Regine thought it was only a "symptom of his melancholy," which she with her "happiness and affection had for a long time vainly fought against." She rushed to his flat on Nørregade, but he was out. When he returned he found a note from her begging him "in the name of Christ and your deceased father" not to leave her. This injunction made a strong impression upon him, and he resolved "to repel her with all my powers" by a cruel pretense of indifference. Two months later the final break came. In Kierkegaard's words:

> From her I went immediately to the theater because I wanted to meet Emil Boesen. (In time this gave rise to a story that I looked at my watch and asked the family please to hurry if they had anything more to say, as I had to go to the theater.) The act was finished. As I left the stalls the *Etatsraad* came from the first parterre and said: "May I speak with you?" We went together to his home. She was desperate, he said: "It will be the death of her; she's completely in despair." I said: "I shall calm her down, but everything is settled." He said: "I am a proud man and find it hard to say, but please, I beg you—don't break off with her."
>
> He was indeed a fine man; he had shaken me. But I held my course. I had dinner with the family and spoke with her when I left.
>
> The next morning I got a letter from him saying that she had not slept all night and that I must come and see her. I went, and tried to persuade her.
>
> She asked me: "Will you never marry?"
>
> I answered: "Sure. In ten years when I've sown my wild oats I'll need some young thing to rejuvenate me." (That was a necessary cruelty.)
>
> She said: "Forgive me for what I've done to you."
>
> I answered: "It is for me to ask forgiveness."
>
> She said: "Promise to think of me."
>
> I did so.
>
> She said: "Kiss me."

I did so—but without passion. Merciful God!

So we separated. I spent the nights crying in my bed but the days as usual, wittier and in better spirits than ever. It was necessary.

Just how disturbed Kierkegaard really was after his break with Regine is suggested by his niece. The Lund children were visiting Peter Christian at Nytorv No. 2 when Uncle Søren made a sudden appearance:

He looked terribly upset and instead of his usual teasing, he kissed me so gently on the hair that I was touched to the heart. A moment later, when he was waiting to talk to us, he burst into violent weeping, and without really knowing what there was to weep about—at least, that was so in my case— we were soon all sobbing with him, gripped by his grief, as though under the weight of a deep sorrow.

Uncle Søren pulled himself together, and told us that one of these days he was going to Berlin, and perhaps would be away a long time. We must therefore promise to write him diligently, since he would long to hear how each of us was. With many tears we gave him our promise.

Only a few days after this meeting with his nieces and nephews, and two weeks after his final break with Regine, Kierkegaard did leave for Berlin. His brother and Emil Boesen accompanied him to the pier, waving as the Swedish steamer cast off her lines and slowly eased out into the channel. Kierkegaard himself, thinking back on this bright autumn day, later wrote: "When I left her I chose death."

CLOISTER

11

MY SORROW IS MY CASTLE

IN the year 1848 much of Europe teetered on the edge of revolution. Denmark was involved in a war with Germany, and crowds of 15,000 roamed the streets of Copenhagen. Kierkegaard's response was to complain that his faithful Anders had been drafted into the army just when he was needed, that his stocks had declined 700 rd., and that the turbulence would prevent him from taking a foreign tour. When his young friend Hans Brøchner suggested that he might volunteer in order "to gain experience, especially self-experience," Kierkegaard replied that "this way of learning from actual life was necessary for most people, but that he himself received a far richer reward ideally through imagination and reflection." In a journal entry a few years later he compared "the whole business of world history" to "the uproar and hubbub which children make in their playroom instead of sitting still and reading their books, as their parents would like." ·

In the years following his break with Regine, Kierkegaard came to withdraw further and further from the world. Like street noises muffled by shuttered windows and many layers of curtains, the affairs of the world came only faintly to his indifferent ears. Insulated from the harsher realities by the comforts of wealth, his life took on the shape of an aesthetic hermitage, one whose outlines, he said, had already been apparent to

him as he stood on the deck of the Stralsund packet in 1841 and
waved goodbye to his brother and Emil Boesen.

> I was so deeply shaken that I understood perfectly well I
> could not possibly succeed in striking the comforting and
> secure *via media* in which most people pass their lives: I had
> either to throw myself into despair and sensuality, or to choose
> the religious as absolutely the only thing—either the world
> in a measure that would be dreadful, or the cloister. That it
> was the second I would and must choose was already deter-
> mined. . . . Personally, . . . I was already in the cloister.

Until his final assault on the Danish state church in the last
year of his life, the contours of his external existence are barren
of change or movement. In 1846 he thought for a while of becoming a country parson but soon abandoned the idea. A few
years later he hoped for a kind of Platonic reconciliation with
Regine, but abandoned this too when her husband refused to
deliver his letter to her. In 1848 he considered petitioning the
King (whom he knew personally) for a government pension, but
the draft of the petition never went beyond his desk. He often
thought of going on an extended tour abroad, but except for
three short jaunts to Berlin (in 1843, 1845, and 1846), he never
left Copenhagen. Even his celebrated attack on a local paper, the
Corsair, occurred more in his mind than in public; after provok-
ing the editor to attack him, he filled his desk with polemic drafts
but in the end retired without firing a shot.

In contrast to the lack of eventfulness in his external life there
is the enormous richness of his journal. Covering some fourteen
volumes in the present Danish edition, it demonstrates what
Brøchner called Kierkegaard's ability to "think a trifle up into
a matter of world-historic significance." It is filled with polemics against the daily press and the public, complaints about
money matters, interminable debates on whether to seek a position in the church, and agonized reflections over how clearly he

ought to speak his mind. But the biographer must approach this material with the greatest circumspection, always mindful of the warning sounded by Kierkegaard's secretary and copyist, Israel Levin:

> He who would treat SK's life should take care that he doesn't burn himself, so full of contradictions is it, so difficult to reach bottom in that character. . . . He was preyed upon by all sorts of moods and was such a creature of mood that he often stated things that were not true, imagining them to be true.

Many of the claims Kierkegaard made in his journal and elsewhere turn out to be false when compared with external evidence. He complained often about the cost of publishing his works and at one point declared, "As an author I paid out money and reaped no profit." But research has shown that he actually made substantial sums on his publications—in all, 5,000 rd. [$35,000] between 1843 and his death in 1855. Likewise the claim in the posthumously published *Point of View* that the master plan for his books was in his mind from the beginning is contradicted by contemporary letters and journal entries. Kierkegaard himself seemed to be occasionally aware that he was injecting fantasy into the confessions and self-descriptions scattered through his *Papers*; in 1852 he confessed:

13 Oct.

About Myself

In all that I wrote about myself in the journals from '48 and '49, something of the literary often slipped in. It is not so easy to keep that sort of thing segregated when one is poetically productive to the extent that I am. Strangely enough, deep inside I understand myself clearly. But as soon as I go to write it down, I immediately become "productive."

With this man, who is so "poetically productive" that he himself comes to doubt the veracity of his own attempts at self-definition, it is "difficult to reach bottom" really because there is no bottom in his character. His claim that "deep inside I understand myself clearly" is no more to be respected than what he wrote about himself "in the journals from '48 and '49," where "something of the literary often slipped in."

Hans Brøchner caught something of the exotic climate in which his friend lived during a chance meeting in Berlin. Invited to dine with Kierkegaard in his hotel, Brøchner found that everything in his rooms was arranged with ingenious calculation to contribute to the right mood for his work: the lighting, the communication between the rooms, the arrangement of the furniture. And these were only hotel lodgings; back in Copenhagen not a detail was neglected to construct an environment perfectly suited to Kierkegaard's wishes.

Between October 1844 and April 1848 he lived alone in 2 Nytorv, and some of his greatest works were written in the lonely rooms of this house which held so many memories for him. But in the period 1841 to 1855 he also lived in five apartments. One of these, Østerbro 108A, lay just outside the city walls near one of the lakes that provided Copenhagen's water supply. But the others were all located in the center of the city within a block or two of Nytorv. When he moved, it was always because of an annoying distraction in the immediate neighborhood. He left a fine apartment at the corner of Tornebuskgade and Rosenborggade to escape the smell from a nearby tanner's yard, and he moved out of Nørregade 35 because of a light reflection from across the street and a barking dog on the floor below. Within the confines of the apartments themselves, however, he could at least ensure the right surroundings for his work.

Of first importance was the temperature. His rooms were always kept a very cool 13¾°C (57°F), and if Anders let them overheat while his master was out there was hell to pay. Israel Levin relates how Anders had instructions to open the windows

wide when Kierkegaard and Levin left the apartment and to
see that the temperature was exactly 13¾°C when they returned.
"When we came home," Levin recalled, "there was fresh air;
Kierkegaard walked up and down the room, waved his handker-
chief, and looked at the thermometer. . . . The devil knows how
they managed it, but it was always just as it should be, exactly
13¾°C. Each of us then took a flask of Eau de Cologne and
sprayed it on the stove, and so to work." Kierkegaard preferred
to live on the first floor up from the street, which got much less
sunlight than the higher floors. But Levin remembered that he
was not content until he had also "closed out the sun and
shielded the windows (both the outer and inner ones) with
white drapes or tapestries." Even when he went for his strolls in
the city, Levin continued, "he always walked in the shadows,
and, just like the trolls, could never be induced to step over a
sunlit patch."

In addition to coolness, Kierkegaard also liked space. Until
he ran out of money in the 1850's his apartments were always
large—six, seven, or eight rooms—and he wanted all the rooms
heated and illuminated, which was a real luxury in those days.
For furniture he preferred expensive woods of dark grain (rosewood and mahogany) worked into the graceful shapes of the
Empire style. In each room a table or sideboard held ink, paper,
and pen so that he could jot down any idea that came to mind.
He did most of his work at a huge mahogany stand-up desk.
Anders recalled that he often "came home from the city and
went immediately to his high desk, where he would stand for a
long time with his hat on, his cane or umbrella under his arm,
and write." Near the desk was the rosewood cabinet in which he
kept two copies of his own works, all especially printed on
vellum paper edged in gold, and bound with great elegance by
his personal bookbinder, N. C. Møller. Also near the high desk
lay several tin boxes containing his manuscripts; in case of fire

Anders had been told to save only the tin boxes, because everything else was insured.

Levin remarked that "Kierkegaard's style of living cost him
surprising sums," and this is supported by some of his account
books preserved in the Royal Library. Food prepared by a "Fru
Andersen" and delivered to his apartment between April 6,
1847, and March 28, 1848, came to 267 rd. The food itself was
a gourmet's choice: In November 1847, Kierkegaard ordered
roast duck four times, salmon twice, and stuffed lamb (*Sprængt
Lam*) four times. In other months he also ate roast pigeon, roast
goose, and breast of goose with spinach. He seemed especially
fond of bouillon; in August 1847 he had it on 29 days—and on
22 days for two meals. Levin tells us that at one time he ate at
Kierkegaard's apartment every day for five weeks.

> Every day we had soup, enormously strong; fish and a piece
> of lemon; in addition, a glass of fine sherry. Then the coffee
> came in: two silver coffee pots, two silver cream pitchers, and
> a bag of sugar which every day was filled anew. Then he
> opened the cabinet, where he had at least 50 cups and saucers,
> but only one pair of each pattern, and said: "So which pair
> will you have?" I was indifferent but it was important to him,
> so I told him which I would have. "Why?" One should
> always say why. At long last we were finished and got the
> cups. (He also had an incredible number of canes.) Now the
> sugar was put in until it almost came up over the rim, and
> the coffee was poured over it; every day it pleased him to
> see the sugar melt—then he was quite happy. The coffee was
> awfully strong; he destroyed himself with it. It was excellent.
> Minni [a restaurant frequented by SK] provided the beans
> for a princely sum. The sugar was from Sundorph, and ex-
> actly on the first of the month he paid his bills.

There is probably an element of teasing in these elaborate
rituals; one senses Levin's annoyance and in the background,
Kierkegaard's enjoyment of that annoyance. But one senses

something else here, for not only the ritual elements but also the studied regularity of the meals—bouillon on 29 out of 31 days—points to a life that has withdrawn into an aesthetic cocoon. Protected from distractions and interruptions by his faithful Anders, his rooms kept a constant 13¾°C with just a trace of Eau de Cologne in the air, Kierkegaard has succeeded in keeping that "infected" world he hated at a distance. We picture him, for example, living on Nørregade in the early 1840's, in a series of rooms so brightly lit they attracted notice from the street, as he worked into the late evening, first at this desk and then at another, trying to catch with pen and ink the precise nuance of his mood. A young acquaintance who was only sixteen or eighteen at the time recalled how strangely he had been received on one of these evenings. Seeing the lights from below, he thought a party might be in progress and rang the bell. Kierkegaard answered the door in evening dress, but when the young man asked if he were expecting guests, he replied: "No. I never have people in, but now and then it occurs to me to pretend as if I were, and so I stroll back and forth through the rooms imagining that I am entertaining my fictitious guests."

Kierkegaard's greatest luxury was neither the stuffed lamb nor the coffee beans from Minni, but rather his carriage drives through the woods and near the lakes and beaches of northern Sjælland; he called them his "airbaths." While he was engaged to Regine he had learned to ride a horse, principally for the exercise but also to permit him to take short excursions without a coachman. He never, however, became comfortable on horseback. According to Brøchner: "One saw from his posture that he did not trust his ability to control the horse if it should decide to act up. He sat stiffly upright, and one got the impression that all the time he was trying to remember his riding master's instructions." But, as Brøchner points out: "He soon gave up horseback riding and preferred a carriage when he wanted to

visit his favorite spots in the woods around Copenhagen. . . .
On horseback he could scarcely have had much freedom to pur-
sue his thoughts and fantasies." It was, of course, precisely this
freedom that he sought on excursions. If his work became
knotted up or his mind empty, a quick coach trip was a sure cure.
The motion of the coach, the changing scenes, the enforced idleness all combined to produce a mood of easy lassitude. "I won't
ride," he once wrote in his journal. "It is too violent an exercise
compared to my apathy; I only want to drive, to let a number of
objects glide by me while I'm comfortably and easily shaken, to
linger in beautiful places and feel my own languor."

He took these drives often until his money ran out in the
1850's. He always seemed to prefer the same destinations: Fredensborg, Lyngby, Klampenborg, and Røjels Inn at Ny Holte.
The coachman's receipts, which have been preserved for certain
years, show a considerable expenditure. The average drive cost
over 5 rd., and he took forty-three drives in 1844 and thirty-two
in 1845. On most of them he traveled alone, huddled under a
robe, watching the clouds skidding by overhead, listening to the
steady trot of the horses' hooves and the occasional flick of the
coachman's whip. Driving through the Deer Park or Grib's
Forest in the early autumn, he could hear the great beech trees
groaning in the wind, scattering their leaves along the coach's
path. The world would slide by as the coach gently rocked,
lulling its passenger not to sleep but into a kind of trance.
Suddenly would come the brisk commotion of a country inn; the
clatter of hooves on the courtyard as the coachman reined in,
his call inside—"The Magister"—and the burst of activity this
prompted. After a brief stroll through the grounds, Kierkegaard
would enter to dine, usually on soup and chicken or duck. There
would be deferential smiles all around, as the Magister was
known to be a liberal tipper; and soon another clatter of hooves
would mark his departure. The frail, round-shouldered man
would once again hunch down under his robe and top hat to

watch the familiar scenes pass: the last view of Fredensborg
Castle as they left the village, the rolling hills north of Grønholt
with its windmill, Hørsholm with its church and lake, then south
along the coast road—Vedbæk, Skodsborg, Taarbæk, Charlot-
tenlund—until he could see approaching on his right the string
of lakes, then hear the rumble and clatter as they entered the
city proper through Østerport. Whatever stretch of road it was,
he would have ridden it not long before. Now, as the scenes
fell into place like beads on a necklace, it would no longer be
clear what he remembered and what he perceived. The two
orders of experience slid together, since what was remembered
would soon be reexperienced—just around the next bend. Lulled
into reverie by the regular rhythm of the hooves and the equally
regular appearance of familiar scenes, the world took on the
nuance of image. Refreshed by his drive, he could now return
to his apartment, possibly to take up once more the entertainment of his absent guests.

It is hardly surprising that Kierkegaard ran out of money in
the 1850's. When he entered the hospital to die in the autumn
of 1855, he had exhausted his inheritance of 33,594 rd. He had
only enough money left to pay the hospital and possibly to cover
his funeral. After his death three legends grew up to explain
the disappearance of his wealth, some spawned by his own remarks, others by the recollections of friends and family: (1) He
spent it on publishing his own works; Troels-Lund thought half
his fortune had been eaten up in this way. (2) On Old Testament grounds he refused to accept interest on his capital; Georg
Brandes backed this explanation in his full-length study of
Kierkegaard. (3) From Christian compassion he gave away
much of his money to the poor; Hans Brøchner seemed to favor
this theory.

It was not until eighty years after Kierkegaard's death '
that Frithiof Brandt and Else Rammel shattered all three
legends by giving a close accounting of his income and expendi-

tures in their fascinating book, *Søren Kierkegaard and Money*.
He had not spent great sums to have his books published; on
the contrary he had received a rather nice income from their
sales. His royalties of 5,000 rd. probably covered the rent on his
various apartments and the wages of the secretaries he engaged
for copying and proofreading during his most productive years.
Nor could the disappearance of his fortune be laid to gifts to
the poor or to a refusal to accept interest. Kierkegaard's gifts to
the poor were small amounts presented to the occasional beggar
who happened by his door; in all of 1847 he gave away exactly
31 rigsdaler, 2 marks, 3 shillings—the cost of six carriage drives.
Moreover, Kierkegaard managed his money with great skill,
making a tidy profit when it became necessary to sell 2 Nytorv,
collecting sizable interest from mortgages, and even floating
loans from his brother or the national bank in the period 1843 to
1848 when the market for securities was poor. The fact is that
Kierkegaard simply spent his fortune on the carriage drives, exquisite furniture, elegant bindings, stuffed lamb, and good wine;
30 bottles of which were found in his apartment at his death.

To say that Kierkegaard squandered his fortune would be to
miss the point. He did not spend his money carelessly, but used
it up with great deliberation to construct the "cloister" in which
he could work fruitfully, without interruption or distraction.
Having rejected the world early in life (he told Emil Boesen in
1841, "You lack one thing that I have; you have not learned to
despise the world, to see how small everything is"), he used his
money simply to sustain that rejection. An early section of his
first major work, *Either/Or*, contains a haunting description of
his situation:

> My sorrow is my castle, built like an eagle's nest upon the
> peak of a mountain lost in the clouds. No one can take it by
> storm. From this abode I dart down into the world of reality
> to seize my prey; but I do not remain there. I bear my quarry

aloft to my stronghold. My booty is a picture I weave into the
tapestries of my palace. There I live as one dead. Everything
I have experienced I immerse in a baptism of forgetfulness
unto an eternal remembrance. Everything temporal and con-
tingent is forgotten and erased. Then I sit like an old man,
grey-haired and thoughtful, and explain picture after picture
in a voice as soft as a whisper. And at my side a child sits
and listens, although he remembers everything before I tell it.

It was in building this castle that Kierkegaard's fortune was
expended."But for my extravagance," he wrote in 1850, "I
would never have been able to work on such a scale."

But he did not spend all his time cloistered behind
servants and thick drapes. Anders had strict instructions
about callers (only family, Emil Boesen, and the poor were
to be admitted) and followed them rigorously. On most days,
however, Kierkegaard would leave his high desk and manuscripts, select an umbrella or Spanish walking cane, don
his hat (a high topper in the early 1840's, a wide
low-brimmed model later on), and go for his daily stroll—
"immersion in humanity," he called it. If he was in a solitary
mood he would make his way up to the ramparts that encircled
the city or wander through Rosenberg Park. If he was feeling
strenuous, he might walk outside the city's walls to Josty's garden restaurant in Frederiksberg Park. Most often, however, it
was not solitary exercise but company he sought, and he was a
well-known figure on many of Copenhagen's most traveled thoroughfares. "The streets of Copenhagen were in fact a large reception room for him," Henriette Lund wrote, "where he
wandered early and late, and talked to everybody he wanted to."
An umbrella or cane under his arm, well-tailored jacket buttoned
tightly across his thin chest, high white collar and shirt frill
peeking through, he could usually be seen in animated conversation with one of his acquaintances. He would grip his compan-

ion by the elbow, sometimes gesticulating with his cane, all the
while weaving up the street in zigzag. As Brøchner said, "Because of his crooked figure his movements were so irregular that
you could never walk straight when he was with you. You were
successively pushed in toward the houses and cellar holes, and
then out toward the gutter."

But Kierkegaard's conversation made it all worthwhile. He
had a droll sense of humor that delighted in puncturing pom-
posity. Once he encountered a German scholar who had been
told that he should not fail to meet this great Danish personage
while he was in Copenhagen. Kierkegaard behaved toward him
with deference and politeness but assured the visiting professor
that there must be some mistake. "My brother," Kierkegaard
said, "has a German doctorate and is an extraordinarily learned
man whom it would certainly interest you to meet. I, however,
am only a beer retailer." On another occasion he was walking
with J. A. Ostermann when they met Meyer Goldschmidt, a
newspaper editor who had just been imprisoned and put on
bread and water for some censorship violation.

KIERKEGAARD: Are you staying any longer at the hotel?
GOLDSCHMIDT: I'm out in the city, but I'll move in again.
KIERKEGAARD: How are the amenities?
GOLDSCHMIDT: Considering the circumstances, good.
KIERKEGAARD: But the food has not improved?
GOLDSCHMIDT: (*Laughing*) No! Not in any way.

These walks through town were not taken simply for relax-
ation; they were also an important stimulus for Kierkegaard's
imagination. On the streets of Copenhagen he found the "prey"
that he then carried back to "weave into the tapestries of my
palace." Brøchner told how Kierkegaard carried out psychological experiments on passersby during their walks together:

I once walked through a whole street with him while he explained how one can make psychological studies by putting

oneself *en rapport* with passersby. As he explained his theory, he put it into practice with almost everyone we met. There was no one on whom his glance did not make an obvious impression. . . . His smile and his eyes were indescribably expressive. He had a way of greeting one at a distance with a look. It was only a little movement of the eye, and yet it meant so much. There was at times something infinitely gentle and loving in his look, but also something goading and irritating. . . . Anyone meeting that glance was either attracted or else repelled, made embarrassed, uncertain, or irritated.

Not only his eye but also his tongue was busy as he moved through the streets gathering material. According to Brøchner, Kierkegaard talked with all sorts of people, sometimes starting where an earlier conversation had left off and carrying it forward to a point where he could pick it up again as opportunity served.

Yet it would be wrong to think of these walks as designed only to give him character studies for his work. Frederik Hammerich told how, while they walked together, Kierkegaard "worked out in his head exactly what he wrote down later," and Kierkegaard declared that "nearly everything I have written was written *currente calamo*, as they say, . . . because I finish everything while walking about." In his walks Kierkegaard sought to grasp those smells, sounds, textures, and sights that would be grist for his imaginative mill. According to Brøchner, these outings were all quite limited in purpose and extent: "Only such a preamble of enjoyment was taken as could be ideally worked out later."

Considering the ease with which he talked to people in the streets of Copenhagen, why did none of his many acquaintances ever turn into friends? Brøchner saw Kierkegaard often but never broke through a fundamental reserve. He said that Kierkegaard had basically "two methods of conversation," neither of which encouraged much intimacy: "One was essentially a reporting, meant to rouse and stimulate. The other was essentially an ironic questioning, meant to confound through its dialectic." Israel Levin ends his recollections of his employer with the judgment that "on the whole Søren was not lovable. His disciples did not like him. He was sarcastic and could bear a grudge." The fact is that after his student days Kierkegaard had no one whom he could call a friend. Emil Boesen, his boyhood companion, had taken a pastorate in the country. His brother, never close to him in any case, had remarried and taken a church in Pedersborg in 1842. He was *persona non grata* in the Olsen home and notorious in the rest of polite society. For a time in the late 1840's he tried to draw near to a university professor, Rasmus Nielsen, but they clashed and nothing came of it. He remained very much "the strange one . . . the peculiar one," he had been in childhood.

Yet if he never seemed capable of forming a genuine friendship with an adult, he was a delightful friend to children. His sense of magic and zest for fantasy enabled him to insinuate himself into their world at will. Henriette Lund told of an enchanted evening he prepared for her and a young cousin: Arriving by special invitation at Kierkegaard's apartment on Nørregade, they were presented with bouquets of lilies of the valley, together with carefully chosen individual gifts. Next Anders announced that a coach was waiting. " 'Then we must go,' cried Uncle Søren, 'Where to?' But that no one discovered until we arrived at the different stopping places, all prearranged, where some of the sights were pointed out to us." Returning to the apartment, the two girls played children's games with their host until the evening meal was served. "It consisted of *Smørrebrød*, a cake of marzipan with a specially wonderful flower covering, and champagne. Uncle Søren was our attentive and indefatigable host, and Anders an equally attentive waiter."

There is a touching, almost Lewis Carroll–like quality to this image of the author of *Either/Or* and the *Postscript* going to such pains to provide two young girls with a magic evening they would never forget. On another occasion the children of Pastor Spang, knowing that Kierkegaard loved flowers, brought him a large bucket of lilies of the valley. After the youngest child presented the flowers, he "became gay, rubbed his hands, and walking up and down the room, said: 'Let me see now, do I have a piece of candy. No, I don't. But perhaps my maid has one.' Then he laughed, and the package came out, and we went happily away."

Children recognized Kierkegaard as one of their own; like his contemporary Hans Christian Andersen, he remained in many ways a child throughout his life. Troels-Lund, half brother to Henriette, remembered examples of his playfulness:

> He [Kierkegaard] was an unseen witness to a conversation between two poorhouse inmates. The first said: "It's the devil that one never is happy."
> The other: "Nonsense! What's happiness?"
> The first: "It would be if an angel dropped down from heaven and gave me a 'blue one.' "
> This Kierkegaard could not resist. He took a five-dollar note (a "blue one") from his purse, stepped up, presented it with a deep bow, and disappeared without saying a word.

On another occasion Troels-Lund saw his uncle early one summer morning:

> I was walking over the ramparts to school. On the bastion near Nørreport I met him, and we walked together along the ramp to Nørregade. Laughingly he asked me if I was certain that the school was still where it used to be. "Yes, unfortunately."—"But it could have, for example, burned down last night." He had heard the watchman pipe. That possibility put

me in an especially good humor. . . . Together we sketched
out all the advantages that would accrue had the school
burned down. I spared none of the teachers. When the in-
structors in Latin, French, and German and the Principal
came fleeing out of the burning door, I had them shot down
with grapeshot.

Our story had got this far when we reached
Nørregade. Though ecstatic over all the possibilities we had
sketched, I had to say goodbye. While he was still on the
middle of the ramparts I waved to him again, and he smiled
back happily. Then I was alone in reality. Everything became
heavier the lower I descended. Not a whiff of smoke at the
corner of Nørregade. No crowd at all.

Thus Troels-Lund went down to the street and to a world
heavier, duller, more mundane than the land of possibility he
had left behind with his uncle on the ramparts. And in spirit
Kierkegaard did, at least until the last year of his life, remain
on the ramparts, preferring solitude and the private interstices
of imagination to the public world around him.

· To understand Kierkegaard is to understand the double image
of a man who knew many yet was known by none, who chatted
with everyone yet really talked with no one, who made the
streets of Copenhagen his own reception room yet lived in a
cloister. He talked not to reveal but to conceal. He lived in the
world but was never at home in the world. His real life was
solitary and withdrawn, situated in that private territory where
percept and image merge. Thus his carriage drives, his pauses by
the flowers in Frederiksberg Gardens, his attenuated domestic
life, his similarly attenuated excursions into the streets, where
he solicited "only such a preamble of enjoyment . . . as could
be ideally worked out later." In all these ways Kierkegaard was
seeking the elusive coincidence with self-as-image that Narcissus
sought as he peered into his darkened pool—the tranquil mo-

ment when consciousness and its object become one, when the
world, purified of its alien elements, reflects back only oneself.
By choosing the cloister instead of the world, Kierkegaard was
in fact choosing to "live as one dead." Yet this seeming death-
in-life was the necessary condition for the aesthetic act by which
experience was to be transmuted into image—or as he put it in
Either/Or, the act by which "everything I have experienced I
immerse in a baptism of forgetfulness unto an eternal remembrance."

It should come as no surprise, then, to find in Kierkegaard's
art the evidence of his lifelong struggle to shape experience into
image. For it was the act of writing that betrayed his purpose
most clearly. It is no exaggeration to say that in the years following his break with Regine, his life was his writing. Lacking job
or family, friends or confidants, writing became his only serious
activity. And write he did, turning out in the four-year period
1842 to 1846 no less than twenty-one religious discourses, one
book of literary criticism, and eight pseudonymous works (three
of them over 350 pages, one over 800 pages). In itself the
pseudonymous production would be a respectable body of work
for an ordinary writer. But what matters is not the quantity of
his books, but the way in which they were produced. For there
was nothing of the entertainment, of the pleasant diversion, in
Kierkegaard's literary production. It was wrung from the very
"abscess" of his suffering as a man:

> When I am sunk in the deepest suffering of melancholy, one
> thought or another becomes so knotted up for me that I
> cannot loose it, and since it is related to my own existence, I
> suffer indescribably. And then when a little time has passed,
> the abscess bursts—and inside lies the richest and most won-
> derful material for work, and just what I need at the
> moment. . . .
> I suffer as a human being can suffer in indescribable melan-

choly, which always has to do with my thinking about my own existence.

This is no isolated admission, but a familiar theme of his journal. "Only when I am producing do I feel well," he wrote in 1846. "Then I forget all life's discomforts, all suffering, then I am absorbed in my thought and happy. If I let my work alone for a couple of days I immediately become ill, overwhelmed, troubled, my head heavy and burdened." It was due to his melancholy, he tells us, that he "discovered and poetically traveled through a whole fantasy world." His writing was not an agreeable amusement, but "the product of an irresistible inward impulse, a melancholy man's only possibility." "As Scheherazade saved her life by telling stories," he confessed, "so I save myself or keep myself alive by writing" (*ved at producere*).

Kierkegaard joking and playing with children, dining with Israel Levin, or taking a stroll through downtown Copenhagen is not a man idling away a frivolous or leisurely existence. The calculated aestheticism of his daily life permitted him to carry out his work. His life and work, inextricably joined, exhibited with rare purity the lineaments of the aesthetic project. From childhood on he sought that "imperceptible transfiguration" of which Mallarmé speaks when he tells how, in his own person, "the sensation of lightness is melting little by little into one of perception." Not surprisingly, it was this sense of lightness which Kierkegaard knew in the act of writing: "So I require the magic of artistic production in order to forget all of life's crude trivialities." Thus in the last third of his lifetime, it is impossible to distinguish his life from his work. His carriage drives through the Sjælland countryside, his "immersion in humanity" in the streets of Copenhagen, and the endless hours of scribbling at his stand-up desk were part of one comprehensive project—that of re-presenting the world through imagination.

When he left Regine, he felt he had chosen "death." But what he had really chosen was his vocation as artist—the unremitting, day-to-day labor of producing some thirty-six works of literature. The lesson he learned in his relationship with Regine—that for him the world was uninhabitable—did not compel him to retire into indolence, but provided the driving energy behind his work. For eight, ten, twelve hours a day he pushed himself to the narrow limits his fragile body could sustain. All this he told Emil Boesen in a letter from Berlin:

> At the beginning I was ill, now I am well in a manner of speaking—that is, my mind is expanding and presumably killing my body. I have never worked as hard as now. During the morning I go out for a little while. Then I come back and sit in my room uninterruptedly until about three o'clock. I can scarcely see out of my eyes. Then I shuffle by the aid of my cane to the restaurant, but am so weak that I believe if anyone were to call my name aloud, I should fall over dead. Then I go home and begin again. During the past months I have been pumping up a real shower bath, now I have pulled the cord. The ideas stream down upon me—healthy, happy, plump, merry, blessed children, easily brought to birth, yet all of them bearing the birthmarks of my personality.

The vital center of Kierkegaard's existence during his last fourteen years was his work—"to produce," he wrote, "was my life." Since this production is the sum and meaning of his life, we turn now to the "merry, blessed children" each of which bore the birthmarks of his personality.

12

MASTER OF IRONY

I

ON the next to last day of 1845 the manuscript of Kierkegaard's final pseudonymous work, *Concluding Unscientific Postscript*, was delivered to the printer Bianco Luno. Three sheets were kept back—"in order," Kierkegaard wrote, "not to be left lying around the printshop"—and were delivered only when the printing was nearly complete. Along with these sheets came instructions in Israel Levin's handwriting to bind them, unpaginated, into the end of the book as endpapers. This odd document, slipped furtively into the *Postscript* at the last moment, was entitled "A First and Last Declaration." It began with the admission that Kierkegaard was "the author, as people would call it" of the long series of pseudonymous works published over the preceding three years. As the Declaration quickly made clear, however, its purpose was not simply to acknowledge authorship but to speak for the autonomy of the pseudonyms:

> What is written is indeed my own, but only insofar as I put into the mouth of the poetically actual individual whom I *produced*, his life view expressed in audible lines. . . . So in the pseudonymous works there is not a single word which is mine, I have no opinion about them except as a third person, no knowledge of their meaning except as a reader, not the

remotest private relation to them. . . . My wish, my prayer, is that if it occur to anyone to cite a particular saying from the books, he do me the favor to cite the name of the respective pseudonym.

Historically speaking, this injunction has proved difficult to follow. In the century since Kierkegaard's death hardly an essay written on the pseudonymous series has lacked some reference to their real author and his twisted life. When we ourselves try to follow his plea, we recognize immediately why it has been so often ignored. With his words ringing in our ears ("in the pseudonymous works there is not a single word which is mine") we pick up the first pseudonymous work, *Either/Or*, and dutifully note his absence from the title page. We sort through the complicated web of multiple pseudonyms in which the secret of its authorship is wrapped, and agree not to identify Kierkegaard with any of his creations. Yet as Stephen Crites has pointed out, this does us no good: "For there he is on every page, the spindly figure with the umbrella, the hypochondriacal young man born old, with his eccentricities, his love affair that we are sick of hearing about, his abysmal melancholia." No matter how willingly we try to follow Kierkegaard's wishes, we discover that we cannot leave his actual life out of account. He implores us to forget about him and pay attention to his characters—but he *is* his characters in so many ways. His ironic glance is theirs, and so too is his isolation, his hyperconsciousness. It is as if his life had been refracted by a powerful prism into a multitude of images, each of which retained some mark of the original, some spoor of "the spindly figure with the umbrella." This may be what he had in mind when he wrote to Boesen of his "merry, blessed children," each of which bore the birthmarks of his personality.

What is it that in spite of Kierkegaard's claim to the contrary makes the paternity of the pseudonymous works so clear? He did, of course, use some material from his journal in his writings. Twenty-seven of the first twenty-eight "diapsalmata" (a Greek word meaning "refrain") in *Either/Or* were lifted verbatim from his journal, and the young man in *Stages on Life's Way* repeated word for word Kierkegaard's letter to Regine returning her ring. But these are isolated instances; the borrowing of an idea here, a simile there, cannot alone account for the Kierkegaardian flavor of the books. To find the origins of his identifying signature we must look elsewhere, examining the style of the works, the character of the pseudonyms, and the predicament they share.

Today most Danes first read Kierkegaard in the *Gymnasium*, where he is studied as a master stylist. The remarkable lightness and flexibility he brought to Danish, his ear for the music of words, his eye for the limpid image, the pure metaphor, his ability to dress the most abstract idea in the garments of concreteness, to unravel complexity into simplicity—these characteristics of his extraordinary style are duly noted and admired by successive generations of seventeen-year-olds. Indeed it cannot be denied that Kierkegaard is a clever, even brilliant, writer and that his works are lit at points with stylistic fireworks. What is most Kierkegaardian, however, is not the pyrotechnics but the background against which they explode. For in essence Kierkegaard is an enormously diffuse writer.

There are passages in his books—the "Unhappiest Man" essay in *Either/Or*, parts of *Fear and Trembling* and the *Postscript*—and at least one complete work, *Philosophical Fragments*, that are masterpieces of concision. But Kierkegaard's basic style is extravagantly prolix, flooding the reader under a torrent of words. Loosely moving from theme to theme, he sometimes finishes a train of thought before beginning another, but not always. What he called "the vegetative luxuriance of my style" cannot be ascribed to any particular pseudonym, for it burgeons in almost all of them. It also characterizes the "edify-ing discourses" he was simultaneously publishing under his own name.

Part of his exceptional verbosity can be attributed to the con-ditions under which his books were published. Kierkegaard had no editor, and all his writings through August 1847 were issued on a commission basis—he paid the printer himself and then gave the bookseller a percentage of the list price to sell them. Since his funds during these years were ample, there was no external check on his production; publishing a book of 300 in-stead of 200 pages simply meant that both the copyist and the printer had to be paid more.

Kierkegaard's prolixity, however, is not to be confused with mere loquacity. His writing, he told us, "was the prompting of an irresistible inward impulse"; it was a "necessary emptying-out" (*Udtømmelse*). During the years of his pseudonymous produc-tion his journal remained small; in all of 1843, 1844, and 1845 it amounted to only 145 pages. (On the other hand, in 1848 it grew to 349 pages, and in 1850 to 671.) Without friends, fam-ily, or confidants Kierkegaard was emptying out his thoughts and feelings through his pseudonyms. His pen rushed across the page not because he enjoyed it but because he felt he *must* write, must drain the watershed of ideas and fancies that had built up over the years. And so the shower descended, a great flow of arguments, images, stories, and characters: in February 1843, *Either/Or*, a massive two-volume work of 838 pages; eight months later, two shorter works, *Repetition* and *Fear and Trembling*; eight months later, three more, *Philosophical Frag-ments*, *Prefaces*, and *The Concept of Dread*; ten months later in April 1845, the large (383 pages) *Stages on Life's Way*; and finally, in February 1846, the even larger (480 pages) *Conclud-ing Unscientific Postscript*. In this time he also published twenty-one religious discourses under his own name. No wonder, then, that the enormous productive outpouring sometimes seems out of control, cascading over the reader like a waterfall. In much of it one feels the author's intoxication with language, and remembering his remark that "to produce was my life," one also feels a certain chill. For indeed these works were his life, and all his life was concentrated in them.

Kierkegaard's style, of course, cannot be disentangled from our impressions of the pseudonyms he created. For what we are given in his books are not the activities of a group of characters, but rather the essays, diaries, letters, commentaries, and lyrical outbursts of the pseudonymous authors. And they are a talkative lot: Judge William rambling through 70,000-word "letters" to his young friend; the aesthete A running on through page after page of pseudo-Hegelian criticism; Frater Taciturnus's long-winded commentary in *Stages on Life's Way*; Johannes Climacus's tour de force of humorous philosophizing in the *Postscript*. But this general garrulity is not their most outstanding characteristic, nor is it what gives them and their works a Kierkegaardian signature.

Georg Brandes has remarked on the "hothouse" quality of Kierkegaard's imagination, how his pseudonyms are "bloodless" and "brain-figment-like." But here Brandes partially misses the point, for it is not that Kierkegaard has failed in producing characters who are bloodless, but rather that he has succeeded in deliberately producing them. When the aesthete of *Either/Or* observes that his Johannes the Seducer seemed to live in "a world of gauze, lighter, more ethereal, qualitatively different from the actual world," the description might apply to any of Kierkegaard's pseudonyms. Like their author they seem inordinately "ghostly," purely mental, never rooted in the physical world through their bodies, without physical desire or suffering. They all are disembodied hermits lacking parents or home, wife or job, appetite or fear. In a single case (Judge William) we encounter a pseudonymous spokesman who has a family, but his wife and child function more as poetic reference points than as flesh-and-blood relations. Lonely, intelligent, sometimes witty, these pseudonymous figures appear most often as "strangers and aliens in the world," happy (when they are happy) only in their thoughts and reveries.

Their ghostly character is suggested by their names. There is first of all Victor Eremita, whose last name, Kierkegaard tells us, places him "in the cloister." Next is Constantine Constantius who, mired in his "constant constancy," cannot receive the thunderstorm of "repetition" that revives his young friend and restores him to life. Then there is Johannes de Silentio, that "knight of infinite resignation," who can only stand astonished before the imagined faith of Abraham. Next is Vigilius Haufniensis, the pedantic psychologist, whose name is a Latin transcription for "the watchman of Copenhagen." There is William Afham, who describes himself as " 'pure being' and therefore less than nothing," and in the same volume, Frater Taciturnus, the taciturn priest of the final stage anterior to faith. Finally there is Johannes Climacus who, although unable to make the movements of faith, nevertheless can set up the ladder (Latin: *climacis*) leading to it. From their names can be read their characters— hermetic, constant, silent, taciturn, and watchful. Nonparticipants in life, they are its critics and spectators. '

Their actions are as revealing as their names. For the odd thing about all these Kierkegaardian children is that their primary activity seems to be imagining still other characters, thinking of the thoughts they might think and of the arguments they might profess. Victor Eremita imagines an aesthete and then produces a series of essays as they might be written by him. Not to be outdone, the aesthete mimics his creator by imagining still another character, Johannes the Seducer, and proceeds to write his 150-page diary. Johannes de Silentio embroiders various themes on the Biblical story of Abraham and completes his reflections by imagining a modern hero: the knight of faith as

tax collector. Constantine Constantius finally admits that the
"young man" whose letters he has presented is really a figment
of his imagination. Frater Taciturnus likewise reveals that the
"Quidam" whose diary the reader has just finished is not an
actual person but a "thought experiment."

The remaining pseudonyms content themselves not with in-
venting fictional characters, but with producing arguments concerning the nature of original sin, the difference between the
Socratic and the Christian standpoints, the distinction between
objective and subjective truth. Like their author, all these
pseudonyms are cloistered from the world, and in their respective
monastic cells they all mimic his life-activity—thinking and
imagining. Removed thus from the world, they are alive without
feeling alive, they are human but only abstractly so. And it is
the abstraction of their lives that haunts them. Each, troubled
by his ineradicable "thinness," keeps returning to the image of
a life that has been made lively, a humanity richly and passion-
ately fulfilled. And here their thoughts are drawn into a fatal
dialectic. For, like insomniacs proposing sleep, they imaginatively
propose to themselves an actuality of selfhood which is flawed
by the very fact that it is imaginary. Like the insomniac they
remain ever wakeful, ever conscious of the ideality of their
dream, and thus end where they began—in the cloister. More
than anything else it is this steadfast refusal of the pseudonym
to be taken in by his dream that gives these works their characteristic flavor.

II

To point out the Kierkegaardian signature of the pseudonymous
writings is not finally to refuse Kierkegaard's injunction to regard the pseudonyms as independent beings. On the contrary, it

is only by scrupulously complying with his plea that we can be led to the central meaning of the works. There is an all-important correlation, a kind of doubling, that characterizes Kierkegaard's relation to his pseudonyms. For precisely in the same way that the pseudonyms maintain their distance from their imaginative creations does Kierkegaard maintain his distance from the pseudonyms. He tells us he is absent from their compositions, that in their works his own voice is silent. And it is true that the views of the pseudonyms are not Kierkegaard's. If anything, they are the views he has outlived or outthought. As certain well-to-do matrons hand on their old clothes to their maids, so Kierkegaard handed on his old, outworn visions to his pseudonyms. Thus it requires no special prescience to recognize in the portrait of the aesthetic life painted in *Either/Or* only an extrapolation of the life Kierkegaard tried to live in the late 1830's, or to understand that later in the same work, when Judge William sings the praises of marriage, he is only dressing up the hopes Kierkegaard earlier entertained for himself and Regine. In 1848 he characterized his pseudonyms in this way:

> One will perceive the significance of the pseudonyms and why I must be pseudonymous in relation to all aesthetic production: because I led my own life in entirely different categories and understood from the beginning that this productivity was something interim, a deceit, a necessary emptying-out.

In *The Point of View*—the posthumously published piece from which this citation is drawn—Kierkegaard never made clear just what these "entirely different categories" were. In a journal entry from the same year he was more explicit: looking back over the work of the last seven years, he wrote: "As poet and thinker I have represented all things in the medium of imagination, myself living in resignation."

Thus the distance that Kierkegaard maintains between himself and his pseudonyms is meant to indicate (at least in part) his own incapacity to believe the content of their visions. Just as the pseudonyms remain ever wakeful in their irony, so Kierkegaard's silence—his absence from these works—indicates a similar wakefulness. The central focus of the pseudonymous writings is not ethics or religion or aesthetics, but rather the dialectic of the life of imagination. Their achievement lies in the construction of a literature of self-reference, a series of works that comment repeatedly on the imaginative act involved in their own creation. They are a "deceit," then, only to the extent that they are not about what they appear to be about. To take them seriously is not to take them seriously. To paraphrase them, to earnestly elucidate the philosophy expounded or the metaphysics presupposed in this or that work, is to miss the point that ultimately they seek to show the vanity of all philosophy and metaphysics.

Regarding these works, John Updike has remarked that "duplicity was the very engine of Kierkegaard's thought," that he was a "man in love with duplicity and irony and all double-edged things." In the pseudonymous writings we find pseudonyms curled within pseudonyms like Chinese puzzle boxes. We find elaborate hoaxes that disappear in an eye blink as the pseudonym admits his ploy. We see Kierkegaard going to extreme lengths to conceal his authorship at the same time that he writes a tongue-in-cheek letter to *Fatherland* asking, "Who is the author of *Either/Or?*" The world of the pseudonyms is a world of stratagem and pretense, of "acoustic illusion" and "thought experiment." It is a world of artifice and subterfuge, a world of trapdoors and hidden panels, of sudden surprises and shapes only half-recognized in a mirror. Thus we have pseudonyms pretending *not* to be other pseudonyms—Constantine Constantius pretending not to be "the young man" (and then admitting it),

Frater Taciturnus pretending not to be Quidam (and then admitting it), the aesthete A pretending not to be Johannes the Seducer (and then implying that the two are identical).

More important, through the device of parody we find books pretending to be books that they are not. *Either/Or* comes on the scene dressed in the familiar trappings of the romantic novel —the letter, the aphorism, the essay are all very much in evidence. It would seem to have been staged on the same platform as *Wilhelm Meister*; but as Louis Mackey has pointed out, it is in reality a parody of Goethe's great universal novel—"a *Bildungsroman* but without *Bildung*." The *Concluding Unscientific Postscript*, that massive work of 480 large pages, is a postscript to a tiny work of 164 small pages. A glance at its complicated table of contents leads the casual reader to suspect that here the philosophical urge to system building has run amok. Yet the target of the book is really systematic philosophy. In the pseudonym's absurd conclusion that the difficulty of belief can itself become a criterion of true belief, we recognize that the attempt to save philosophy from the philosophers has itself become a target of satire. Finally, in the comic profusion of pseudonyms and the transparency of their stratagems in *Stages on Life's Way*, the device of pseudonymity itself is parodied.

The ambience of all these works is that of duplicity, and their essential theme is the inherent volatility of human consciousness. In their elaborate hoaxes and sudden surprises, in their trickery and satire, there is an underlying black humor. For finally the joke is on the reader, and the smarter he is, the sooner he realizes it. But to see through all the pseudonyms, to recognize that the vision of any one is not to be preferred to that of any other, is finally to join Kierkegaard in his cloister. It is to share with him that peculiarly modern laceration—"I must believe, but I can't believe"—which since his time has become ever more painful.

The essentially duplicitous character of the pseudonyms is, then, essential to their meaning, and is founded on the simple yet all-important fact that in the pseudonyms, Kierkegaard is absent.

But how can a man be absent from his words? Years before, in the master's thesis that won him the whimsical sobriquet "Master of Irony," Kierkegaard gave the answer. Moreover, in the last part of this work, written in 1841 as he slowly and painfully disengaged himself from Regine, he laid out the problematic that was to order the pseudonymous series. As Georg Brandes pointed out a century ago, *The Concept of Irony* is the real point of departure for Kierkegaard's writings.

The ironist, of course, is the man who is absent from his words. In ordinary speech, writes Kierkegaard, a person can be pinned down in what he says. The ordinary speaker means what he says and hence is bound to that meaning. But "the ironic figure of speech cancels itself," since the speaker's meaning is not in what is said. "If . . . what is said is not my meaning, or the opposite of my meaning, then I am free both in relation to others and in relation to myself." The ironist, absent from his words, is epitomized by Socrates, whose ironic turn of speech was not just a conversational gambit but rather expressed a life view culminating in "infinite negativity."

In the last third of the book Kierkegaard turns from a consideration of Socratic irony to the concept of irony itself. It is here, in his portrait of the ironist's ultimate refusal of the world, that we can discern the outlines of the problematic that will later guide the pseudonymous series. Praising Hegel's characterization of irony as "infinite absolute negativity," he goes on to point out that the ironist must live among his contemporaries as "a stranger and an alien." "The whole of existence has become alien to the ironic subject," he says. "He in turn has become estranged from existence, because actuality has lost its validity for him as he too, to a certain extent, has become unreal." This

theme of the hostility of the ironist to actuality, his attempt
to poetically derealize it (and the derealization of self which
necessarily follows), becomes the guiding idea of the book's final
section. "Irony is free," we are told, "free from all the cares of
actuality. . . . When one is free in this way, only then does one
live poetically, and it is well known that irony's great demand
is that one should *live poetically*." ·

But what does it mean, to live poetically? Choosing Hegelian
terminology (perhaps not without a trace of irony), Kierkegaard
suggests that the project of "living poetically" is really the attempt to translate the *an sich* (in-itself) character of the world
and the self into *für sich* (for-itself): "But really to live poetically, to be able poetically to create himself, *the ironist must
have no an sich.*" The ironist's project is then one of perpetually .
remaking himself and his world. Repeatedly he seeks to extirpate the otherness of the world so that he can stand unencum-
bered in the presence of his own image:

> As he is not inclined to fit himself to his surroundings, so his
> surroundings must be shaped to fit him, that is, he poeticizes
> not only himself but his surroundings as well. . . . When
> the given actuality loses its validity for the ironist, this is not
> because it is an outlived actuality which shall be replaced by
> a truer, but because the ironist is the eternal ego for whom no
> actuality is adequate. ·

The "eternal ego for whom no actuality is adequate" is, of
course, no one else but that solitary individual we have come
to know in the journal entries of the 1830's and 1840's. As the
outlines of Kierkegaard's sketch of the ironist are filled in, it
comes more and more to resemble a self-portrait:

> The ironist stands proudly withdrawn into himself; he lets ·
> mankind pass before him, as did Adam the animals, and finds
> no companionship for himself. By this he constantly comes

into conflict with the actuality to which he belongs. . . . For him life is a drama, and what engrosses him is the ingenious unfolding of that drama. He is himself a spectator even when performing some act. . . . He is inspired by the virtues of self-sacrifice as a spectator is inspired by them in a theater; he is a severe critic who well knows when such virtues become insipid and false. He even feels remorse; but aesthetically, not morally. In the moment of remorse he is aesthetically above his remorse, examining whether it is poetically correct, whether it might be a suitable reply in the mouth of some poetic character.

Because the ironist poeticizes both himself and his surroundings with the greatest possible license, because he lives hypothetically and subjunctively, his life finally loses all continuity. With this he sinks completely into mood. His life becomes *sheer mood.* . . . The ironist is a poet. . . . He poeticizes everything, especially his feelings. . . . He imagines that it is he who evokes the feeling, and he keeps on imagining until he becomes so spiritually exhausted that he must cease. Feeling has therefore no reality for the ironist, and he seldom gives expression to his feelings except in the form of an opposition. His grief hides itself in the incognito of the jest, his joy is wrapped in lament. ´

The term "ironist" may appear somewhat strange for describing a person who tries, despairingly, to poeticize all existence. Even in this passage, Kierkegaard at one point calls him a poet and at another (not in the excerpted portion) notes that he lives "metaphysically" and "aesthetically." Somewhat later in the same chapter he remarks, "Throughout the discussion I use the expressions *irony* and the *ironist*, but I could as easily say *romanticism* and the *romanticist*. All designate the same thing."´Again in offering a commentary on Friedrich Schlegel's novel *Lucinde,* he indicates that the subject of his portrait is really the man who "allows imagination alone to rule": "When the imagination is allowed to rule in this way it prostrates and anesthetizes the soul, robs it of all moral tension, and makes of life a dream."

The great importance of Kierkegaard's dissertation on irony lies in the clarity with which it shows Kierkegaard's grasp of his own position. The standpoint of irony (inferentially his own) is not a point of destination but of departure; in the closing pages of *Irony* it is revealed as a stage to be overcome. The ironist is really the naysayer, the man who negates in its very foundations the actuality of the world. Not only absent from his words, he is also absent from himself: He does not "possess himself in infinite clarity" but has "his infinity outside himself." He has become "intoxicated by the infinity of possibles." The task of the ironist, Kierkegaard suggests, is to master irony, indeed to overcome it. And this stage of mastered irony is described in the final section of the dissertation as a stage where actuality is again actualized. "Actuality will therefore not be rejected," Kierkegaard writes, "and longing shall be a healthy love, not a kittenish ruse for sneaking out of the world."

Significantly, Poul Møller charged Kierkegaard with being "so polemical through and through that it's just terrible," and Kierkegaard's mind kept drifting back to this remark for nearly twenty years. In some primordial sense, Kierkegaard was a man absent from himself. "Each time I wish to say something," he complained in 1837, "there is another who says it at the very same moment. It is as if I were always thinking double, as if my other self were always somehow ahead of me."

The dissertation on irony ended with the demand that irony be overcome so that actuality can be realized. This, in essence, was both Kierkegaard's desire and his problem. Experience had become for him a kind of sieve through which actuality seeped. Like the ironist, his mind had become "intoxicated" by possibilities, escaping, like a leak of gas, into the imaginary. His problem—and ultimately the problem of the pseudonyms—is how to stop that leak, how to prevent consciousness from "sneaking out of the world." In *Either/Or* (parts of which were written simultaneously with *Irony*), this problem is given flesh and substance.

III

Kierkegaard's name appeared nowhere on the title page of *Either/Or*, and in the months following its publication on February 20, 1843, there were few in Copenhagen who knew its author's identity. Its pseudonymous "editor," Victor Eremita, complicated the question by likewise disclaiming responsibility for its authorship, claiming that he found the manuscript in the secret drawer of a desk. By studying the handwriting, he says, he concluded that the manuscript was the work of two persons: a civil magistrate named William (whom Victor designates "B") and a nameless "young friend" of the magistrate (whom Victor designates "A"). The papers of Judge William consist first of two long letters (really treatises) on the subject of marriage and ethics. They are followed by a sermon written (so Judge William tells us) by an obscure Jutland priest.

Together, the sermon and the two letters make up the second volume of *Either/Or*, while the first consists of the scattered papers of A. These cover a wide range. There are a number of aphorisms and lyrical outbursts grouped under the rubric "diapsalmata." There are several essays of literary criticism as well as speeches written for a private club of aesthetes. Finally there is the famous "Diary of the Seducer," for which A disclaims authorship, claiming in his preface to the diary that he stole it from a friend named Johannes. But A's disclaimer is denied by Victor Eremita, who in *his* preface to the entire work tells us that Johannes the Seducer is most likely a creature of A's imagination and that A's attempt to pass himself off as only the editor is "an old novelist's trick." Victor then hints that his own "editorship" may be a novelistic ruse and that he himself may very well be the true author of the whole book.

Why this deception and masquerade? Why is pseudonym wrapped in pseudonym "like parts in a Chinese puzzle box"? If we ask for the real author of *Either/Or*, Søren Kierkegaard presents himself. But his figure soon merges with his pseudonym, the hermetic Victor, who is so volatile that he quickly splits into other characters: the aesthete, equally given to turning into still further pseudonyms, and the judge. Instead of a person we are likely to be given a persona, whose interior world, once entered, is found to be in motion, spinning off through fantasy into yet another persona. We search in vain for actuality, for substance. All we find is a volatile human consciousness continually on the move. And it is precisely this volatility that is the central focus of the book.

Like both Kierkegaard and the ironist, the aesthete is presented to us as living *beyond himself*, a characteristic made ironically clear in his preface to "The Diary of the Seducer." The Seducer's life, the aesthete points out, has been "an attempt to realize the task of living poetically." The diary reflects this fundamental project in its odd use of the present tense, a use which "is neither historically exact nor simply fictional, not indicative but subjunctive." Again and again the Seducer describes incidents as if they were occurring before his very eyes. But as the aesthete remarks in his preface to the diary, this is impossible, since everything in the diary "is recorded, naturally, after it has happened." The deliberate mixing of present with past, however, has a point. It is in fact the essence of the aesthetic project, whose final goal is not just a new or more intense experience, but (as the aesthete makes clear) the reproduction of "experience more or less poetically." "How can we account for the fact that the diary has acquired such a poetic coloration?" he asks. "It is explained by . . . [the Seducer's] poetic nature, which, we might say, is not rich enough, or perhaps not poor enough, to distinguish poetry and reality from one another." The Seducer's act in writing the diary hence exemplifies that deliberate mixing of immediate experience with imaginative reconstruction which is the core of the aesthetic project.

But now the irony inherent in the "Chinese puzzle box" structure of the book makes itself felt. For the aesthete ends his preface to the diary by concluding that the Seducer's project must fail:

> Many people who appear bodily in the actual world do not belong in it. . . . But the fact that a man can thus dwindle away, almost vanish from reality, may be a symptom of health or of sickness. . . . He did not belong to reality, and yet he had much to do with it. . . . He was not unequal to the weight of reality; he was not too weak to bear it, not at all, he was too strong; but this strength was really a sickness.

As readers of Victor Eremita's original preface, we know that the diary is not the product of the Seducer's recollection; both Seducer and diary are products of the aesthete's imagination. We know that in describing the Seducer, the aesthete is really describing himself, and that in pointing out the necessary failure of the Seducer's project, he is also remarking the necessary failure of his own life. Fundamentally, then, the aesthete is presented to us as *beyond himself*. "Your thought was hurried on ahead," the Judge admonishes him in *Either/Or*, Volume II. "You have seen through the vanity of everything, but you have got no further. . . . So you are constantly beyond yourself, that is, in despair." The Danish term for despair, *Fortvivlelse*, signifies more, philosophically, than its English counterpart, since it bears within it the morpheme *tvi* for "two," signaling the doubling of consciousness. (*Tvivl* in Danish means "doubt"; *Tvivlesyg* "scepticism"; *Tvetydighed* "ambiguity.") Thus to speak of the aesthete as "in despair" is to ascribe to him a doubled consciousness; he perseveres in his project, but at every moment he is beyond it, recognizing its nullity. It is this recognition that is communicated ironically through his preface to the Seducer's diary, and it is this recognition that makes of him (like the ironist) a man *absent* from himself.

A portrait of the man who is "always absent, never present to himself" is sketched with algebraic brevity in a little essay from *Either/Or* entitled "The Unhappiest Man." Originally intended by the aesthete A as an address to be delivered to the *Symparenekromenoi* (a Greek coinage meaning "society of co-deceased ones"), it catalogues the ways in which one can be absent from oneself either in the future or in the past, either in hope or in recollection. But the uniquely unhappy man is he whose partial presence in both past and future prevents him from having a life in the present at all: "When the forward-looking individual sees a future which can have no reality for him, or when memory presents a past that has no reality, then we have an essentially unhappy person." For the unhappy man, "It is memory which prevents him from being present in hope, and hope which prevents him from being present in memory." The consequence of this separation of self into two mutually repellent temporal modes is the loss of temporality:

> His life is restless and without content. He is not present to himself in the moment. He is not present to himself in the future, for the future has already been experienced. He is not present to himself in the past, for the past has not yet come. . . . Alone, he has the whole world over against him as the Other with which he finds himself in conflict. . . . In one sense he cannot die, for he has not really lived; in another sense he

cannot live, for he is already dead. . . . He has no time for
anything, not because his time is taken up with something
else, but because he has no time at all.

Although it may not be apparent from this brief description,
the "unhappiest man" is really the aesthete. For it is the aesthete
who above all wants to recapture the past. "The first kiss," he
remarks at one point, "is qualitatively different from all others."
On page after page of *Either/Or* we see him in search of those
inimitable "firsts"—not only the first kiss, but also the first love,
the first dance, the first sensation of falling in love. "Like the
Spanish knight of the doleful countenance," the Judge cautions
him, "you are fighting for a vanished time." Vainly trying to
recapture in the future the "firstness" of things that now lie
buried in the past, he is a creature of nostalgia. The desperation
of his search, moreover, soon becomes apparent in his removal
from time itself. "I feel the way a chessman must," he complains,
"when the opponent says of it: that piece cannot be moved." At
another point: "Time flows, life is a stream, people say, and
so on. I do not notice it. Time stands still, and I with it." His
world has become a "still life" where time, change, and growth
are hauntingly absent. In place of vitality and movement we encounter only a paralysis of emotion and purpose, an all-embrac-
ing indolence: "How terrible tedium is . . . I lie stretched out
inactive; the only thing I see is emptiness. The only thing I feed
on is emptiness. I do not even suffer pain." Immersed in this
great emptiness which muffles the sounds of the outside world, he
is left alone with a consciousness that never changes. Through
all the essays of *Either/Or*, Volume I, runs the complaint of
the aesthete: Life is trivial and empty; he has seen through it;
boredom is everywhere.

This is a complaint we recognize not only from Kierkegaard's
journal, but also from the pages of *The Concept of Irony*. The
true novelty of *Either/Or* lies not in its painting this familiar

portrait in deeper colors, but in its profile of the development that culminates in the aesthetic life. Oddly, the absence from self which so torments the aesthete turns out also to be the motivating force behind his development. Or to put it another way: If it is important to recognize that the aesthetic life ends in despair (*Fortvivlelse*), it is equally important to acknowledge that it begins in dread (*Angest*).

The first essay in *Either/Or*, entitled "The Immediate Stages of the Erotic," offers a description of the stages which end in the full-blown aesthetic life. Briefly, they might be indicated by the terms "dreaming," "seeking," and "desiring." Dreaming, the first stage, is exemplified by the Page in Mozart's *Figaro*. In him desire is not yet qualified as desire; it is "present only as a presentiment about itself, is without movement, without disquiet, only gently rocked by an unclarified inner emotion." The first stage evolves into seeking, a more definite condition midway between dreaming and explicit desiring. This second stage—also exemplified by a Mozart character, Papageno in *The Magic Flute*—manifests itself in a yearning after a yet unspecified object. The two earlier stages culminate finally in explicit desiring, symbolized by Mozart's Don Juan. Finding its object, desire now becomes determinate. It is this stage of outright desiring which constitutes the aesthetic life.

The three stages clearly plot an ascent through varying levels of consciousness. The signal characteristic of this movement up the scale of consciousness is its inspiration by what Kierkegaard calls dread. A year later Kierkegaard devoted an entire volume to the analysis of dread, which he described as "a qualification of the dreaming spirit. . . . When awake the difference between my self and my Other is posited; sleeping it is suspended; dreaming it is a nothing vaguely hinted at." In dread, consciousness is dreaming in man, and this dreaming state (parallel to its description in *Either/Or*) is both painful and sweet. "Dread,"

Kierkegaard continues, "is a sympathetic antipathy, an anti-pathetic sympathy. . . . If we observe children, we find this dread more definitely indicated as a seeking after adventure, a thirst for the prodigious, the mysterious." And finally (again as suggested in *Either/Or*), in the state of dread one dreams, but one dreams of nothing: "In this state there is peace and rest, but at the same time there is something else, which is not dissension and strife, for there is nothing to strive with. What is it then? Nothing. But what effect does nothing have? It feeds dread."

The vague apprehension of dread rests in the very bosom of the dawning consciousness. It is this apprehension which provides the energy for the ascent to consciousness. In the dreaming state man is aware of a vague lack, an emptiness. He feels as if the tiniest of cracks has opened in the pure substance of his being; a nothingness has intruded, and with its entrance there has arisen the possibility of movement. With the first vague hints of a "homesickness for himself" he turns outward to the world to recover the closure which was his, and now is lost. The vague yearning of the dream becomes a thirst for adventure, a quest of discovery:

> The longing breaks away from the earth and starts out wandering; the flower gets wings and flits inconstant and unwearied here and there. . . . Swiftly the objects vanish and reappear; but still before every disappearance is a present enjoyment, a moment of contact, short but sweet, evanescent as the gleam of a glowworm, inconstant and fleeting as the touch of a butterfly. . . . Only momentarily is a deeper desire suspected, but this suspicion is forgotten. In Papageno, desire aims at discoveries.

In each isolated moment of discovery the dreamer-become-seeker experiences a moment of contact—a brief, poignant taste of the original unity that was his. For a moment he savors it; but then in a flash it is gone. Yet no matter; he can find another object, another scintillation of enjoyment to replace the present one. And so he skips from moment to moment, from sparkle to sparkle, with hardly a glance toward the deeper desire which lingers in the background.

In the next stage—the stage of outright desiring exemplified by Don Juan—the deeper desire becomes more pressing. For Don Juan is inspired by dread: "There is a dread in him, but this dread is his energy. In him it is not a subjectively reflected dread, but a substantial dread. Don Juan's life is not despair; it is the whole power of sensuousness which is born in dread, and Don Juan himself is this dread."

What should be clear from Kierkegaard's developmental account is that the aesthete is fundamentally a Narcissist. Like the young Camus, he can "never forget that part of the self that lies sleeping in the world." From the very beginning it has been the vague awareness of absence—of his self as somehow lost "out there" in the world—that has propelled him from dreaming to desiring, and ultimately to despairing. Tormented by the memory of a primordial unity that once was his and now is lost forever, he tries to recover it in the world. But the world is other than the self, opposed to it, unutterably alien. Still the aesthete perseveres, seeking to reduce all experience "to a sounding board for the soul's own music." Yet here his project enters a fatal dialectic. For he both requires otherness and seeks its destruction. The Seducer requires his young fiancée's freedom (otherwise there could be no seduction), but his aim is to sub-jugate it. More generally, the aesthete seeks not actual experi- ence, but actual experience lit up with ideality, the world made image. Ultimately what he pursues is a kind of unconsciousness, the absorption into "a single mood, a single color," yet he seeks it deliberately, consciously. The wound he has tried to close is therefore exacerbated; consciousness grows; he becomes not

less but more wakeful. Finding the world recalcitrant, he slips
deeper and deeper into a dream world where immediate sensa-
tions are muted, and where he is stimulated only by the fantastic
shapes of his imagination. To use the words A applies to the
Seducer: "He comes to dwindle away, aye, almost vanish from
reality. . . . He soon discovers that he is going about in a circle
from which he cannot escape. . . . Like a startled deer, pursued
by despair, he constantly seeks a way out, and finds only a way in,
through which he goes back into himself."

The way out of this labyrinth of self is proposed by Judge
William in the second volume of *Either/Or*. In an analysis pre-
figured in the closing paragraphs of *The Concept of Irony*, he
sees A's problem as a lack of actuality. In refusing the actuality
of the world (its resistance and otherness) A has drained
actuality from his own person, has permitted it to bubble off into
the imaginary. Faced with this problem, the Judge's advice to
A is deceptively simple. How is A to achieve actuality and
reverse the diaspora of his life? By *choosing* himself, says the
Judge:

> He who chooses himself ethically chooses himself as this de-
> finite individual. . . . The individual thus becomes conscious
> of himself as this definite individual with these talents, these
> dispositions, these instincts, these passions, influenced by these
> definite surroundings, as this definite environment. But being
> conscious of himself in this way he assumes responsibility for
> all this. He does not hesitate as to whether he shall include
> this particular trait or the other. . . . He has his place in the
> world, and with freedom he chooses his place, that is, he
> chooses this very place. He is a definite individual; in the
> choice he makes himself a definite individual, for he chooses
> himself.

In choosing himself, according to the Judge, the ethical man
affirms his identity in all its concreteness. He is *this* person,

born in *this* town, of *these* parents, at *this* time; *this* is his situation, and in choosing himself he accepts it unconditionally. Yet curiously, this very choice of the situation transforms it. For by his freely taking it on, it is, according to the Judge, transferred from the realm of necessity to the realm of freedom: "All that has happened to me or befallen me is by me transformed and translated from necessity to freedom." What previously was alien and unwanted, the ineluctable evidence of one's factual existence, is now penetrated with freedom. "He who lives ethically," the Judge remarks, "has seen himself, knows himself, penetrates with his consciousness his whole concretion."

This choice of oneself *in situ* has yet another dimension. For the fact that the ethical man chooses himself concretely involves a necessary transformation of his relation to the future—of his possibilities. "He who chooses himself ethically has himself as his task, and not as a possibility, not as a toy to be played with arbitrarily. He can choose himself ethically only when he chooses himself in continuity, and so he has himself as a manifestly defined task."

For the aesthete, the future and possibility are blank and open. They are, A admits in one of his "diapsalmata," like the empty space into which a spider hurls itself. But in the Judge's portrait of the ethical man this empty space has been transformed into the firm outlines of a life task. It is as if in discovering his identity in the act of ethical choice, the ethical man also discovered how this identity should be realized. "Although he himself is his aim, this aim is nevertheless another, for the self which is the aim is not an abstract self which fits anywhere and hence nowhere, but a concrete self which stands in reciprocal relations with these surroundings, these conditions of life, this natural order." The self he chooses is the historically given, but the emphasis is on vectors toward the future: gifts, talents, potentialities. By this choice the ethical man knits past and future together and ceases to be passive in his despair. The future flows out of the past naturally and confidently; the personality is consolidated; the individual attains mastery over himself: "The fact that the individual sees his possibility as his task expresses precisely his sovereignty over himself."

It is this aim of gaining sovereignty over himself which summarizes the ethical man's project as it is pictured by Judge William. The individual wills to penetrate his whole being with the consciousness of his choice. "Only when in his choice a man has assumed himself," the Judge continues, "is clad in himself, has so totally penetrated himself that every movement is attended by the consciousness of a responsibility for himself, only then has he chosen himself ethically."

We can think of the ethical man's choice of himself as a curious kind of marriage vow—a vow which marries him not to another person but to life itself. The Judge speaks of "the consolidation, the penetrating shudder through all thoughts and joints which is marriage," and this description might as aptly be applied to the ethical man's choice of himself. For above all it is a "deed," an act which only the individual can perform for himself, an act by virtue of which *uno tenore* he can break free of the chrysalis the Judge calls despair: "Behold, my young friend, this life of yours is despair. It is as though you were caught and ensnared and could nevermore either in time or eternity slip free." The only escape lies in the healing act of choice whereby the individual once and for all becomes concrete by marrying himself to life.

This marriage to life results in an idyll described by the Judge in the closing pages of *Either/Or*, where he speaks of his own existence as husband, father, and man of affairs. He admits that he too now and then comes to "subside into himself," permitting a "melancholy" to gain ascendancy over him. But swiftly the presence of his wife resuscitates him. "I take part in everything she undertakes," the Judge remarks, "and it ends with my being again reconciled with time, finding that time acquires significance for me, that the instant moves swiftly." Here are the rich tones, the luminous atmosphere, the romance of the commonplace so characteristic of a Vermeer interior. The Judge tells how he returns from work to the beautiful tones of his wife's lullaby, how he enters to "hear the cry of the little one," which to his ear "is not inharmonious." There is a peace here, a feeling of time passing happily, of a harmony of individual and world that is quite touching. Here is the ideal of the ethical life, the husband, father, and man of affairs who has become fully actual through contracting a binding commitment to life:

> So our hero lives by his work, his work is at the same time his calling, hence he works with pleasure. The fact that it is his calling brings him into association with other men, and in performing his job he accomplishes what he could wish to accomplish in the world. He is married, contented with his home, and time passes swiftly for him, he cannot comprehend how time might be a burden to a man or an enemy of his happiness; on the contrary, time appears to him a true blessing.

This is indeed a touching picture—and when we stop to think of it, a picture false to the core. For this is not Judge William's own existence, but an image of the bourgeois life as idyll that he is imagining. Even his supposed "descriptions" of his wife are poetic fancy, for we never meet her directly but only through his refraction of her into the ideal wife, the eternal feminine with her exemplary "comprehension of finiteness." As we consider the Judge's letters as a whole, we come to recognize his fundamental volatility. They do not bear witness to a character firmly anchored in the concrete through action, but to an extravagant bourgeois who has substituted a romance of the commonplace for the aesthete's diary of seduction. His mind is filled with visions of a life that has become lively through self-choice, of a wife whose sole function is to cure his melancholy with her cheerful innocence, and finally of a lonely religiosity that takes form in the sermon of a nameless Jutland priest. Much as "Diary of the Seducer" closes *Either/Or*, Volume I, by pointing beyond the aesthete's romantic fancies, so this sermon ends Volume II by pointing beyond the Judge's bourgeois idyll.

The title of the sermon is "The Edification Implied in the Thought That as Against God We Are Always in the Wrong," and it takes its departure from Luke XIX, 41: Christ's prophecy of the sack of Jerusalem and the consequent suffering of guilty and innocent alike. The lesson of the sermon is the disastrous result of trying to calculate one's own moral worth, an attempt that leads inevitably to self-doubt and ultimately to despair. "One does what one can?" the Jutland priest asks (using one of the Judge's favorite expressions). "Was not this precisely the reason for your disquietude? Was it not for this reason your dread was so painful . . . , that the more earnestly you desired to act, so much the more dreadful became the duplicity in which you found yourself, wondering whether you had done what you could." But the Judge meant to vanquish "dread" and "duplicity" by unifying the personality once and for all. In a preface to this sermon—allegedly a gift which the Judge is sending along to his "young friend"—he gives a hint that in sending the sermon he means to acknowledge the failure of the ethical life. "Take it," he implores his young friend. "I have read it and thought of myself—read it then and think of yourself."

If the Judge had thought of himself while reading (or even writing) the sermon, he could have seen clearly why his notion of ethical choice must turn out to be a chimera. For how can it be brought about that "all which has happened to me or befallen me is by me transformed and translated from necessity to freedom?" How can the accidents of a person's birth, the fact that he was born in one century and not another, that his parents were white or black, that his body is ugly or beautiful, his mind quick or slow—how can such facts be "translated from necessity to freedom"? For the individual does not cause his givenness; it stands outside him, supporting the only freedom he can aspire to—the possibility of determining its meaning. One can vaguely understand what it might be like to achieve such a translation: the resistance of the world, its otherness, would have been banished. But in understanding this, one also understands that such a proposal is only an imaginative fancy, the wish of a mind that still desperately wants to escape its worldly condition.

Then too, there is the Judge's supposition that the self can, so to speak, pull itself up by its own bootstraps, banishing despair and becoming actual through one mighty act of will. His dream is of an act of will that suddenly, and paradoxically, annihilates the distinction in the self between will and anything else. But the individual must use his will to will the concentration into will, and at just this point the project becomes contradictory. For when nothing is left to confront the self as alien or other, the will itself becomes impossible. Judge William's dream of a self become actual as pure will is revealed as exactly that—a dream, a romantic fancy. His dream is distinguished from the aesthete's project only by its content, not by its form. Both remain essentially *dissipated* individuals, their minds ablaze with visions they cannot fulfill, their lives volatilized into plans, justifications, theories, arguments, fancies.

It becomes possible now to understand more clearly the charade of pseudonymity in which the book is wrapped. The point is that Victor Eremita is lucid; he is no more taken in by the aesthete's paean to enjoyment than he is by the Judge's vision of marriage. "Strictly speaking," Kierkegaard later confided, "*Either/Or* was written in a cloister, which thought is hidden in the pseudonym: *Victor Eremita*." Smiling ironically,

Victor stands apart from the visions of both Judge and aesthete. Both, assuredly, are products of his imagination, and he recognizes this—they are his creatures; they are *only* imaginary. Yet here lies the secret of the Chinese puzzle boxes. For Victor has labeled them "imaginary," and thus separated himself from them, precisely by suggesting that they are real persons whose papers he found in a desk. For both Victor and Kierkegaard the device of pseudonymity is a means to detachment. Each pseudonymous character detaches himself from his creation by disclaiming paternity, and in so doing each means to teach an important lesson: "These are only ideas and images, personae, not persons," they seem to be saying, "not to be confused with the real." At the end of the book we are left only with questions and embodied philosophical possibilities. Is the Seducer real or imaginary? And the Jutland priest? The Judge himself? The aesthete? The curtain falls on this book to the accompaniment of laughter from the wings. To use the aesthete's own words: "The curtain falls, the play is over; only the situation's fantastic shadow play, which irony directs, remains for contemplation. The immediately real situation is the unreal situation; behind this there appears a new situation which is no less false, and so forth."

IV

Inevitably, our lives slip away from us. We try to grasp actuality, but it seeps away. Tantalized by possibilities, we become fantastic even to ourselves, our minds teeming with endless theories we can never validate, plans we can never realize, doubts we can never assuage. The wound of consciousness remains.

In brief, this is the outlook presented by *Either/Or*. Both aesthete and Judge are presented as existing *beyond* their own standpoints. Each exemplifies a definite life view, but both have transcended the views they represent. Both remain in "despair," since neither has been able to extirpate his own essential volatility. The failure of the aesthete's and the Judge's projects, however, should come as no surprise; as early as *The Concept of Irony* Kierkegaard had suggested that only religion offered an antidote to despair. "The true happiness," he wrote, "wherein the subject no longer dreams but in infinite clarity possesses himself . . . is possible only for the religious individual. . . . Only the religious is capable of effecting this true reconciliation [between self and actuality], for it renders actuality infinite for me." In the works which followed *Either/Or* Kierkegaard explored with deepening intensity the notion of a religious cure for the sickness of despair. Man is divided against himself, a split creature whose life boils off endlessly into the imaginary. Experiencing his consciousness as a wound that begs for closure yet resists it, he seeks a reintegration of self that lies always beyond his grasp. This is the image that emerges from the remaining books of Kierkegaard's pseudonymous authorship—an image etched with special vividness in the work of Johannes de Silentio, "author" of *Fear and Trembling*, and Johannes Climacus, "author" of *Philosophical Fragments* and the *Concluding Unscientific Post-script*.

"Not merely in the realm of commerce but in the world of ideas as well, our age is organizing a regular clearance sale," Johannes de Silentio begins in *Fear and Trembling*. A hundred pages later he ends on a similarly commercial note: "One time in Holland when the market was rather dull for spices, the merchants had several cargoes dumped into the sea to peg up prices. . . ." This frame of commercial metaphors around the book is not accidental but a device intended to suggest an essential polarity. On the one side is the world of commerce and sanity—the commercial men with their dollar calculi and the

academics who, according to Johannes de Silentio, "live secure
in existence . . . [with] a *solid* position and *sure* prospects in a
well-ordered state; they have centuries and even millennia between them and the concussions of existence." On the other side
are those singular individuals—Mary, mother of Jesus; the
Apostles; above all, Abraham—who in their own lives have
suffered such concussions. These special individuals, their psyches
stretched on the rack of ambiguity, have become febrile. Minds
inflamed with absurdity, their lives burn with an unearthly glow.

   In all Kierkegaard's writings there is nothing so powerful or
so characteristic as the opening Prelude to *Fear and Trembling*.
Here Johannes de Silentio pursues the story of Abraham
through a series of variations, each one attempting (yet failing)
to make clear the ambiguity of Abraham's position. In each
version Abraham rises early, saddles the donkeys, and, accompanied by Isaac, makes his way to Mount Moriah. In the first
version Abraham turns away from his son: "And when Isaac
saw Abraham's face it was changed, his glance was wild, his
form was horror. He seized Isaac by the throat, threw him to
the ground, and said, 'Stupid boy, dost thou then suppose that
this is God's bidding? No; it is my desire.' Then Abraham in a
low voice said to himself, 'O Lord in heaven, I thank Thee.
Above all it is better for him to believe that I am inhuman,
rather than that he should lose faith in Thee.' " In all versions
Isaac's life is saved by the appearance of the ram, but the effects
on father and son are different in each. In the second version,
Abraham's "eyes were darkened . . . because he could not forget
that God had required this of him." In the third version, Abraham could never forget that it was a sin to be willing to sacrifice
Isaac. In the fourth version, Isaac saw that Abraham's left hand
"was clenched in despair, that a tremor passed through his
body," and this was sufficient for Isaac to lose his faith. None of
these versions, however, adequately characterizes the ambiguity

of Abraham's position. "The ethical expression for what Abraham did," Johannes de Silentio points out, "is that he was about to murder Isaac; the religious expression is that he was about to sacrifice Isaac; but precisely in this contradiction lies the dread which can well make a man sleepless; and yet Abraham is not what he is without this dread." But perhaps the most dreadful consequence of the contradiction is the radical solitude it enforces on Abraham. For strictly speaking, "Abraham cannot talk." That is, he cannot talk about the one thing that most concerns him, his faith: "The dread and distress in this paradox are that, humanly speaking, he can in no way make himself understandable."

Another way of expressing the central polarity of the book is to see it as tensed between sanity and madness. On the one hand we have the world of society, language, and justification. This ultimately is the home of the ethical man, who "translates himself into the universal, who edits a pure and elegant edition of himself, as free from errors as possible, and readable by everyone." The ethical man can justify himself in terms of allegedly universal norms, and therein lies his security. But the man who has stepped beyond good and evil has no such comfortable resting place. "He knows," writes Johannes de Silentio, "that it is beautiful to be born as the individual who has the universal as his home, his friendly resting place. . . . But he knows also that higher than this there winds a lonely path, narrow and steep; he knows that it is terrible to be born outside the universal. . . . Humanly speaking he is mad and cannot make himself intelligible to anyone." Beyond language, beyond justification, beyond understanding, the religious man makes his solitary way. He lacks even the security of the true madman who is wholly and irrevocably mad, whereas the man of faith is a failed madman who never puts behind him the temptation of sanity. He is "kept sleepless," remarks Johannes, "for he is constantly tried, and

every instant there is the possibility of being able to return re-
pentantly to the universal."

It is the religious man's state of tension which is the central
focus of the book. Johannes de Silentio admits that he has never
met in person what he calls "a knight of faith." Johannes is, by
his own admission, "a shrewd fellow, the kind who always has
great difficulty in making the movements of faith." Unable to
understand the faith of an Abraham, he must rest content to
stand "astonished . . . paralyzed . . . blind" before him. Yet if
Johannes cannot understand Abraham, he can at least understand what it is that he cannot understand. And here we are
returned to the concepts of ambiguity and tension. For what
attracts Johannes to Abraham and also appalls him is the way
Abraham's life seems to have been both intensified and unified
by tension. This applies to every knight of faith. Many people,
suggests Johannes, read the New Testament with a kind of romantic longing, but "what they leave out is the distress, the
dread, the paradox." To be Mary, mother of Jesus, or to be one
of the twelve Apostles, is to participate in the mutilation of
one's sanity. Religiosity is to be defined by that unique heightening of consciousness—"the holy, pure and humble expression of
the divine madness which the pagans admired"—where the
individual dwells in ambiguity as his element. If consciousness
be a wound, then the religious man is he who has deliberately
exacerbated it, salted it with paradox. Yet in his very pain, his
"fear and trembling," he may discover an ambiguous sign of his
election. "The knight of faith," writes Johannes, "feels the pain
of not being able to make himself intelligible. . . . The pain is
his assurance that he is on the right course."

Kant once suggested that it was his intention "to deny knowledge in order to make room for faith." This phrase more aptly
describes the efforts of Kierkegaard's next pseudonym, Johannes
Climacus, than it does any endeavor of Kant's. For if faith points

toward the trammeled madness of Kierkegaard's Abraham, then
it is sanity and sanity's world (noon in bourgeois Copenhagen)
that is faith's enemy. Consequently the task of a true defender
of the faith is the undermining of sanity—and of sanity's step-
child, language. This task Johannes Climacus undertakes in two
books, *Philosophical Fragments* and *Concluding Unscientific
Postscript*. Equipped with a dialectical wit and a wry sense of
humor, he sets out to show that both the man in the street's hovel
of common sense and the speculative philosopher's palace of
thought are built in the sand. As principal weapon he chooses a
traditional scepticism.

"The Greek sceptic," Johannes Climacus reminds us in *Philosophical Fragments*, "did not deny the validity of sensation or
immediate cognition. Error, he says, has an entirely different
ground, for it comes from the conclusions I draw. If only I can
refrain from drawing conclusions, I will never be deceived. If
my senses, for example, show me an object that seems round
at a distance but square near at hand, or a stick bent in the water
which is straight when taken out, the senses have not deceived
me. But I run the risk of being deceived when I draw a conclusion about the stick or the object." The most obvious and
least justified conclusion man is inclined to draw, according to
Climacus, is that something *exists*. He peers through a telescope
at a distant star. The pinprick of light recorded on his retina is
indisputable, but "the star becomes involved in doubt the moment . . . [he seeks] to become aware of its having come into
existence. It is as if reflection took the star away from the
senses." But this is a necessary consequence, since existence is
always a postulate and never a conclusion:

> Thus I always reason from existence, not toward existence
> . . . I do not, for example, prove that a stone exists, but that
> some existing thing is a stone. The procedure in a court of
> justice does not prove that a criminal exists, but that the ac-

cused, whose existence is given, is a criminal. Whether we call existence an *accessorium* or the eternal *prius*, it is never subject to demonstration.

If we can never demonstrate the existence of anything, how can we know anything exists? You cannot *know* it, argues Climacus; you must *believe* it.

In the uncompleted draft for a book by Johannes Climacus entitled *De Omnibus Dubitandum Est*, Kierkegaard gave a fuller account of his understanding of doubt. Climacus suggests that doubt comes in with reflection, with speech:

> Cannot consciousness remain in immediacy? If man could not speak, then he would remain in immediacy. . . . Immediacy is actuality. Speech is ideality. Consciousness is opposition or contradiction. The moment I express reality, the opposition is there.
>
> The possibility of doubt, then, lies in consciousness, whose very essence is to be a kind of contradiction or opposition. It is produced by, and itself produces, duplicity.

Climacus goes on to make the point that "the word 'doubt' [*Tvivl*] stands connected etymologically with the word 'two,'" and suggests that this duality springs from the opposition within consciousness between actuality and ideality. Not just to sense the world, but to think it (i.e., be conscious of it) means to suffer this opposition, and with it, doubt. Doubt, then, is an essential attribute of consciousness, since it makes evident nothing less than the fundamental opposition which *is* consciousness. "If ideality and actuality," Climacus says, "could enter into partnership with each other in all innocence and without opposition and friction, then there never would be any such thing as consciousness. For consciousness only appears when they collide." If doubt be defined in this way, clearly it can never be overcome, since to overcome doubt would be to overcome consciousness itself. The opposite of doubt must then be an act of the mind that lets the opposition of consciousness abide, but somehow robs it of its bite. This act Johannes Climacus calls "belief."

In *Fragments* Climacus makes clear that he means to give the Danish term for belief, *Tro*, a double sense. "In the most eminent sense" it will refer to the Christian's *faith*, his capacity to believe against reason the awful paradox of God's entry into time through Christ. As the mental act that somehow holds together oppositions of incalculable severity, *Tro* in this sense is "the category of despair." But there is another "direct and ordinary sense" of *Tro* that refers not to the relationship of the mind to the Christian paradox, but to "the relationship of the mind to the historical." In this second sense of belief, *Tro* is "the category of doubt." In both senses *Tro* is founded on opposition, ultimately on the opposition which is consciousness itself. Also in both senses, *Tro* is seen as a mental act that respects yet defeats the opposition upon which it is founded. "Defeat" may be too strong a word, for uncertainty (just another name for the opposition) is never really defeated by *Tro*, but only ignored, uncoupled, put out of circuit. Thus Climacus argues that "in the certainty of belief there is always a negated uncertainty, in every way corresponding to the becoming of existence. Belief believes what it does not see; it sees that the star is there, but what it believes is that the star has come into existence."

The essential claim, then, is that the existence of anything cannot be known, but must be believed. Surely there must be a part of us that resists this claim, since in our lives we constantly and easily distinguish between existent and nonexistent entities. Would we, for example, be inclined to believe in the existence of something which could not be apprehended publicly, in different circumstances, by different observers? Is not "publicity" itself a criterion of existence? Climacus never directly takes up the question of existence criteria, but his answer is not difficult to frame. He would point out simply that whatever criteria we choose, we must still *believe* their legitimacy. And if we choose to say that legitimacy itself has criteria, we have only moved our belief to a second level. This is precisely the thrust of his long discussion of the uncertainty of all historical knowledge. Certain knowledge, he says, can only be found within the structures of logic and mathematics; but outside their precincts, in the coming-into-being and passing-away of life in the world, we must be satisfied with belief.

Earlier, in *Fear and Trembling*, Johannes de Silentio observed that reason was the "broker" of the "whole of finiteness." This finite whole has now been brought into question. For it is reason which has populated this whole with supposed real, existent entities (reason is constantly making inferences about rocks and criminals and philosophers), and now the reality of all these entities has been questioned. Suddenly the daylight world of Copenhagen, the world of commerce and sanity, has been revealed in its insubstantiality, hanging as it does from the thread of belief.

In *Concluding Unscientific Postscript*, his sequel to *Fragments*, Climacus explores some of the consequences of this argument. "The apparent trustworthiness of sense," he reiterates, "is an illusion. . . . The trustworthiness claimed by a knowledge of the historical is also a deception." But if this be true, the life of the ordinary citizen can only be seen as a kind of comprehensive forgetfulness. Immersed in his habitual round of activities, perpetually justifying himself in terms of rights and duties, the bourgeois turns out not to be living an authentic life of his own, but rather to be fleeing life, shielding himself from awareness of its ambiguity and terror. If consciousness consists in being divided against oneself, if simply to think about the world means to grasp it duplicitously, then a full human life must witness this duplicity. Hence Climacus urges not that the hypertension of consciousness be relaxed, but that it be tightened to ever greater levels of intensity. In a metaphor resonant with significance, he says of his hero—the "existential" or "subjective" thinker: "He is conscious of the negativity of the infinite in existence, and he constantly keeps the wound of the negative open, which medically is sometimes the condition for a cure. The others let the wound heal over and become positive; that is, they are deceived."

The essential polarity of the *Postscript* is between the deceived and the undeceived. But now the deceived are no longer (as in *Fear and Trembling*) those who "live secure in existence [with] a *solid* position and *sure* prospects in a well-ordered state," but rather the speculative philosophers who, infatuated with their orotund formulations, have rushed headlong out of existence. "Philosophy and the philosophers simply desert existence," Climacus writes, "leaving the rest of us to face the worst." Their desertion is accomplished by means of a sleight-of-hand trick that substitutes ideal being (*Væsen*) for factual being (*Væren*). Climacus has already pointed out in *Fragments* how this threadbare magic made possible the ontological argument—obviously the more perfect a thing is, the more it is; however, its being is not factual but ideal, quintessential. In the *Postscript* he pushes the distinction further, arguing that the principles of speculative philosophy ultimately reduce to tautologies. The speculative philosopher, according to Climacus, pretends to a finality and certainty of judgment which is misplaced, since his statements, if properly understood, turn out to be either empirical generalizations (hence uncertain) or logical truths (hence necessarily irrelevant to existence).

In his drive toward a systematic understanding of the world, the philosopher "fantastically dissipates the concept *existence*." Even more important, by imagining that he grasps everything *sub specie aeternitatis* he dissipates his own existence and himself becomes, according to Climacus, "a phantasm rather than a human being." His "so-called pure thought is in general a psychological curiosity, a remarkable species of combining and construing in a fantastic medium, the medium of pure being." Unfortunately for him, he cannot live wholly in that medium, but must emerge regularly to pick up his paycheck. Thus he remains a kind of duplex entity, "a fantastic creature who moves in the pure being of abstract thought, and on the other hand, a sometimes pitiful professorial figure deposited by the former, as one puts down a walking stick."

On the one hand the speculative philosopher is a comic figure who has simply forgotten what it means to exist. On the other hand he manifests a pronounced morbidity in attempting to reduce being to thought, actual life to a kind of "shadow existence":

> The politicians have pointed out that wars will ultimately cease, everything being decided in the cabinets of the diplomats. . . . If only the same sort of thing does not also happen in daily life, so that we cease to live, while the professors and academics speculatively determine the relationship of the different factors to man in general. It seems to me that there is something human in the horrors of even the bloodiest war in comparison with this diplomatic stillness; and likewise there seems to me something horrible, something bewitched, in the dead insensibility by which actual life is reduced to a shadow existence.

Like Johannes the Seducer, such a professional "comic unreality" who has "either been terrified or tricked into becoming a phantom," eventually "dwindles away, aye, almost vanishes from reality."

On the other hand, the subjective thinker accepts existence in all its pain and ambiguity. His "scene is not the fairyland of the imagination," Climacus cautions, but "the inwardness of existing as a human being." The first step toward nurturing this inwardness lies in recognizing what Climacus calls the "doubleness characteristic of existence." Doubleness springs from the fact that one must both think and exist, although thinking directs itself toward the common and the universal, while existing is particular. "The subjective thinker," writes Climacus, "is an existing individual and a thinker at one and the same time; he does not abstract from the contradiction and from existence, but lives in it while thinking." What he thinks about is himself; he tries to "understand himself in existence." It is for this reason that the content of his thought lies within the boundaries of what we might call the ethico-religious. Only those ideas that can be expressed by being lived can have relevance. "All essential knowledge," says Climacus, "relates to existence . . . [and] only ethical and ethico-religious knowledge has an essential relation to existence." The subjective thinker is not the moralist or the preacher who seeks to "edify." Rather he is the solitary individual who tries to express in his own life the content of an ethical or religious norm. "To abstract from existence," cautions Climacus, "is to remove the difficulty. To remain in existence so as to understand one thing in one moment, and another thing in another moment, is not to understand oneself. But to understand the greatest oppositions together, and to understand oneself existing in them, is very difficult." The subjective thinker chooses to live the dissonance of these oppositions. Knowing that he can never justify or secure the ideality he lives, he perseveres. The ethical life "consists of that true hypertension of the infinite in the spirit of man," and it is this hypertension that the subjective thinker accepts. His activity "consists precisely of his active interpenetration of himself by reflection concerning his own existence, so that he really thinks what he thinks by making a reality of it."

Climacus uses various terms to describe his hero. Sometimes he is the "subjective thinker," at other times the "existential thinker," at still others the "concrete thinker." But the basic definition is clear. In contrast to the ghostlike presence of the speculative philosopher, the subjective thinker is a fully actual, richly alive human being. Opposed to the dissipation of the philosopher, his life has become progressively concentrated and dense. His subjectivity has suffered an "infinite concentration into itself" relative to his *telos*. "Purity of heart," Kierkegaard later wrote, "is to will one thing," and it is this purity and concentration of self that the subjective thinker gradually realizes. But since his activity is directly proportional to the passion with which he holds together the contradictory elements of existence, his project will depend in part on what ideas he chooses to actualize. Hence the famous definition of subjective truth: "An objective uncertainty held fast in an appropriative process of the most passionate inwardness is the truth, the highest truth attainable for an existing individual." Presumably this definition of truth would apply to all the ideals the subjective thinker might try to realize. Objectively they are uncertain, unfounded, unjustified—made actual only by people choosing to live them. But most ideals, if uncertain and unjustified, are not in themselves paradoxical, offensive to reason. What if one took as the *telos* of one's life an ideal, that was not just objectively uncertain, but impossible, contradictory—in short, a paradox? Might not one's passion be inflamed exponentially by the abrasion of such an ideal, and consequently might not one's life be annealed by the heat of that passion?

Here, according to Climacus, is where "Christianity fits perfectly into the picture." For the focus of Christian belief is not just an objective uncertainty, but a paradox—in fact, the "Absolute Paradox." The Christian believes that God—the infinite, the immortal, the omnipotent, the eternal—entered into time to suffer and die in the person of Jesus of Nazareth. This is not merely an uncertainty, it is a radical impossibility. "God," Clim-acus points out in *Fragments*, "is a concept," and concepts do not suffer and die on crosses in obscure Near Eastern kingdoms. To believe this (which is after all the central contention of Christianity) is to believe against understanding and reason; it is to suffer the "crucifixion of the understanding" on the cross of the Paradox. Yet the passion of that crucifixion will lead to a final "fixing" of the individual in existence.

"In the same degree that time is accentuated," writes Clima-cus, "we go forward from the aesthetic, the metaphysical, to the ethical, the religious, and the Christian religious." Socrates exemplified the position of the subjective thinker in the ortho-dox sense, and his irony betrayed his conviction that objectively everything is uncertain. But the position of the Christian is a move beyond Socrates. For the last escape hatch out of existence —the Platonic doctrine of recollection—has been blocked by the notion of original sin. "Let us now call the untruth of the individual *sin*," suggests Climacus. "The more difficult it is made for the individual to take himself out of existence by way of recollection, the more profound is the inwardness that his existence may have in existence; and when it is made impossible for him, when he is held so fast in existence that the back door of recollection is forever closed to him, his inwardness will be the most profound possible." In this way, then, "Christianity de-cisively accentuates existence" by placing the individual "be-tween time and eternity in time, between heaven and hell in the time of salvation."

It would seem that Climacus has rounded out his vision into a complex whole. He has articulated a metaphysic that will de-stroy the secure and certain outlines of bourgeois sanity. To exist is to doubt, since to be conscious is already to involve oneself in duplicity and contradiction. Through belief we hold polarities together, living their contradictions, drawing from them our passion. To exist in the most eminent sense is to raise contradiction to its highest intensity by attempting to live a paradox. To do this is the Christian way. It means permitting oneself to be led through despair to faith in its highest sense. Clarity, certainty, common sense all are shattered. Our universe has become a duplicitous and dreadful one, a land of "twos"—*Tvivl* (doubt), *Fortvivlelse* (despair), *Tvetydighed* (ambiguity)— where the individual's most insistent wish is to become integral, to overcome the cleavages of existence. That wish becomes his passion (*Lidenskab*) and also his suffering (*Lidelse*). Ultimately it also becomes his salvation. For it is Climacus's vision that in the end, the very negativity of existence—the gap between ideal and actual, infinite and finite, universal and particular, eternal and temporal—will permit the individual to realize actuality. With his pipeline to the imaginary finally blocked, confined to the "straitjacket of existence" with no chance of escape, his mind crucified on the cross of the Paradox, Climacus's hope is that the individual will be annealed in the fire of his suffering, and that his life, like Abraham's, will be set alight. "Christianity," Climacus imagines someone remarking, "has set my soul aflame."

V

The other works of the pseudonymous series add nothing essential to Climacus's vision. In *Repetition* Constantine Constantius follows his imaginary "young friend" through the trauma of an unhappy love affair to the onset of a religious "repetition." In *The Concept of Dread* the pedantic Vigilius Haufniensis traces the theological category of sin to its origin in the psychological category of dread. In *Stages on Life's Way* the familiar characters of *Either/Or* appear once more, only now they make their speeches and sound their complaints against the background of an explicitly religious alternative. Although fascinating in their own right, these books only buttress and amplify the central argument that runs from *Either/Or*, through *Fear and Trembling* and *Fragments*, to its searing conclusion in the *Postscript*. It would seem, then, that in tracing the development of Climacus's vision we have also traced the outlines of what, lacking a better word, we might call Kierkegaard's "philosophy."

This would be reassuring and correct except for two salient omissions—it leaves out both Johannes Climacus and Kierkegaard. For at the end of the *Postscript* Climacus revokes it, and his revocation is followed by "A First and Last Declaration" wherein Kierkegaard revokes all the pseudonyms, including Climacus. How then are we to take these works? Do they articulate a single outlook, a philosophy, so to speak? Or have we been tricked, made the victims of an elaborate joke?

First, to Climacus and his revocation. "As in Catholic books," he remarks in a final appendix, "one finds at the back a note which informs the reader that everything is to be understood conformably with the doctrine of the Holy Catholic Mother Church—so what I write also contains a rider to the effect that everything is to be understood as revoked; thus the book has not only a Conclusion, but a Revocation." He points out that although he has in effect offered an apology for Christianity, he himself is not a Christian but only a humorist. "My attempt," he remarks, "is *eo ipso* without importance and only for my own diversion." The reader who has just slogged through 550 pages of convoluted prose may not welcome this announcement, but he cannot claim that he was not forewarned. Earlier, Climacus had made clear why he wrote the book; it was out of boredom. He had been a student for many years and had found his life

afflicted with an enervating "indolence," "a glittering inactivity."
He had read a lot and then spent the rest of the day "idling and
thinking, or thinking and idling." At last it occurred to him that
he might occupy his time with an intellectual puzzle. "I thought
to myself, 'You are now tired of life's diversions, you are tired
of the maidens, whom you love only in passing; you must have
something to occupy your time fully. Here it is: to discover
where the misunderstanding lies between speculative philosophy
and Christianity.'" What we have been reading as a serious
philosophical treatise is in fact a "thought experiment." "I have
nothing to do here with the question of whether the proposed
thought determination is true or not," Climacus observes, "I am
merely experimenting."

His "experiment" is really only another attempt to explore
the way toward salvation. Like the Judge, like Johannes de Silentio (and too, like Constantine Constantius, Vigilius Haufniensis, and Frater Taciturnus), Climacus has imagined a life
of superior intensity, a richer humanity. The "existence" he refers to is not the common quotidian life, but rather an intensification, a concentration which makes life larger, denser, richer
than anything we have ever experienced. His portrait of existence is really of an existence lit up with value; in short, it is
imaginary, like the love affair the Seducer envisages but never
experiences. The salvation Climacus longs for is actually no
more "realistic" than the "salvation" earlier proffered by the
Judge. In both, the intensification is achieved by a heightening
of consciousness, as shown in the Judge's remark that "he who
lives ethically . . . has penetrated with consciousness his whole
concretion," and in Climacus's contention that "really to exist
. . . [is] to penetrate one's existence with consciousness." Both
meet shipwreck on the same reef. For when the ethical man has
penetrated his whole being with consciousness and so has become
pure will, his project must collapse, since will requires some-

thing other than itself to function and therefore be. Likewise, at just the point when the Christian has succeeded in "willing one thing," in concentrating all his mind and heart on the Medusa-like Paradox, at just that point does the essential duality of faith collapse, humbled by the sudden absence of temptation. Just as the ethical man requires competing inclina- tions to be ethical, so the religious man requires distraction of mind to be religious. Remove either—that is, grant either man his "salvation"—and you are really granting him only his death.

Like the aesthete alive only in his dream of beauty, like the Judge alive only in his dream of duty, like the speculative phi- losopher alive only in his dream of reason, Climacus too seems to come alive only in his dream of passion. It is easy to turn his dream into a "philosophy" or even a "metaphysic." And this, sadly, is what many modern theologians and philosophers have done, using Climacus to accent their trumpetings for a new "phi- losophy of existence." But Climacus, at least, was not taken in by his own words, and in his humorous asides he meant to re- mind his readers that any alleged "philosophy of existence" must remain a contradiction in terms, another way of sneaking out the back door, a dream. The real import of these humorous asides is to remind us that he has not fallen asleep in his dream. As with all the pseudonyms before him, one eye remains open, reminding both us and himself that what he is doing is only a diversion, a way to "occupy time." For those who would take his work as important and serious, he has only the laughing refrain, "This sounds almost like seriousness."

Behind Climacus's laughter sounds Kierkegaard's, echoing through the *Postscript* from the four-page Declaration slipped furtively into its conclusion:

> What is written therefore is indeed my own, but only insofar as I put into the mouth of the poetically actual individual whom I *produced*, his life view expressed in audible lines. For

my relation is even more external than that of a poet, who poetizes characters, and yet in the preface is himself the author. For I am impersonal, or am personal in the third person, a *souffleur* who has poetically produced the *authors*, whose preface in turn is their own production, as are even their own names. So in the pseudonymous works there is not a single word which is mine.

What are we to say of this authorship that turns out to be an extended mystification? Certain critics, having grasped the point that the authorship cannot be taken as "serious" or "philosophical," have used Climacus's own theory of "indirect communication" to explain it.

According to this theory no direct communication on existential matters is possible between man and man. Since these matters must be communicated indirectly, Kierkegaard has created a "marionette theater" of personae whose dramatizations of existential alternatives may spur the reader to personal reflection and appropriation. The real action of the pseudonyms will then be performed offstage in the privacy of the reader's study. As Stephen Crites puts it:

> In these aesthetic works Kierkegaard had to find a way of pointing to the existential movements. . . . The attempt to describe them directly would falsify what is essential. For again, as in Kierkegaard's view of art, an idea can be brought forth only in its own medium. Only in this case the medium is the temporality of human existence itself: a life time. As the Don Juan idea can only be rendered in music, and not in poetry, an existential movement can only be realized in the life of an individual.

In this theory Kierkegaard becomes a maieutic trickster who lures his reader into the kind of "double reflection" that will permit him to discover his own "subjective truth." Kierkegaard ironically, even dispassionately, uses his works to manipulate his reader's subjectivity. In essence, this view accepts Climacus's discussion of "subjectivity" and "inwardness" and sees the pseudonymous authorship as a clever strategy for bringing about precisely such inward changes. But Climacus's discussion is only part of the charade, while Kierkegaard has already told us that his works are not the products of dispassionate reflection, but are wrenched from the very "abscess" of his suffering as a man. Nor are there any "existential movements" which the reader can and should be induced to make. For if the pseudonymous works have shown us anything, it is that *all the so-called "existential movements" end in failure.* If failure is the outcome of all attempts to make these movements, then how can their stimulation be the aim of the books—unless, of course, the objective is the recognition that failure is inevitable?

This, I suspect, is precisely the aim of the pseudonyms: not to get the reader to make some impossible "existential movements," but to make the point that all such attempts at self-direction must fail. It is *failure*, I submit, the necessary failure of all human projects, that is the central meaning of the pseudonyms, as well as the source of their deepest religious import.

At various points in the pseudonymous writings the reader is reminded of God's elusiveness. In the *Postscript* God is compared to an ironic writer (*pace* Climacus and Kierkegaard) who never reveals himself to his reader. "For no anonymous author," writes Climacus, "can more cunningly conceal himself, no practitioner of the maieutic art can more carefully withdraw himself from the direct relationship, than God. He is in creation, and present everywhere in it, but directly He is not there." But if God is not directly apprehensible, how can He be encountered? Under what circumstances, through what refractive lenses, is the individual permitted to see God?

In *Fragments* God is defined as "the Unknown." "What then

is the Unknown?" asks Climacus. "It is the limit to which reason repeatedly comes. . . . It is the different, the absolutely different." God is the unsurpassable limit against which man's reason flings itself: "Reason cannot advance beyond this point, and yet it cannot refrain in its paradoxicalness from arriving at this limit and occupying itself therewith." Here God is defined relative to reason, but there is nothing to prevent us from generalizing the definition. For there must be a limit to every human project—to desiring, to willing, to loving, to imagining. Generalizing the definition we arrive at this result: God is revealed to man only negatively, as man's limit. Man encounters God only by encountering his own finitude and incapacity. God is *deus absconditus*, never present, always absent, an inhabitant of dark places, God the spider.

It is God who ultimately haunts the world of the pseudonyms. He lurks not in their words, but between their words, in their silences and failures. Theirs is an ambience of duplicity and illusion. They are tricksters and playactors, speaking evasively and ironically. They talk in a characteristic rhythm in which the systole of their affirmation is matched by the diastole of its revocation, followed by a relapse into irony or resignation. But this revocation is not just a maieutic device to encourage the reader to make those "existential movements" none of us can talk about. On the contrary, it is a confession of our incapacity to pull ourselves up by our own bootstraps. "You shut your eyes, you seize yourself by the neck," writes Climacus jokingly of the speculative philosopher, "and then—and then you stand on the other side."

But all of us know that we will never (at least in this life) "stand on the other side." With the pseudonyms we share the incapacity to live our images, to give them being, and in our joint failure we express an unsurpassable limit of our condition. Our finitude is reflected back to us in the "elsewhere" character of the image, in the evident quality that it *is not, is not here*. This is the secret of the pseudonym's world. For it is finally the world of human consciousness itself, and its negativity—individual characters and whole works pretending to be other than they are, pseudonymity masking irony, parody piled on satire—is again that of consciousness. What the pseudonyms illustrate is the failure of all attempts to prevent our lives boiling off into the imaginary. Like us, the pseudonyms never succeed in becoming integral, never overcome a fundamental dissipation. Yet precisely in that failure can be glimpsed, ambiguously, like a shape half-seen in a mirror, the face of God.

Thus the full austerity of Kierkegaard's vision can only be grasped when the pseudonyms are understood self-referentially. What they seek to demonstrate is not the adequacy of a new philosophy, but the nullity of all philosophy. What they seek to exhibit is not the possibilities of a new literary genre, but the final impossibility of all genres. What they are really about is not ethics or aesthetics or theology or philosophy, but rather the imaginative act which founds all these disciplines. Since this is also the act by which the pseudonyms themselves come into being, they are ultimately about themselves. Their achievement lies in the construction of a literature of self-reference, a series of works that comment repeatedly on the imaginative act involved in their own creation. And their repeated and austere comment is that the act must inevitably end in failure. We are permitted to imagine, it would seem, precisely that which we cannot create.

Finally, we are returned to Narcissus staring fixedly into his darkening pool. From the beginning he has refused the world in order to re-create it, but creation has proved to be beyond his grasp. He would grasp the world as his reflection, but what he succeeds in grasping is only a reflection. The judgment of the pseudonyms is that he must look more deeply into his reflection. For he may, if he looks long enough, discover in the reflectivity of his image the absence of divinity. It is that absence, as we have seen, that makes ironists of both God and man.

13

AN UNWILLING POET

IDLENESS is a dangerous condition for small boys and writers, and in late December 1845 Kierkegaard was idle. During the previous four years he had worked with uninterrupted energy on book after book, beginning a new manuscript as soon as the old one was sent to the printer. But now, with the manuscript of his last pseudonymous work, *Concluding Unscientific Post-script*, safely deposited at Bianco Luno's printshop, his pen lay idle for the first time since his break with Regine. Looking around, his eye fell naturally upon a slim volume of literary criticism published on December 20 by the young aesthete P. L. Møller. One article, entitled "A Visit to Sorø," related Møller's conversations with various literary figures living in Sorø, and described at length an evening party where the conversation turned to the recent writings of Søren Kierkegaard. In substance it was a sharp attack on Kierkegaard's most recently published work, *Stages on Life's Way*.

Kierkegaard knew things about Møller that were not known to the reading public—most importantly, that for several years Møller had maintained a *sub rosa* association with a satiric weekly called *Corsair*. He frequently contributed articles and on several occasions had taken over the duties of its regular editor, Meyer Goldschmidt. *Corsair* usually sided with the liberal opposition, and this political stance together with the unremitting ridicule it directed at Copenhagen's notables won it a place on many café tables and secured for Goldschmidt several short jail terms. But it was not a reputable or even very witty paper, and Møller, who was angling for a professorship at the university, had kept his connection with it a secret. Knowing that this alliance was Møller's Achilles' heel, Kierkegaard aimed his counterattack at it. Writing under his pseudonym of Frater Taciturnus, he closed an article in *Fatherland* (December 27, 1845):

> If only I might soon get into *Corsair*. It is really hard for a poor author to stand so singled out in Danish literature, that he (assuming that we pseudonyms are one) is the only one who was not abused there. My boss, Hilarius Bogbinder, has been flattered in *Corsair*, if I remember correctly; Victor Eremita has even had to experience the disgrace of being made immortal—in *Corsair;* and yet I really have already been there, for *ubi spiritus, ibi ecclesia: ubi P. L. Møller, ibi Corsair.**

As the citation suggests, two of Kierkegaard's pseudonyms— Victor Eremita and Hilarius Bogbinder—had been praised in *Corsair*, but this earlier commendation could not blunt the present offense. "One can engage *Corsair* to abuse," Kierkegaard remarked two weeks later in *Fatherland*, "just as one can engage an organ grinder to make music . . . *Corsair*'s faded spirituality should and ought to be ignored from a literary standpoint, just as prostitutes are in ordinary life. Anyone who is insulted by being praised in this paper, if he accidentally gets to know it, can . . . retort: 'Please abuse me, for it is really too much to be made immortal by *Corsair.*'"

Just as Kierkegaard had teased bigger boys twenty years earlier in the school playground, so now he baited *Corsair* and dared its editors to attack him. And attack they did, although at first in a mild and almost amiable manner. The January 2, 1846, issue carried a tongue-in-cheek reply to Frater Taciturnus entitled, "How the itinerant philosopher found the itinerant

* Wherever the spirit, there the church: wherever P. L. Møller, there *Corsair.*

real editor of *Corsair*." There is more whimsy than malice in the article, and its generally light tone evidences some of the affection in which Kierkegaard was held by *Corsair*'s editor, Meyer Goldschmidt. Goldschmidt respected Kierkegaard's work and felt sympathetic toward him personally, but he was a combative man himself, and soon nearly every issue of *Corsair* carried something spiteful on Kierkegaard and his pseudonyms. Besides articles there were drawings that caricatured Kierkegaard's peculiarities—his bent back and thin legs, his perennial walking stick or umbrella, his crablike gait, his uneven trousers, one leg shorter than the other. The joke about the trousers caught the public imagination. Small children would run up to him and stare at his pants, and once he sat down in church only to find two young men studying his legs and mocking him. Even his tailor began to wish that Kierkegaard would take his business elsewhere. *Corsair* embroidered the joke with an announcement on February 19 that "the author of *Either/Or*, Mr. Victor Eremita, won a prize at the Industrial Union for an essay on the manufacture of clothing in Denmark. The motto to the essay was as follows: 'We all know from experience that *either* the two legs of trousers are equally long, *or* that one is longer than the other. *Tertium non datur.*' "

But as winter turned to spring, *Corsair*'s references to Kierkegaard and his trousers came less frequently, and by summer his name appeared only rarely in its columns. P. L. Møller's chances for a professorship had been destroyed by Kierkegaard's disclosure of his connection with *Corsair*; he soon left Denmark and died abroad in poverty and obscurity. For Goldschmidt too, Kierkegaard's attack marked the beginning of the end of his association with *Corsair*. Later that year the two men passed in the street. "He went by me," Goldschmidt remarked in his memoirs, "silently, with an extremely bitter glance. There was in that look's bitterness, as in Kierkegaard's whole appearance, something almost comical. . . . His great wild look had something about it which accused and depressed me. *Corsair* had won the battle, but I myself had achieved only a Pyrrhic victory. Before I got home, I had decided to give up *Corsair*."

The consequences of this literary feud for Kierkegaard were enormous, because it brought him an unprecedented notoriety in Copenhagen. Previously he had been known only to the educated world as an odd but gifted writer and wit; now he was familiar to all as an easy target for ridicule. "Every butcher's boy thinks himself justified in being offensive to me on *Corsair's* order," he wrote. "Students grin and giggle, glad that a prominent person has been trodden down, and professors are envious and secretly sympathetic with the attacks, adding, of course, that it's a shame." His formerly easy passage through the streets of the city, his occasional conversations with servant girls and cab drivers, his delight in observing the everyday life of everyday people—all had been taken from him. "In a sense," he wrote, "I live like a fish that has been put into polluted water, so that it cannot breathe. Someone has poisoned the air I breathe. What I need in order to rest is lonely isolation among the masses. But I can't get it anymore, and I despair."

His journal entries of the time abound with self-pity—"God knows they have treated me scurvily enough, yes, mishandled me like children mishandling a costly present"—and there is some doubt whether all the looks and insults he claimed to see were really there. In March 1846, for example, Kierkegaard met Lieutenant J. C. Barth, adjutant of the Hussars, and Barth's young son on the street and described in his journal the "almost excessive politeness" he had been shown, taking it to mean that Barth and his son (as avid readers of *Corsair*) were secretly mocking him. Some years later Georg Brandes asked Barth's son about the encounter. The boy could not recall it but told Brandes that both he and his father had been earnest admirers of Kierkegaard, and that neither had ever laid eyes on *Corsair*.

As might be expected, Kierkegaard kept his anger to himself.

No additional articles followed the second blast in *Fatherland*, although a number of drafts quickly accumulated on his desk: "The Dialectic of Contempt," "The Serious Result of a Literary-Police Matter," "A Literary Signal Shot," "A Courteous Hint," "Literary Contempt." Some of these drafts are witty, but their general tone is testy and malicious, and it is fortunate for Kierkegaard's reputation that none was published. Sometimes he vented his annoyance in his journal, as in this outburst from March 1846: "Now listen little *Corsair*! Be a man! It's womanly to keep running after someone to scold them; be a man and keep quiet." More often, his anger was sublimated into comments about the vulgarity of the time and the depravity of journalists.

Yet by far the chief importance of the *Corsair* episode was to suggest to Kierkegaard a new understanding of himself—that is, a revised scenario for the remaining years of his life. At first, he saw quite well that the feud had come about more through an accident of timing than from any deliberate decision on his part. In September 1846 he admitted that Møller's article had caught him in an idle period just after finishing the *Postscript*. "Had P. L. Møller's article come a month earlier," he said, "it would have gotten no reply." But as time went on, he forgot the accidental origin of the affair, and his role in it became more heroic. He began to think of himself as "the only one who dared to act when the 'plebs' raged and triumphed," and came to speak of his decision to intervene as "unselfish . . . almost heroic . . . my cause was pure, consecrated by God." Three years after the event, he offered this description of the "victims" of *Corsair*'s attack:

> There have been sacrifices, and tears have been shed by women in silence (the wives and daughters of the persecuted), and meanwhile the grins broadened and the circulation rose. The

victims went to the side and died, and no one remarked it; the women hid their tears and no one remarked it. . . . Then I offered myself as a victim. I dared believe that Denmark was a little too big for the way I died to pass unnoticed. Only a dead man can arrest and revenge the baseness of which a whole country is more or less guilty.

Of course these crying wives and daughters, these victims sneaking off to die in silence, existed only in Kierkegaard's imagination, but to sustain the myth of his own heroism he had to raise the stakes. Where in reality people were only laughed at, in the revised scenario they die of their wounds. Where in reality the whole affair was a literary spat, in the revision it has world-historical significance. The new scenario, of course, was designed to present a drama in which Kierkegaard could appear once again in his primordial role of martyr. As a very young man he had "got the notion that my life's destiny was to be offered up," and this notion had entered into his earlier view of himself as the victim of a familial curse. Now his brush with *Corsair* seemed to confirm these long-dormant suspicions. More, it appeared to be a revelation of his true identity. "From now on," he wrote in January 1847, "it must be said that I am not only running into uncertainty but going to certain destruction, and in confidence in God, that is precisely the victory. That is how I understood life when I was 10 years old, from which came the terrific polemic in my soul. Thus I understood it when I was 25 years old and also now that I am 34. It was for that reason that Poul Møller called me the most polemical of men."

In 1845 and 1846 he had thought of retiring from Copenhagen to the tranquillity of a country parsonage. But the *Corsair* episode changed all that. "God be praised that the attack of all which is vulgar came upon me," he wrote on January 20, 1847. "Now I've had time to learn from within and to assure myself that it was a melancholy idea to want to live in a country parsonage. Now I stand at my post, determined in quite a different way than I ever have been." Standing alone, he came to see himself as precisely the kind of person the times required. He felt he was like the stormy petrel which appears with the thunder, or like Socrates, he was the "gift of God" to his people. The times were becoming confused, he wrote, and "the question is whether literary, social, and political conditions do not require an *extraordinarius*, and whether there is anyone in the kingdom as well fitted as I am for the role. . . . It is clear enough that I'll be sacrificed." And so the thought of martyrdom gained ascendancy in his reveries: "What the age needs is not a genius—it has had geniuses enough—but a martyr, one who, in order to teach men to obey, would himself be obedient to death." It was God, moreover, who was preparing this martyrdom for him; in suffering it he would be God's instrument. "What our age needs is education," he wrote. "And so this is what happened: God chose a man who needed to be educated, and educated him *privatissime,* so that he might be able to reach others from his own experience." He was sure, he said, "to be offered up for what, in truth, is truth." But what surprised him was how "perfectly Providence has led me in order to develop me for that purpose."

But if God was using him as an instrument, then it was not just his writings that were important. His life itself now gained the resonance of a dramatic action; it became a gesture of communication. "My whole life," he wrote in 1848, "is an epigram calculated to make people aware." Now he must take pains to make sure his life was not misunderstood. And so in the same year he jotted down just what he conceived its meaning to be in an essay entitled *The Point of View for My Work as an Author.* Here he announced that his authorship from first to last was a complicated maieutic project designed to lead the Danish people to Christianity, and as such, was directed by Providence. He never published this self-interpretation during his lifetime, but put it away in a drawer to be published after his death by his brother. "The book [*The Point of View*] is true and in my opinion, masterly," Kierkegaard said in his journal. "But it can be published only after my death. If my penitence, my sin, my guilt, my inner suffering are all stressed a little more: then it will be true."

The reader of Kierkegaard's journal for these years tends to tire quickly, for the will to martyrdom, the self-pity, the incessant worrying of insignificant details make for irritation rather than admiration. But it is Kierkegaard's personal greatness as well as his most private cross that he could never successfully deceive himself. Just as his pseudonyms remained ever wakeful, never taken in by their illusions and dreams, so at this time did Kierkegaard himself remain only partially under the spell of his vision of a divinely sanctioned martyrdom. His prodigious intelligence made him subject both himself and it to criticism. And criticism is a ready solvent for dreams.

Although it is not apparent at first sight, much of his self-criticism took the form of an analysis of the extraordinary case of a Danish priest named Adler who claimed to have received a revelation from God. Kierkegaard pursued Adler's case with great intensity beginning in June 1846, and he finally wrote a diffuse essay of over two hundred pages on the issues raised by it. The essay was never published, but its results were summarized in a short treatise called "On the Difference Between a Genius and an Apostle" (1849). According to Kierkegaard, the crucial distinction turns on the question of divine authority. "An Apostle is not born," he wrote. "An Apostle is a man called and appointed by God, receiving a mission from Him. . . . The doctrine communicated to him is not a task which he is given to ponder over. On the contrary, he is on a mission and has to proclaim the doctrine and use authority."

It was precisely this obstacle of divine authority that Kierkegaard could never surmount in thinking about his own "task." He
had been careful from the beginning to distinguish between
"sermons" (which carried the authority granted the priest in
ordination) and his own unordained "discourses." As early as
1843 he had written in his journal: "By ceasing to have authority, by becoming in the highest degree unreliable in the eyes of
men, I present the truth and also put them in a contradictory
position from which they can only save themselves by making
the truth their own." He would not at this late date take on an
authority he had earlier eschewed. In 1848 he offered this description of himself:

> I am quite sure that with our age's confusion of concepts
> someone might have come forward with the idea that I was
> an apostle. Good God, instead of helping to honor Christianity
> I would have ruined it. A charming affinity for apostles—for
> me to be an apostle. Indeed, a charming result for my life to
> have established the masterly thought—that I was an apostle.
>   From the beginning I have watched with the eyes of a
> lynx for that frightful confusion. . . . Was it not the aspiration
> of Magister Adler? I have tried to prevent it with fear and
> trembling. Hence my constant use of the expression "without
> authority"; hence the treatise "On the Difference Between a
> Genius and an Apostle."
>   As an author I am a genius of a special sort—neither more
> nor less, unconditionally without authority and therefore
> continually assigned the task of destroying himself so as not
> to be authority for anyone.

Though the age "had geniuses enough" and might really need
a martyr or an apostle, Kierkegaard recognized that he was
neither: "I wonder if this impatience for martyrdom may not
have something to do with another sort of impatience, my
reluctance to take up the humiliating work of looking for a

position, and all the mortifications involved in that step and its whole way of life. Moreover, perhaps I am a little sick of life. Perhaps too it is an exaggerated way of saying that I suffered injustice, so that as a result I wish they would put me to death."

In the deepest recess of his heart Kierkegaard may have longed for the integrity of the martyr, for a consciousness annealed through act and suffering. Yet his critical faculty, shunning the claim of divine authority, intervened: "I'm still not ready to become a martyr for Christianity," he wrote in 1848, "for to such a high degree I dare not call myself a Christian. I'm really a genius who possibly could become a martyr for the truth, in order truly to present what Christianity is." More genius than martyr, he is best described as a kind of unwilling poet.

"Up to now I am a poet," he wrote in 1849, "absolutely nothing more, and it is a desperate struggle to will myself to go out beyond my limits." His fascination with the identity of the poet and his wish to overcome the poet in himself had been with him from the very beginning. In his copy of *Either/Or* he had underscored these words: *"Vainly I strive against it. My foot slips. My life is still a poet's existence. What could be more unhappy? I am predestined. Fate laughs at me, when suddenly it shows me how everything I do to resist becomes a factor in such an existence."* It would be interesting to know when the underlining was done, for the passage seems to express vividly Kierkegaard's own complaints about his "poet existence" in the late 1840's. In *The Point of View* (1848) he remarked, "It is the 'poet' that must be got rid of," called *Either/Or* "a poetical catharsis," and in speaking of his youth, said, "the poetical had to be emptied out." But in spite of the enormous productivity of his pseudonymous period, the poetic had not been emptied out. Again in *The Point of View* he complained that he "had too much imagination and far too much of the poet about me to dare to be called in a stricter sense a witness for the truth," and in a small essay published in 1850, he exclaimed: "If I were in fact a strong ethico-religious character—alas, I am hardly more than a poet."

Translated into another idiom, this "struggle" to get beyond the poetic may be seen as central to his life. For his wish (expressed as early as the Gilleleje entry of 1835) to find a postulate in which he can "live" is really only another way of saying that he wants desperately to overcome the distance that separates the poet from his vision. It was this poetic distance that prevented him from wrapping himself in the authority of the martyr: "If I have always stressed that I was without authority, it is because I have felt there was too much of the poet in me." And it was his poetic distance that ultimately caused him the deepest laceration, his inability to live his vision: "I am essentially a poet. . . . In this respect I only have to humble myself beneath one thing; the fact that I have not the strength myself *to be* that which I understand." Unable to place the martyr's crown of thorns on his own head, he became the martyr's laureate. Unable to become a Christian in the most important sense, he became Christianity's poet:

> Ordinarily the hero comes first, or the ethical character, and then the poet—I wanted to be both. At the same time that I needed the "poet's" repose and detachment from life and the thinker's repose, I always wanted (in the midst of real life) to be what the poet and thinker depict. . . . I remain the unsuccessful lover with respect to *being* myself the ideal of a Christian, hence I became its poet. . . . As in the poet's song there echoes a sigh from his own unhappy love, so will all my enthusiastic discourse about the ideal of being a Christian echo the sigh: alas, I am not that, I am only a Christian poet and thinker.

Indeed, his work during the closing years of the decade does include some writing on purely literary subjects. In 1846 he published a slim essay in social criticism called *A Literary Review*. It contained some of the ideas Heidegger would develop eighty years later in *Being and Time*, but it also offered (just two years short of the paroxysms of 1848) the untimely observation that "in the present age a rebellion is, of all things, the most unthinkable." Along the same line he published an article in drama criticism for *Fatherland* celebrating Fru Johanne Luise Heiberg's return after twenty years to the role of Juliet in a Royal Theater production of *Romeo and Juliet*.

The main thrust of Kierkegaard's authorship after 1846, however, was clearly religious. As before, he turned out a steady stream of "edifying discourses" under his own name: *Edifying Discourses in Various Spirits* (1847), *Works of Love* (1847), *Christian Discourses* (1848), *The Lilies of the Field and the Birds of the Air* (1849), *Three Discourses at Communion on Fridays* (1849). Like the discourses published simultaneously with the pseudonymous works of the early 1840's, their tone is solemn yet intimate, and their counsel is again that of patience in suffering and resignation in adversity. John Updike has written that Kierkegaard's discourses belong with the memorable sermons of fiction, like those of Father Mapple in *Moby Dick* and of Père Paneloux in *The Plague*. They have a literary sheen, and although they are sometimes trenchant and direct, often they seem to be reaching for "poetic" effects. All the earlier ones were dedicated to Kierkegaard's father—"former hosier here in this city"—and they resemble nothing so much as the sermons of Bishop Mynster that Michael Kierkegaard loved and that young Søren often read to him. Although more argumentative than Mynster's sermons, they have the same rhythmic diction and solemn tone. But more than anything else they convey a mood of quiet, tempered resignation, as suggested by their titles: "The Expectation of Faith," "To Acquire One's Soul in Patience," "Patient in Expectation," "The Expectation of an

Eternal Happiness." The standpoint of the whole series of discourses parallels the view expounded at the end of the *Postscript*: God can never be met directly but only obliquely in the
failure of all human projects. Man must suffer his estrangement
from God in guilt, despair, and uncertainty, and ultimately this
estrangement is not to be overcome.

Although as time went on the discourses became more bitingly
Christian, Kierkegaard saved his distinctly Christian reflections
for two other works, *The Sickness unto Death* (1849) and
Training in Christianity (1850). It is in these works, published
under a new pseudonym, Anti-Climacus, that the voice of
Christianity's poet can be most clearly heard. It is no exaggeration to call them incendiary. For the announced intent of their
pseudonymous author was not to present a balanced portrait of
Christianity—much less a poetically attractive one—but to shock
and lacerate a complacent public that had come to associate
Christianity with the sclerotic Christendom of the Danish
bourgeoisie. "Christendom has done away with Christianity,"
Anti-Climacus writes. "One must try again to introduce Christianity into Christendom." And he seeks to bring this about by
stressing the most stringent, even terrifying, elements of the
Christian tradition.

Christianity, according to Anti-Climacus, is not a doctrine, not
a body of propositions that can be agreed or disagreed with, but
a *scandal* that must be believed. There is an infinite gulf between God and man that can never be spanned, least of all by
1800 years of sacred history. One attains "contemporaneity
with Christ," a central theme of *Training in Christianity*, only
by believing against reason in the entry of God into time through
Christ. Thus the historical Jesus fades into the background,
leaving the reader of these works alone with the single fact of
his historicity. "The believer must shudder every time he thinks
of it," Anti-Climacus says, "and yet cannot withhold his eyes

from gazing into that abyss of (humanly speaking) senseless lunacy—God in human form." At the core of Kierkegaard's vision of Christianity lies a fascination with the horrific. For according to him, it is in a paroxysm of terror that one confronts the essential truth of Christianity. A few years later he said that the death's-head, not the cross, is Christianity's "most significant symbol." In *Training in Christianity* he contented himself with pointing out that "because Christianity requires absolute respect, it must and will display itself as madness or terror."

There is a strong pessimism in these works by Anti-Climacus that becomes especially evident in *The Sickness unto Death*. Earlier in *Either/Or*, despair was seen to be a consequence of the aesthete's choice of life view. In *The Sickness unto Death*, it is seen as man's natural state. "The self is a relation which relates itself to its own self," observes Anti-Climacus at the beginning of *Sickness*, only to point out shortly thereafter: "Despair is the disrelationship in a relation which relates itself to itself." As the book proceeds it becomes apparent that this disrelation in the self, this inability to become integral, is man's primordial state. The dualities of finite/infinite, temporal/eternal, freedom/necessity are offered as metaphysical bases for the "double-mindedness" of despair. The volatility made evident in despair is hence inescapably a part of the human condition. "So one might say," remarks Anti-Climacus, "that there lives not one single man who after all is not to some extent in despair, in whose interior there does not dwell a disquietude, a perturbation, a disharmony, an anxious dread of an unknown something, or of a something he does not even dare to make acquaintance with, dread of a possibility in life, or dread of himself." As page follows page Anti-Climacus plots meticulously all the stratagems we use to outwit despair, and shows how each necessarily fails. On the positive side he leaves only the unredeemed promissory note that in some inexplicable fashion Christian faith will overcome despair by grounding the self "transparently in the power which constituted it."

In these final works Christianity's poet articulates a vision of Christianity as the ultimate *horror religiosus*. And in the background of his vision lurks that same ache which prompted Hölderlin to exclaim: *"O du des Aethers Tochter! ercheine dann aus deines Vaters Gärten, und darfst du nicht, ein Geist der Erde, kommen, schröck, o schröcke mit anderem nur das Herz mir."* (Oh Hope, daughter of Air, appear to us out of your father's gardens; but if, a spirit of the earth, you may not come, then find some other way to frighten, oh frighten my heart instead.) Kierkegaard has left happiness behind. It lingers in his mind only as a remembrance of Regine's presence. Now, as Christianity's poet, he tries to articulate a vision of radical terror whose frisson will be life-giving. Yet even here, the distance that separates the poet from his creation denies him its felt reality—hence the decision to publish the two works under the pseudonym Anti-Climacus.

In his Editor's Preface to *Training in Christianity* (his name appeared on the title page of both works) he announced, "In this little book . . . the requirement for being a Christian is strained by the pseudonym to the highest pitch of ideality." Kierkegaard knew that he himself was not an exemplary Christian, could not live up to his own ideal vision. "Anti-Climacus is a Christian to an extraordinary degree," he pointed out in his journal, "whereas I manage only to be quite a simple Christian." Not modesty but incapacity is behind this second pseudonym; in using it Kierkegaard once again betrays his discomfort at being "only a poet." His aspiration is higher than the poetic. In spite of its terror, he seeks not just to announce the vision but to live it. Ultimately this aspiration led him away from poetry, first to silence, then to battle.

14

ONCE AND FOR ALL
SOMETHING GHOSTLY

By 1851 Kierkegaard's major works had been written. *Training in Christianity* appeared in September 1850 and *For Self-Examination*, which he had planned in 1848, was published in 1851. Apart from his pamphleteering attack on the church in 1855, his output in the last five years of his life was restricted to a few minor religious discourses on familiar themes. His enormous productive urge had been stilled; his life was contracting.

It showed even in his dress. In the 1850's the top hats and frilly shirts of his youth were replaced by a wide-brimmed felt pulled low over his forehead and by stiffer, plainer shirts. He still carried a walking stick or cane, but now there was something of an old man in his gait and presence. The youth who had always been "too old" for his fiancée had come in his late thirties to resemble a man twice his age. "I am now elderly and hardened," he wrote in 1854. His portraits showed it, as did the following description by a contemporary:

> Kierkegaard was close to resembling a caricature. Under the wide-brimmed hat worn low on the forehead, one saw his great head with the heavy, dark-brown hair, his still expressive blue eyes against the pale yellow of his face, and his sunken cheeks. Then the many deep wrinkles from the cheeks

down to a mouth eloquent even when it was silent. He
usually carried his head a bit to one side. His back was slightly
bent, and under his arm he carried a cane or an umbrella. His
brown frock coat he kept tightly buttoned across his frail body.
His weak legs seemed almost too uncertain to bear their
burden.

The children of Pastor Spang had known Kierkegaard in the
1840's when he was a young writer who had visited in their
home and played games with them. They recalled how heartily
he had laughed, leaning back in his chair, and how he "rubbed
his hands so that the diamond in his ring glittered in competition
with the deep, soulful eyes that were blue and mild." But later
when they met him on the street in the late 1840's and early
1850's, his look had changed. "When we walked away from
him," the boy remembered, "we often wondered, especially my
sister, that we had dared speak to him, such a strange, piercing,
greyish glare his eyes had taken on in place of the familiar mild
blue radiance we remembered from childhood."

A constricting factor of some importance in Kierkegaard's
circumstances was, of course, the gradual disappearance of his
fortune. In the early 1840's he had paid little attention to the
shrinkage of his capital. He expected to die (like all his siblings
except Peter Christian) before turning thirty-four, and he had
money enough to last until then. But May 5, 1847, came and
went and he was still alive. By the end of that year he had sold
all the shares and royal bonds in his inheritance—something over
17,000 rd.—and was left with a little cash and his interest in
2 Nytorv. In December 1847 he succeeded in selling the house;
Peter Christian retained a 7,000 rd. mortgage, while Søren
received 10,000 rd. in cash and a 5,000 rd. mortgage. He immediately put the cash into insurance stocks and royal bonds,
both of which fared badly in the wartime financial troubles of
1848. By the beginning of 1852 he had cashed all his royal

bonds, and by the end of the year he had sold all his stocks. The mortgage, all that was now left to him, was converted into cash in August 1854.

Kierkegaard complained repeatedly in his journal about his difficult financial situation, but it is hard to know how seriously to take these complaints. For his style of living came only gradually to reflect the diminution of his fortune. After leaving Nytorv in April 1848, for two years he occupied a sunny six-room apartment at the corner of Rosenborggade and Tornebuskgade. The following year (April 1850–April 1851) he lived in an equally commodious flat on Nørregade, after which he moved to an apartment just outside the city walls at Østerbrogade 108A. This was then country, and cows were sometimes brought down to drink at the watering trough opposite his house. The carriages rustled past on their way north to Helsingør, and his windows looked south over Sortedam Lake to the city beyond. But his money was dwindling, and in October 1852 he moved back into the city to Klædeboderne 5-6, just off Nytorv. This final dwelling was not a self-contained flat but only several rooms let out of a larger apartment by the owner, Fru Borries. It was cramped and dark (Klædeboderne was only 9 meters wide and the flat was on the first floor up from the street), and Kierkegaard found the bedroom especially disagreeable.

Other luxuries had to be given up as well. The carriage rides probably stopped sometime before his return to the city in 1852. The last dated receipt from Coachman Lassen is marked March 31, 1851, and in all of 1850 he spent 132 rd. on carriage drives— just two-thirds of what he had spent two years earlier. As for his books, a number of volumes that he had purchased in the late 1830's and early 1840's were not in his library at his death. Some may have been given away, but a good proportion were very likely sold in secondhand shops in the early 1850's. A bill from A. G. Salomon dated June 1, 1850, notes that he received books from Kierkegaard to the value of 6 rd., and there is reason to believe that many others disappeared in similar transactions.

His social life dwindled after the *Corsair* episode, which deprived him of those easy contacts with the general public that he had relished in the early 1840's. As late as 1854 he complained in his journal that he was "continually surrounded by curiosity, always a stranger . . . treated on all occasions not as a person but . . . as a sort of object of interest, something to gossip about." Even among the educated people of Copenhagen he was unable or unwilling to keep up a steady acquaintance, much less form a friendship. For a time in 1848 and 1849 he took regular Thursday afternoon walks with Rasmus Nielsen, professor of philosophy at the university. But this ended when it became apparent that Kierkegaard wanted a disciple rather than an acquaintance.

He had never been close to his brother, but their relationship softened somewhat after Peter Christian's second marriage and the birth of a son. In 1847 Kierkegaard made three trips to Peter's parish at Petersborg ved Sorø, 50 miles west of Copenhagen, and in the same year gave his prized personal copy of *Edifying Discourses in Various Voices* to Peter's wife Henriette. Peter Christian's church, a charming whitewashed stone structure dating back to 1649, stood on a hillock overlooking Sorø Lake. The parsonage next door had flowered arbors and a view over a gentle slope curving down to the lakefront. When Søren arrived on one of his visits, the whole family would eat together *alfresco* under the arbors and in the evening sit in the field watching moonrise over the lake. These friendly relations were short-lived, however; the next year Kierkegaard was raging in his journal: "My brother's smallness and envy have been the only things my family have done for me." By 1855 things had become so bad that Peter Christian could make a ten-day visit to Copenhagen without contacting his brother.

Of all Kierkegaard's personal relationships, Regine remained the most troubling. Having married Fritz Schlegel in 1847, she was now a young Copenhagen matron, but she remained very much in his thoughts. In July 1849 she nodded to him as they passed close by in church. Kierkegaard even then had been dreaming of a reconciliation, yet he could not bring himself to return her nod—instead he kept his eyes cast down. Typically, having passed up this easy and natural contact, he tried to do the same thing in his own way four months later—this time using the awkward device of a formal letter:

To Fru Regine Schlegel:

Cruel I was, it is true; why? Ah, that you do not know.

Silent have I kept, that is certain: only God knows what I have suffered. God grant that I do not even now speak too soon!

Marry I could not; even if you were still free I could not manage it.

Meanwhile, you have loved me as I you. I owe you much— and now you are married. But I offer you again what I can and dare and ought to offer you: reconciliation. [This was changed from "my love, that is, a friendship" to "my friendship," and finally to "reconciliation."]

I do it in writing so as not to surprise or overwhelm you. My personality has perhaps once worked too strongly upon you; it shall not happen a second time. But consider seriously for the sake of God in heaven, whether you dare entertain such a notion; and if so, whether you will speak to me immediately, or first exchange some letters.

If your answer is "no"—then you must remember for the sake of a better world, that I have made this attempt.

In my case, as from the first so to the last, I am,

honorably and entirely devotedly yours,

S.K.

The letter never reached Regine, for Kierkegaard had sent it enclosed with a note to her husband, who was asked to decide whether he could permit his wife any contact with Kierkegaard.

If not, Schlegel was requested to return Regine's letter unopened. Schlegel did so with alacrity, enclosing what Kierkegaard described as a "morally indignant note." This seemed to end the matter, as Kierkegaard noted in his journal: "Now it's done. . . . It's impossible to do anything further. . . . The thing is decided." But of course it could no more be decided now than it had been eight years ago. Her presence in the same town, the same streets, the same church taunted him. In 1851 when he was living on Østerbrogade, he used to leave Østerport at exactly 10 a.m., and she would consistently appear from a side street at just that hour. On Christmas Day 1852 she again passed close to him in church, and turned as if to speak. He recorded the incident in his journal and remarked on its ambiguity: "Perhaps it was another she turned toward in the corridor, perhaps it was me, perhaps it was a little gift from her, perhaps she wished that I would speak to her, perhaps, perhaps." Unable to approach Regine in the everyday world of Copenhagen, he vowed that his life and hers would be joined by posterity. "I shall take her with me into history," he wrote. "There I walk by her side. As a master of ceremonies I introduce her in triumph and say, 'Please be so kind as to make a little room for her, for our own dear little Regine.' " With this in mind he began his *Two Discourses at Communion on Fridays* (1851) with the words: "To one unnamed whose name one day will be named, is dedicated this little work as well as my whole authorship from the beginning."

And so Kierkegaard slipped into still deeper isolation and loneliness. He thought of his cousin Wilhelm Lund far away in Brazil: "How like his life mine is. He lives in Brazil, lost to the world, lost in his search for antediluvian fossils, and I live away from the world lost in my excavation of Christian concepts." Another time he wrote: "And everything goes its busy way, each one taking care of his own affairs, the wind blows, the river flows—it is as if God were infinitely far away; alas, it is

1800 years since Christ lived." Prematurely old and wizened, almost spectral in appearance, Kierkegaard had come to lack every sort of human contact or warmth. In the streets his solitary wanderings were greeted more often with a smirk than a smile of recognition. And among his peers in the literary world he was known as a strange if gifted author who lately had fallen under the spell of a morbid religiosity. Withdrawn, impoverished, he wrote in his journal on September 7, 1849: "Alas, I am now once and for all something ghostly."

Along with this narrowing of personality and life-circumstances there came too a growing intolerance of other points of view. Where earlier Kierkegaard's powerful intellect had made him alert to many viewpoints and his irony had proved a ready solvent for conviction, now his mind settled into a narrow rigidity. "I am so convinced of the rightness of my ideas," he wrote in 1851, "that it never occurs to me to start a discussion." Three years later he enjoined his readers: "Shut your eyes, be blind, for God's sake do not look out, for as the raven lost the cheese through listening to what was being said, so you will lose the absolute if you look out." Together with this intellectual intolerance came an abdication of the role of poet. On Easter Monday 1853, in explaining why he had not been productive in the last several years, he confessed that he now saw his "enormous productivity as a kind of magnificent distraction. . . . The Christian thing is not to produce but to exist." Six months later he remarked: "To produce seems to me almost a folly; to starve, on the other hand, to be Christian." Shortly thereafter he ceased making journal entries altogether.

This terminal silence was, however, a consequence of Kierkegaard's perception of the Christian requirement. In the pages of his journal and in notes scribbled on odd pieces of paper he sketched the outlines of his final vision of Christianity, a vision which both justified and motivated his penultimate withdrawal from the world. Probably due to its morbidity, it has been generally ignored by Kierkegaard scholars. Yet in many ways it is not only Kierkegaard's final vision, but also his most characteristic one.

At the center of Kierkegaard's conception of Christianity stands the Fall. "With eternity's firmness, immovable as the Pole Star, Christianity points to the Fall: this is what it is related to as its presupposition." Yet the Fall, in Kierkegaard's view, is only a metaphor for the human egoism that is concentrated in the sexual relation:

> As the nerve filaments lie under the nail, so human egoism is concentrated in the sexual relation, the propagation of the species, the giving of life. . . .
> So God demanded the giving up of this egoism. . . .
> The celibate is a stranger (and this is just what Christianity wants the Christian to be, and what God wants him to be, so that he may love God). . . .
> The Fall is the satisfaction of this egoism—and this is where the history of temporality properly begins, as the constant repetition of the same fault, constantly opposing or preventing what God has in view, which is to put a stop to this error—by means of celibacy.

To his credit, Kierkegaard does not shrink from any of the consequences of his conviction. For if it is human egoism that is responsible for the continuance of the race, then it must be God's will that the race die out, be "stopped":

> For God this world surely lies in the grip of evil—and that is what Christianity teaches. . . . This whole human existence which dates from the Fall, and which we men are so puffed up about as a devilish tour de force, this whole existence is against Him, it is merely the consequence of a false step. . . .
> This whole human existence is opposed to God, it is a fall

from Him, a false step away from Him, and all the time (for He is love) He pities man, but He also wants to pick a quarrel with him.

This is what Christianity is for—which straightaway bars the way to procreation. This means: Stop! I have put up long enough with this world-historical process, certainly I will have pity, but I do not want any more of the consequences of that false step.

Christianity is salvation but at the same time it is a stopping, · it aims at stopping the whole continuation which leads to the permanence of the world. . . .

And that is why Christianity upholds celibacy. By this the Christian gives characteristic expression to his relationship to the world, which is an obligation to stop it. And this is why the New Testament continually uses words concerning the Christian which indicate this putting a stop to things: for example, to be salt, to be sacrificed.

The race is lost, we have had only too much of it, and we have to be saved out of the race. Consequently a beginning must be made by barring the way for our race. ·

God, then, really desires the human race to die out; in His eyes propagation is a sin, an offense against His omnipotence. Given such hostility toward the sexual instinct, it should come as no surprise to find Kierkegaard railing against women. "Woman," · he writes in 1854, "is egoism personified. . . . The whole story of man and woman is an immense and subtly constructed intrigue, or it is a trick calculated to destroy man as spirit." ·

Yet it is not only hostility to sexuality and woman that Kierkegaard's final version of Christianity teaches. Rather it is hatred of everything worldly, of temporal existence as such: "As a consequence of Christianity, to love God means to hate the world." This hatred of the world is to be carried out by an extirpation of the worldly in oneself that Kierkegaard calls

"dying off" (*at afdøe*). "To become a Christian according to the
New Testament is to become 'spirit.' To become spirit according
to the New Testament is to die, to die off from the world." But
what does it mean, to "die off"?

> Flesh and blood (that is, the life of the senses) and spirit
> are opposites. So it is easy to see what being spirit means: it
> means being free to will that which flesh and blood must
> shrink from.
>
> · Now what do flesh and blood shrink from most of all?
> From dying. Therefore spirit is the willingness to die, to die
> off.
>
> Now it is easy to see that to die off is suffering of a higher
> potency than dying. For dying is merely to suffer, but dying
> to the world is freely to engage oneself in the same suffering;
> moreover, dying is a fairly brief suffering, whereas dying off
> lasts the whole of one's life. ·
>
> To be a Christian is the most terrible of all torments, it is—
> and it must be—to have one's hell here on earth.
>
> What does a man most shudder back from? Surely from
> dying, and most of all from the death throes, which one there-
> fore wishes to be as brief as possible.
>
> ʿ But to be a Christian means to be in the state of dying
> (you must die to the world, hate yourself) and then to live
> perhaps forty years in this state.ʿ[Written in the margin:] One
> shudders to read what an animal must suffer when it is used
> for vivisection; yet this is only a fugitive image of the suffering
> involved in being a Christian—in being kept alive in a state
> of death.

And so the blows fall with unremitting severity: "To love God
is to hate what is human"; the teaching of Christ is to "hate
yourself, forsake everything, crucify the flesh, take up your cross,
hate your father and mother"; "Behind everything there is a
Providence that says, 'This land is morally decayed . . . and they

shall not escape punishment.' " Often it seems as though sickness and death have become the natural habitat of the Christian.
In 1849 Kierkegaard observed: "To lead a really spiritual life
while physically and psychically healthy is altogether impossible." Four years later, when a cholera epidemic broke out in
Copenhagen (sparing Kierkegaard's well-to-do neighborhood
but carrying off 4,700 people from the slums of Regensgade and
Christianshavn), he saw it as a spiritual benefit: "Cholera's significance is in the direction of teaching people that they are
individuals . . . plague splits them up, teaches them—bodily—
that they are individuals."

In Kierkegaard's view it is not just disease and death that are
Christianity's natural habitat. Beauty itself is anathema to the
Christian, whose canon includes the love of ugliness and whose
"most significant symbol" is the death's-head:

To love God—or to love that which is ugly

July 10, 1855

To love the ugly—yes, quite right. For if I am (as indeed
I am) flesh and blood, a being of senses, an animal creation,
then spirit is the most terrible thing for me, terrible as death,
and to love spirit is the most terrible thing of all. So too
Christianity understands it, it teaches that to love God means
to die, to die off, the worst of all torments—blessed is he
who is not offended.

That is why, in times when Christianity was taken seriously,
those who took it seriously made use of a death's-head for
their constant contemplation. Of course one cannot say that
the spirit is like a death's-head, for the spirit is not like any
object of the senses. But a death's-head was its most significant symbol.

Through all the entries from the 1850's runs a deep strain of
world-weariness and disgust. But now this *Weltschmerz*, earlier

denigrated in the aesthete, is elevated to the status of a moral principle—it is what God demands of man:

> A man is born in sin, enters this world by means of a crime; his existence is a crime—and procreation is the Fall.
>
> When this comes by way of a crime, a sin, then it is not difficult to guess where one arrives when one is born—one enters a prison; this world is a prison.
>
> And the punishment—and as always, the punishment fits the sin—the punishment is to exist. Since to exist by way of procreation is what is displeasing to God, the punishment is just this: you will get tired of this life; you will become so sick and weary of this life, that you will thank your God that sometime through death you may get out of it.
>
> God's kingdom is not of this world; a stranger and an alien shall the Christian be in this world that for God lies in the grip of evil, the consequence of a sin which yet for God is committed today.

This phrase, "a stranger and an alien" (*en Fremmed og Udlænding*), carries us back, for "stranger" (*Fremmed*) was the word Franz Welding applied to Kierkegaard as a boy, and Kierkegaard later used it to describe himself as an adult. To Judge William, his young aesthete friend appeared as "a stranger and an alien," and later Johannes de Silentio applied the same phrase to his "knight of infinite resignation." Thus an epithet which had been applied to so many of Kierkegaard's fictional characters trapped in the "still life" of despair was now awarded to the Christian. The world-weariness and ennui that Kierkegaard earlier denigrated he now honored as the very essence of Christian suffering. Himself a spectral and solitary figure, Kierkegaard now embraced the estrangement he had fled as a youth. Here are the last words from his pen, written on a scrap of paper less than a week before he entered Frederiks Hospital to die:

The purpose of life seen Christianly

September 25, 1855.

The purpose of life is to be brought to the highest degree of disgust with life.

He who when, brought to this point, can hold fast . . . he, in a Christian sense, has passed life's test, is ripe for eternity.

Through a crime I came into existence; I came into existence against God's will. The offense which, in one sense, is not mine, even if it makes me a criminal in God's eyes, is: to give life. The punishment answers to the offense: to be deprived of all lust for life, to be brought to the highest degree of disgust with life. Man wanted to imitate the Creator in his handiwork, if not by creating life, at least by passing it on. "You will be made to pay for it, for the purpose of this life is . . . to lead you to the highest degree of disgust with life."

Most people are now so spiritless, so bereft of Grace, that the punishment is not applied to them at all. Lost in this life, they cling to this life; from being nothing they become nothing; their lives are wasted. . . .

Only those who, brought to this point of disgust with life, are able by the Grace of God to hold fast to the thought that God did it from love, so that not even in the innermost recess of their soul lurks any doubt that God is love: only they are ripe for eternity.

These final words are the logical outcome of Kierkegaard's life, a necessary consequence of the position he laid out in the early 1840's. For if, as Johannes Climacus remarks, "the very essence of consciousness is contradiction or opposition," then there is no way man can overcome his estrangement from the world. Man is a being of duplicity, the friction point where ideality and actuality, freedom and necessity, time and eternity abrade each other. Alienation is thus man's primordial and necessary state. This was the message of *Sickness unto Death,* which

presented the double-mindedness of "despair" as man's universal and natural state. Given such a perception of man's ultimate
estrangement, it is no wonder that the world turns out to be a
"prison" from which he longs to escape.

Having tried to make his home in the world but finding it
ultimately uninhabitable, Kierkegaard finally forsakes it, not in
the ambiguous guise of poet or ironist, but unequivocally as a
religious enthusiast. And here, as with everything in his life,
there is a remarkable congruity. For it had been his father's
morbid Christianity that had destroyed his youth and innocence.
Now, in the autumn of his life, his thoughts return to his father.
He remembers the old man twice daily in his prayers, and on the
anniversary of his death makes every effort "to have everything
as it should be on that day." He feels in these years as if his
father's will were becoming his own. "Stealthily, insidiously,"
he notes in his journal, "the dead person's will becomes that
which I want." Christianity had been the vehicle through which
the old man passed on a fundamental estrangement. Now,
finally, this estrangement finds its consummation in Kierkegaard's life and thought. Without friends or acquaintances,
his life running out, he hurls the death's-head of Christianity
at the world.

15

TWO FUNERALS

IN January 1854 Bishop Mynster died. Friend of kings, intimate of generals and cabinet ministers, Jakob Peter Mynster, Bishop Primate of the Danish state church, was given a funeral which in size and magnificence rivaled the last rites for kings and princes. The Crown Prince himself was there, together with many lesser figures in the royal family. The Cultus Minister* naturally attended, and among the crowd in the somber Frue Kirke (Church of Our Lady) one could pick out government officials of every stripe. But above all it was the clergy who gave the occasion its fundamental tone. They had come in by the hundreds from the countryside, their large, pleated "priest-collars" flashing white in the soft illumination of the cathedral's interior.

The rites began shortly after 8 a.m. with a small cortege of theological students bearing the flower-strewn casket across the street from the bishop's palace, up the main aisle of the church, to a catafalque by the choir. The students took up positions around the casket as the funeral procession of notables formed outside and entered the Frue Kirke to the music of bassoons playing a dirge. A particularly distinguished group of clergy—including the Bishops of Fyn, Aarhus, Aalborg, and Lolland/Falster—took places in the choir while four of their number

* Minister for Church Affairs.

relieved the students as guard of honor around the decorated black casket. The university choir sang a cantata by Paludan-Müller, and the dean of the Frue Kirke, E. C. Tryde, delivered a short eulogy. A second choir from the Royal Theater sang one of Mynster's own hymns, and then there were more speeches. Finally the great doors of the Frue Kirke swung open and the procession made its way to the street, moving slowly to the cadence of a boy's choir singing the traditional hymn, "Who Knows How Near to Me Is My End."

It is not known whether Søren Kierkegaard attended the funeral. His rooms were just around the corner, and he had known Mynster all his life. Not only had the old bishop been his father's priest and officiated at all the family funerals, but he had confirmed young Søren in 1828. As a boy Søren had read Mynster's sermons to his father, and as a young man he had read the same sermons to his fiancée, Regine. His own "edifying discourses" owed much to Mynster's style, and he had made regular visits to the bishop's palace until the early 1850's. Lately, however, his deepening religious perspective made him regard Mynster and the church he guided as anathema to genuine Christianity. Both bishop and church would have to be attacked, and soon. He mused in his notes on the collision he knew was coming. In one entry he compared himself to a young artillery officer who sees that the battle can be won if he can succeed in training his battery on one crucial spot: "But just at that spot . . . just there stands his own general, the old Field Marshal Friedland, with his staff." In another entry he compared himself to a passenger on a ship who is the only one to notice a white speck on the horizon that signals storm and danger. But the captain (Mynster) is below and will not listen to his warning. As time went on Kierkegaard became convinced that Mynster symbolized what Christianity had become—a philistine farce—in contradistinction to what it had originally been—a call to martyrdom and suffering.

The funeral is not mentioned in Kierkegaard's journal, since it had fallen silent four months earlier. It was, however, Kierkegaard's response to Hans Lassen Martensen's eulogy of Mynster that catapulted him into mortal combat with Mynster's successor and Mynster's church. Martensen had taken for his text Hebrews XIII, 7 ("Remember them which have the rule over you, who have spoken unto you the word of God: whose faith follow, considering the end of their conversation"), and had characterized Mynster as a true hero of faith, a "witness to the truth." "From the man whose precious memory fills your hearts," Martensen had intoned, "your thought is led back to that long line of witnesses to the truth, which like a holy chain stretches through time from the Apostles up to our own day." What fired Kierkegaard's anger was Martensen's use of the term "witness to the truth" (*Sandhedsvidne*), which at that time could be found in no Danish dictionary for the simple reason that it was a recent Kierkegaardian coinage. Kierkegaard had invented it to characterize those martyrs and apostles who, in their suffering, "witnessed" the truth of Christianity. He had used it in *Works of Love* (1847), *Christian Discourses* (1848), *Two Minor Ethico-Religious Treatises* (1849), *Training in Christianity* (1850), and *For Self-Examination* (1851). And now Hans Martensen, the obvious successor to Mynster and theological tutor of Kierkegaard's youth, had stolen his coinage to eulogize a churchman who stood for everything Kierkegaard opposed in contemporary Christendom. As might be expected, Kierkegaard immediately set to work composing a reply to Martensen. After suggesting that Martensen's "remembrance" of Mynster might have something to do with his "remembrance" that the Episcopal See was now vacant, he went on to describe what he understood a "witness to the truth" to be:

A witness to the truth is a man who in poverty witnesses to the truth—in poverty, in lowliness, in abasement, and so is

unappreciated, hated, abhorred, and then derided, insulted,
mocked. . . . A witness to the truth, one of the genuine witnesses to the truth, is a man who is scourged, maltreated,
dragged from one prison to the other . . . and then at last
crucified, or beheaded, or burnt, or roasted on a gridiron, his
lifeless body thrown by the executioner in an out-of-the-way
place, or burnt to ashes and cast to the four winds, so that
every trace of the filth might be obliterated.

It was thus the height of silliness to apply the title even honor-
ifically to Mynster, Bishop Primate, chaplain to kings and
princes, confidant of the wealthy and powerful. "Precisely in
the sense that the child plays soldier," Kierkegaard wrote, "it
is playing at Christianity to take away the danger (Christianly,
'witness' and 'danger' correspond), and in its place to introduce
power . . . , worldly goods, advantages, luxurious enjoyment of
the most exquisite refinements."

Like the many polemical articles he had written against Goldschmidt in 1846, Kierkegaard did not publish this reply to Martensen immediately but filed it away in his desk. He explained
later that he held his fire so as not to interfere with Martensen's
campaign for Mynster's post. He did not want to be charged
with attacking Martensen out of personal spite. Instead of publishing the article, he took the precaution of trying out its ideas
on people whom he knew would be typical of the Copenhagen
public.

Shortly before Easter 1854, for example, Kierkegaard made
it a point to have lunch every day at the home of his brother-in-
law Ferdinand Lund. After the death of Kierkegaard's sister
Petrea in 1834, Lund had remarried and was now *paterfamilias*
to the children of two marriages. Kierkegaard was very fond of
the Lund children, but the focus of these recent visits was
Lund's second wife, Anna Kathrine, whom Kierkegaard knew
to be a warm admirer of Mynster. Each day Kierkegaard would

turn the conversation to Mynster, making many of the points he had scored in his as yet unpublished reply to Martensen. Each day Anna Kathrine became more annoyed; first she opposed him, then she fell silent, and finally she begged him to stop.

Troels-Lund, the youngest son, was present during most of these discussions and vividly remembered the final meal. Shortly before Kierkegaard's arrival Troels-Lund heard his mother ask to be excused from the table. His father urged her to stay, and their conversation was interrupted by Kierkegaard's knock. At lunch Kierkegaard sat on Anna Kathrine's right, with Ferdinand Lund and the children on the side. At the end of the table the maid silently prepared coffee on the samovar. Ferdinand Lund tried to set a light tone by asking, "Now Søren, can I tempt you today with a small glass of Madeira?" Anna Kathrine then tried to steer the conversation to an innocuous topic, but Kierkegaard immediately raised the question of Mynster. Anna tried to head him off: "Come Søren, let's not take up this old argument again. We know to the bottom each other's opinions, and to discuss it further will only make us angry." But Kierkegaard persisted: Mynster had not been a real Christian, but only a good orator. He had enjoyed his comfortable position too much to know what real Christian suffering was all about. Kierkegaard's tone became bellicose. Then there was a silence as he hesitated, waiting for an answer. Anna said quietly but firmly: "You know that the man you criticize is one for whom we have the greatest respect and gratitude here. I cannot calmly sit and hear him abused. If you will not stop, I can do nothing but leave the room." Whereupon she rose and went out.

Martensen was named to the empty See on April 15, 1854, and installed on June 5. It had been a close thing. The King had backed another theologian, H. N. Clausen, who had also picked up support from the National-Liberal Party and its newspaper. But the extremely conservative Prime Minister, A. S. Ørsted (who at that time was also Cultus Minister), wanted Martensen, and finally had his way. Strangely enough, Kierkegaard remained silent even after Martensen's installation. He gave no satisfactory explanation for the new delay, saying only, "Then again the article could not be published and therefore was not." It may be that he did not wish to mingle his religious attack on Martensen with the political attacks that were raining down on the new bishop from the left. Or possibly it was simple prudence that dictated his delay. In his journal he contemplated paying the costs of a court trial: "If they want to ridicule me, I am ready! If they want me to be imprisoned, I am at their service! If they want to execute me, I am waiting. And I will happily pay all the expenses of the public trial; for human justice is a wearisome waste of time." But he must also have been aware of Section 8 of the *Law of the Use of the Press of January 3, 1851,* which carried a one- to six-month jail sentence for anyone who in print ridiculed established religious teaching and/or practice. With Ørsted simultaneously holding the posts of Prime Minister and Cultus Minister, Kierkegaard could count on swift prosecution under this law. But on December 12, 1854, Ørsted's government fell, to be replaced by a liberal regime under P. G. Bang as Prime Minister and C. C. Hall as Cultus Minister. Six days later, on December 18, 1854, Kierkegaard published his reply to Martensen in *Fatherland.* The time of waiting was over; the battle had begun.

Martensen responded to Kierkegaard's attack with an article in *Berlingske News* on December 28. First, he made the excellent point that even all the Apostles were not witnesses to the truth in Kierkegaard's sense: "The Apostle John, who was neither hung by the neck nor crucified, certainly not thrown away after death by the executioner's assistant, but buried by his congregation, must [then] be excluded from the roll of witnesses to the truth." But as the article continued, Martensen contented him-

self with making trivial debater's points against Kierkegaard:
that it was inappropriate for SK who once wrote a discourse
entitled "On the Work of Love in Remembering the Dead" now
to malign the deceased Mynster; that SK was a Thersites beside
the hero's grave; that SK's own view of Christianity leads to a
kind of "private religion" which leaves out the church, and
hence itself is not "Christian in the most decisive sense." All in
all, the article was rather stuffy and unconvincing, and Kierkegaard renewed hostilities with a series of polemics in *Fatherland*
published on December 28, 1854, January 12, 1855, and two on
January 29, 1855. But now Martensen remained silent, a tactic
which drew from Kierkegaard an article entitled, "That Bishop
Martensen's silence is, Christianly, (1) unjustifiable, (2) comical, (3) low cunning, (4) in more than one respect contempti-
ble."

Kierkegaard was anxious to keep his attack from being interpreted as a personal squabble with Martensen. In one of his
January 29 articles he gave Martensen's eulogy of Mynster a
quick logical turn that revealed the ground of his own position.
Let us go along with Bishop Martensen, he suggested, and take
it for granted that Bishop Mynster was a witness to the truth.
Since Bishop Mynster "was perfectly homogeneous with every
priest in the land . . . so every priest in the land is at the same
time a witness to the truth." But if every priest is a witness to
the truth, then let us put the life and teaching of the Danish
priest alongside that of the New Testament. Immediately we
see the incongruity, the fact that "the Established Church is,
Christianly considered, an impudent indecency." More, "it is
openly an apostasy from the Christianity of the New Testament; it is, Christianly . . . an effort in the direction of making
a fool of God." And how is this foolery brought about? By
hypocritical inversion of the requirements laid down in the New
Testament:

When in His Word He talks about preaching the doctrine for naught, we understand it to mean that of course preaching is a livelihood, the surest way to bread and steady promotion; when in His Word He talks about preaching the Word in poverty, we understand it as making a career, becoming Your Excellency; and by heterogeneity to this world, we understand a royal functionary, a man of consequence; by abhorrence of the use and employment of worldly power, we understand using and being secured by worldly power; by suffering for the doctrine, we understand using the police against others; and by renunciation of everything, we understand getting everything . . . —and at the same time we are witnesses to the truth.

This is the core of Kierkegaard's attack on the established church—that simply by becoming "established" it admitted its bankruptcy from a Christian point of view. The church had become a secular institution with a Cultus Minister in the cabinet, enormous property holdings, and a large bureaucracy of functionaries and priests. As such, the church had become a mockery of its origins in the New Testament.

After so vehement an onslaught it was not surprising that someone soon came forward with the suggestion that the church close its doors to Kierkegaard. Dean Victor Bloch of Lønborg Præstegaard did so in a letter to *Fatherland* in early April. Kierkegaard replied sarcastically in the same paper: "If I do not reform, the Dean would have me punished ecclesiastically. And how? Indeed the punishment is cruelly devised; it is so cruel that I counsel the women to have their smelling salts at hand in order not to faint when they hear it. If I do not reform, the church door should be closed to me. Horrible . . . I should be excluded from the other services of divine worship which the royally authorized . . . spiritually-worldly entrepreneurs have arranged. Terrific! Terrific punishment, terrific Dean!" A more serious response Kierkegaard saved for the following month, when he published his discourse "This Must Be Said, So Let It Now Be Said." What "had to be said" was his ultimate indictment of the established church:

> The official worship of God (with its claim to being the Christianity of the New Testament) is, Christianly, a counterfeit, a forgery. . . .
>
> So I repeat. This has to be said: by ceasing to take part in the official worship of God as it now is (if in fact you do take part in it) you have one guilt the less, and that a great one: you do not participate in treating God as a fool.

As for his own relation to the church, Kierkegaard had decided that issue for himself long before Dean Bloch called for his exclusion. Hans Brøchner says that early in 1855 he had taken to appearing regularly in the reading room of the Athenæum Club at the time when Sunday morning services were held.

In the five-month period December 1854 to May 1855 Kierkegaard published twenty-one polemical articles in *Fatherland*. But it became apparent to him that his attack required its own vehicle, and in late May he arranged with Reitzel to publish a broadside entitled *The Instant*. In issues of 5 to 15 pages *The Instant* appeared at two- to three-week intervals through the summer of 1855. It contains some of the most trenchant and witty prose in all Kierkegaard's writing.

The Instant, No. 6 (August 23, 1855)

In the magnificent cathedral the Honorable and Right Reverend, Privy General Bishop to the High Court, the chosen favorite of the fashionable world, appears before an elect company and preaches *with emotion* upon the text he himself selected: "God hath elected the base things of the world, and the things that are despised"—and no one laughs?

The Instant, No. 3 (June 27, 1855)

As long as here in Denmark there exist 1,000 livings for teachers of Christianity, the most is being done to hinder Christianity. . . .

Take an example. If the State had a mind to put a stop to all true poetry, it would need merely . . . to introduce 1,000 livings for royal poetic functionaries. In this way the goal would soon be attained: the land would be continually flooded with rotten poetry, making the survival of true poetry as good as impossible.

The Instant, No. 4 (July 7, 1855)

The interest of Christianity, what it wants is—true Christians.

The egoism of the priesthood, both for pecuniary advantage and for the sake of power, requires—many Christians. . . .

So this accounts for the millions of Christians, the Christian states, kingdoms, lands, a Christian world. But this is only the first half of the criminal story; we come now to the refinement. The refinement is unique in its genre, altogether without analogy; for those who enrich themselves by counterfeiting the customhouse stamps or the brands of celebrated factories at least do not claim to be the most faithful friends of the customhouse or of those factories. This false claim is reserved for the Christian counterfeiters.

The Instant, No. 6 (August 23, 1855)

"Had the Apostle Paul any official position?" No, Paul had no official position. "Did he then earn much money in other ways?" No, he didn't earn money in any way. "Was he at least married?" No, he was not married. "But then really Paul is not a serious man." No, Paul is not a serious man.

These pamphlets display not only the Kierkegaardian wit and intelligence at its most nimble, but an economy which his rhet-

oric usually lacks. And the very leanness of the prose signals
an important change in Kierkegaard's own person, a collection
of self out of reflection and irony into the unity required for
combat. Gone now is the prolixity of the pseudonymous works,
and the solemn, often sentimental, affectation of the edifying
discourses. What is left is a style where every nuance has been
sharpened to produce the maximum cutting edge. Language has
become again for him what it once was in the courtyard of the
Borgerdydskole. It has become his weapon, a goad and spur
to be used to first tease and then maul his opponents. For here
Kierkegaard is saying what he believes rather than putting atti-
tudes into the mouths of pseudonyms. Totally absorbed in the
controversy he has ignited, for one of the few times in his life
he is happy.

He admitted something of this in the Prelude to the first issue
of *The Instant*:

> To contend with men—well, yes, that does delight me in a
> certain sense. I am by nature so polemically constituted that I
> feel myself really in my element only when I am surrounded
> by human mediocrity and paltriness. Only on *one* condition,
> however: that I be permitted silently to despise, to satiate the
> passion which is in my soul, contempt, for which my life as an
> author has richly provided me with occasions.

Long ago Poul Møller had pointed to this ruling passion in calling him "the most polemical of men." Now, in the autumn of
his life, Kierkegaard released it in flood. The contempt he expressed in his polemic against the church and its hirelings is
only a concrete form of the primordial passion that guided his
life—his contempt for the world, his decision not to live in harmony with it. The rage evidenced earlier in the journals of the
1850's was now redirected against a single target. Instead of de-
nouncing the body, woman, beauty, the senses—all that is

"worldly"—he now attacked a single corrupt and hypocritical institution. Against this target he employed all his powers—his intelligence, his polemical skill, his comprehension of human nature. The result was a tour de force of polemical literature, and for him, a purification of his rage. Purified of spleen, it took on the appearance of a rare yet troubling joy.

The change in him was obvious to his friends and acquaintances. Regine saw him for the last time in April, and the impression he made upon her was so strong that she remembered it for half a century. She was leaving for the West Indies with her husband, and on the morning of her departure she passed Kierkegaard in the street. There was something about his look that made her say to him, "God bless you. I hope things go well for you." And he, for the first time since their engagement, raised his wide-brimmed hat and gave her a warm greeting. Hans Brøchner saw him later that summer and noticed a similar transformation. They exchanged pleasantries one evening as Brøchner was making his way from Højbroplads to Vimmel-skaftet. In the fading light they talked of the controversy Kierkegaard had ignited. Brøchner thanked him for what he had done and told him how many people sympathized with his cause. They chatted for a few moments as they made their way toward Nytorv, Kierkegaard speaking "with the greatest clarity and calm of the situation he had evoked," Brøchner listening. What struck Brøchner was his companion's extraordinary "calm and confidence," and the fact that in all this turbulence he could preserve his good spirits and wit. As they neared Klædeboderne, they took leave of one another, Kierkegaard, with a twinkle in his eye, telling Brøchner a slightly ribald story. It was the last time Brøchner saw him alive.

The fact that Kierkegaard had gained a measure of happiness through his attack did not mean that it was succeeding. By late September with the ninth issue of *The Instant,* it was obvious to everyone that Kierkegaard's campaign was becoming increasingly repetitive. It had created something of a stir in intellectual and student circles—Troels-Lund recalled that several students gathered regularly in his brother's room to read and discuss the latest issue of *The Instant*. But the general public had been left offended and uncomprehending. Part of its bewilderment followed from the very nature of the attack. For the first thing which must be said about it is that it was not a political action at all; there were no reforms (short of ceasing to exist) that the church could carry out to satisfy Kierkegaard's criticism. Not really designed to bring about a definite change in the social order, his attack had the quality of an abstract gesture. Suspecting this, churchmen kept silent and counted on the fact that sooner or later Kierkegaard would tire and his polemic cease. At a convention of clergymen held that July in Roskilde, the chairman of the meeting noted that since the "case" of Kierkegaard had been put on the agenda, he must mention it, but that he did not wish to say anything further on the subject. The next speaker announced that since the matter had been dealt with by the chairman, he saw no reason to comment. Partly due to the clergy's silence, by the end of the summer Kierkegaard's attack was losing momentum. His fortune almost used up, his polemic spent, Kierkegaard's life was nearing the end of its fifth act. At this moment, with a sense of timing more characteristic of the stage than of life, he fell ill and was taken to Frederiks Hospital.

As we have seen, Kierkegaard's health had never been robust. In his youth he had coughed blood on several occasions and his digestion had always been finicky. But he had always managed to muddle through, and had never been sick enough before to need hospitalization. In late September he was afflicted with a series of spells that became progressively severe. The first had come during an evening party at J. F. Giødwad's. Another guest remembered: "He was sitting on the sofa and had been so gay, amusing, and charming, when he fell to the floor; we helped him up: 'Oh, leave—it—'til the maid—clears it away—in the morning,' he stammered, exhausted." He had not lost consciousness but simply experienced an overpowering sense of weakness. The same thing happened the next day while he was dressing. But he recovered soon enough and kept working on the next issue of *The Instant*.

A few days later, however, Kierkegaard collapsed in the street and was carried back to his small flat in Klædeboderne. He lay there for a few days until on October 2, 1855, an ambulance was called to take him to Frederiks Hospital. Just before it arrived he sent 300 rd. to Giødwad, who as coeditor of *Fatherland* was the closest thing he had to a friend. (This money, the remains of his fortune, paid his hospital bills and possibly covered the funeral expenses.) He pulled on his coat, for the last time adjusted the wide-brimmed hat, and supported by an ambulance attendant, shuffled out the door. His landlady, Fru Borries, was watching from her door across the hall. When he saw her he tipped his hat and gave her a cheerful look. Arriving at the hospital, he told the attending doctor that he knew his death was approaching but that he had no regrets; his death might even advance the cause for which he had been struggling. He laid the cause of his illness to "the enjoyment of cold seltzer water in the summertime," and to the combination of an exhausting work schedule with the bad air of his apartment.

It may be tempting to see Kierkegaard's sickness and death as brought on by the exertions of his attack on the church. Walter Lowrie conceived it this way and made Kierkegaard into a kind of modern religious hero who attacked the church "at the cost of his life." However dramatically satisfying such a view might be, there is also the less romantic fact that Kierkegaard most likely succumbed to a staphylococcus infection of the lungs. Even in our day of antibiotics and advanced lung surgery, this illness kills 14 percent of its victims. Danish figures show that in 1934 it was fatal in 34 percent of the cases, and in 1855, sixteen years before the bacillus itself was identified by Ogden, it was a desperate malady. Kierkegaard was given the best care then available. Dr. Seligmann Trier was one of the great men of Danish medicine, and it was to his ward that Kierkegaard was admitted. But little could be done for him. The lung membrane attacked by the staphylococcus germ remains in constant movement as the patient breathes, so that even if the infection subsides, it never gets a chance to heal properly. The patient coughs unremittingly, sometimes bringing up a yellowish phlegm, and finally dies of the by-products of infection and of simple exhaustion. This was Kierkegaard's case—gradual deterioration from his admission to the hospital until his death forty days later on November 11, 1855.

There were times, however, when the coughing subsided, the weakness abated, and Kierkegaard seemed much like his old self. From the reports of his visitors we get the impression that he not only expected death but welcomed it. One friend mentioned that he seemed "quiet and relaxed and said that he wanted to die." What impressed most people was his composure and the quiet radiance of his eyes. His niece Henriette Lund recalled that as soon as she entered his room she was "met by the gleam of light which radiated from his face. . . . Never have I seen the spirit break through its earthly frame and give it such a radiance." On another occasion Troels-Lund, then a fifteen-year-old, accompanied his uncle Christian Lund to Kierkegaard's room. They found the patient sitting pale and bowed in an armchair. Asked how he was, Kierkegaard replied: "As you see me—I myself know nothing more." Standing by the door, Troels-Lund listened to his uncle's sickroom chatter: "You know what, Søren? There's nothing the matter with you but your silly habit of holding yourself round-shouldered. Just straighten your back and stand up and your sickness will be over!" Kierkegaard did not answer, but as Troels-Lund recalled, his glance said everything:

> It radiated through its sadness such a quiet forbearance, coupled with a playful, provocative gleam of humor and fun, that it captivated me in an instant, and our glances came together in happy understanding. . . .
>
> Then the patient became more animated, more like himself from earlier days. At the same time it became clearer to me what the difference was between those days and now. It was as if all expression had fallen away from the movements of his emaciated body, yes, even from the features of his face, and with augmented power had gathered in his eyes alone. They shone with a soulfulness that made an indelible impression.

Later, Troels-Lund shook hands with Kierkegaard and made ready to leave. He remembered how the older man took his hand in both of his, and "how small, thin, and transparently white they were." "Thanks for coming, Troels," Kierkegaard said, "and now farewell." Then once again he turned his look on the boy. "These ordinary words," Troels-Lund said, "were accompanied by a look the likes of which I had never seen before. . . . It seemed to me to make the whole room light."

But Kierkegaard's quiet beneficence did not extend to the clergy. He would not receive his brother, partly because of old and confused antagonisms, partly because Peter Christian was a clergyman. It was suggested that he might like to take Holy Communion, but when he declined to receive it from a clergyman—a "royal functionary"—the idea was dropped. The one clergyman whom he did permit to visit was his boyhood friend, Emil Boesen. Pastor Boesen arrived in Copenhagen from Jutland in mid-October, and his notes of their conversations paint a vivid picture of the dying Kierkegaard.

Wednesday, October 17 How are you? "Badly, it is death. Pray for me that it will come quickly and easily. I'm discouraged. . . ."

Have you made any decision about your papers? "No, let come what may, it's all in the hands of providence. Then too I'm financially ruined and now have nothing; only enough to pay for the burial. I began with a little something over twenty thousand, and saw that it would last for some time— ten or twenty years. Now it has lasted seventeen. . . ."

Frøken Fibiger [the nurse] had sent him some flowers; he had shut them up in a drawer. "It's bad. Pray for me that it will soon be over." He looked at the flowers, but would not have them put in water: "It's the fate of flowers to bloom and smell and die."

By Thursday, October 18, he was very weak. He said that he could collect his thoughts clearly the greater part of the time. Was there anything he still wanted to have said? "No; yes, remember me to everyone. I was much attached to them all, and tell them that my life is a great, and to others unknown and incomprehensible, suffering; it all looked like pride and vanity, but it wasn't. I'm no better than others. I've said that and never anything else. I had my thorn in the flesh, and therefore did not marry and could not take on an official position."

Boesen asked if he did not wish to modify his harsh statements about the church; Kierkegaard said no, they must stand as they are, "otherwise it doesn't do any good. It has to burst like a bombshell. Do you think I ought to tone it all down, first of all wake people up and then calm them? How can you want to confuse me like that? . . . You must not forget that I have seen everything from the inmost center of Christianity; it's all very poor and clumsy. . . . It pleases me so much that you've come here. Thank you, thank you."

Friday, October 19 He had slept for a couple of hours the evening before and was in a good mood.

Don't you wish to receive Holy Communion?

"Yes, but not from a priest; from a layman."

That would be difficult.

"Then I'll die without it."

That's not right.

"That can't be disputed. I've made my choice, have chosen. The clergy are state functionaries, and functionaries have nothing to do with Christianity."

But that's not true. It doesn't agree with truth and reality.

"Well, you see God is the sovereign. But then there are all these people who want to make comfortable lives for themselves, so they get hold of Christianity. There are all these thousands of priests, and no one in the country can die blessed without belonging [to their club]. So they become the sovereign, and it's all over with God's sovereignty. But He shall be obeyed in everything."

Then he sank down, his voice became weak, and he was physically uncomfortable. I left soon afterwards. . . .

Thursday, October 25   Why hadn't he moved from the apartment in Klædeboderne, where the air was so bad for him?

"I was too tired. I still had some numbers of *The Instant* to get out and several hundred rigsdaler for that purpose. So I could either lay it away and save myself, or continue and then fall. Rightly I chose the latter, and so I'm finished."

Did you publish the numbers of *The Instant* you wanted to?

"Yes."

How much in your life has turned out just right!

"Yes. That's why I'm very happy, and very sad that I cannot share this happiness with anyone."

Boesen saw him for the last time on October 27. Only the hospital record charts the final downward trajectory of Kierkegaard's life. It tells a simple tale of rapid loss of physical strength, though his mental powers remained unimpaired and his appetite good until November 5. He died on November 11, at 9 p.m.

A week later on Sunday, November 18, Kierkegaard's niece Henriette Lund sat in the gallery of the Frue Kirke and looked down on her uncle's coffin. Dressed with wreaths and covered in black velvet, it lay where Mynster's casket had rested twenty-one months earlier. She watched as "the tightly packed mass of people heaved like a tossing sea." Gathered around the coffin on its catafalque in the choir was a ring of "sinister-looking characters," most likely some of the anonymous "little" people who had tormented him so often during his life. Ironically, they had taken him to their hearts after his attack on the established church—for all the wrong reasons, from Kierkegaard's point of view. The church doors soon opened, and a group of university students made their way down the main aisle and took up positions as a guard of honor immediately around the coffin.

Down on the main floor Henriette's half-brother Troels-Lund could not tell what was happening. He had gone alone into the second pew. A few moments later the large figure of Professor Rasmus Nielsen entered the pew and shut the door so forcefully that the latch fell. Together the two of them sat sheltered from the pushing, elbowing mass in the main aisle and chancel. A stronger movement began to develop and Troels-Lund, fearing that a group had shoved their way forward to remove the coffin, looked up worriedly at Henriette in the gallery. He could see from her face that something good was happening, and the students then made their appearance.

The occasion differed from Mynster's funeral in that the clergy were conspicuous by their absence. Only two appeared in their vestments—Peter Christian Kierkegaard and the dean of the Frue Kirke, Eggert C. Tryde. The latter, a small red-faced man, was obviously ill at ease. His face showed disapproval and he kept pushing his little skullcap back and forth on his head, stopping only when the dead man's brother rose to speak.

Peter Christian began by saying that he was the only surviving member of Michael Pedersen Kierkegaard's family. He told how his father tended sheep on the Jutland heath, and how in his twenty-second year he had become a citizen and hosier in Copenhagen. He pointed out that his brother had gone astray in recent years and had tried to shake what no power on earth can shake—the church. Alas, no clergyman had been able to take Søren aside in these last years and hold him quiet until he got the rest he so desperately needed. As for this gathering as such, Peter Christian had "absolutely nothing" to say to it; he could not even thank the guests for coming. The man on the catafalque, as they well knew, was no friend to crowds or their hangers-on, and he had hated all ostentation. So he would pray one prayer. Descending a few steps to the coffin, Peter led the congregation in a long prayer asking God's mercy for his brother, and praying forgiveness for his "bewildered and perplexed soul."

The casket was carried out of the cathedral by its honor guard of students and placed on a bier for its trip beyond the city's walls to the family plot in Assistens Cemetery. The family climbed into carriages, and the rest of the multitude, undeterred by Peter Christian's rebuke, followed on foot. Out Nørregade the procession moved, passing directly under the windows of the flat to which Regine had rushed in panic fourteen years earlier, passing northward through Nørreport, between the ramparts where Kierkegaard had wandered so often early in the morning. It crossed Nørrebro with its lakes to either side, as yet unwreathed in ice, but dark and cold. A kilometer beyond the city's walls the procession turned into the cemetery, having followed the same route as Mynster's cortege.

With difficulty the heavy casket was carried up the wet path to the grave site. The mourners followed as best they could, slipping on the wet leaves, spilling over railings and grave-stones, until they stood in a huge circle around the open grave. The railing had been removed and was piled just to the right of a fresh mound of yellow-grey soil. Dean Tryde—Royal Confessor, member of the Silver Cross of the Order of Denmark, Knight of Denmark, Archdeacon of the Frue Kirke—gave the committal: "From earth hast thou come, to earth shalt thou return; from earth shalt thou rise again." He stepped back from the grave. While the coffin was being lowered into the ground a discontented murmur ran through the crowd. Someone shouted: "That was no good!"

Suddenly a large young man stepped forward from the crowd and asked permission to speak. Dean Tryde objected, but several shouted: "Yes, let us hear!" The young man said he was Henrik Lund, nephew of the deceased, and out of friendship for his uncle he wanted to say a few words. Kierkegaard's reputation, he went on, would stand or fall on what he had written. But there was one thing that must be protested, and that was the way the established church was treating him this very day. Kierkegaard had declared often in his writings that he was not a Christian. (A voice from the crowd: "That's a lie.") He refused to be a Christian of the official sort, where all are Christians. Yet official Christendom had done something no other religion would have done—they had taken him by force and buried him as one of their own. But in doing this the state church had profaned itself. For what baptized Jew would be buried by Jews? And what Turk who had defected to another religion would be buried as a Turk? The state church was the great whore with whom all kings and princes of the earth had committed fornication. Here he read from Revelations XVIII. As for himself, he would follow Kierkegaard's advice: "Whosoever does not take part in the official worship of God has certainly one sin the ress." He only wanted to protest the use to which Kierkegaard's body had been put. By bringing it here under official auspices against the declared wishes of the deceased, the state church had committed a kind of rape.

Lund stepped back from the open grave to a chorus of angry voices: "Stop the thief; he is desecrating holy places!" In small groups arguments broke out as to who was responsible for this "scandal." Professor Rasmus Nielsen appeared about to speak, but then turned and walked away in vexation. Beads of moisture collected on the casket and on the clothes of the mourners. Some half-tipsy fellow called: "Let's go home, Christian." A student shouted: "Nobody else is speaking, so let's go home!" Troels-Lund, standing in the crowd, suddenly recognized that he was shivering. The mourners turned from the grave, raised their collars against the damp November chill, and started trudging back to the city. Slowly they dispersed, heading across the lakes to the slums of Christianshavn and Nørrebro. Here and there carriages rumbled past, windows rolled against the damp cold, carrying the more distinguished mourners back to their parlors and drawing rooms. In the cemetery the gravediggers' spades bit deep into the yellow-grey earth, casting it in narrow arcs to thud wetly on the black-draped casket.

NOTES

BIBLIOGRAPHY

INDEX

A GUIDE TO
ABBREVIATIONS AND SHORT TITLES
USED IN THE NOTES

DANISH SOURCES

X⁵ A 132
(Papers)

Søren Kierkegaards Papirer. Second Edition. Edited by P. A. Heiberg, V. Kuhr, and E. Torsting. In 20 Volumes. Copenhagen: Gyldendal: 1909–48. X, Part 5, Section A, Item 132.

SV, XIII, 183

Søren Kierkegaards Samlede Værker. First Edition. Edited by A. B. Drachmann, J. L. Heiberg, and H. O. Lange. In 14 Volumes. Copenhagen: Gyldendal; 1901–6, XII, p. 183.

Breve og Akstykker
(Letters)
I, 345

Breve og Akstykker vedrorende Søren Kierkegaard. Edited by Niels Thulstrup in 2 Volumes. Copenhagen: Munksgaard, 1953–4. I, p. 345.

Archives

Søren Kierkegaard Arkivet, Royal Library, Copenhagen.

TRANSLATIONS OF KIERKEGAARD'S WORKS

Age

The Present Age. Translated by Alexander Dru. London: Oxford University Press; 1940.

Climacus

Johannes Climacus or, De Omnibus Dubitandum Est. Translated by T. H. Croxall. Stanford University Press; 1958.

Discourses	*Edifying Discourses.* Translated by David F. and Lillian Marvin Swenson in four volumes. Minneapolis: Augsburg Publishing House; 1943–6.
Dread	*The Concept of Dread.* Translated by Walter Lowrie. Princeton University Press; 1946.
E/O, I, II	*Either/Or.* Translated by David F. Swenson, Lillian Marvin Swenson, and Walter Lowrie in two volumes. Garden City: Anchor Books; 1959.
Fear	*Fear and Trembling.* Translated by Walter Lowrie. Princeton University Press; 1968.
Fragments	*Philosophical Fragments.* Translated by David F. Swenson. Revised Edition. Princeton University Press; 1962.
Irony	*The Concept of Irony.* Translated by Lee M. Capel. London: Wm. Collins Sons & Co.; 1966.
Postscript	*Concluding Unscientific Postscript.* Translated by Walter Lowrie. Princeton University Press; 1944.
Repetition	*Repetition.* Translated by Walter Lowrie. Princeton University Press; 1946.
Sickness	*The Sickness unto Death.* Translated by Walter Lowrie. Princeton University Press; 1968.
Stages	*Stages on Life's Way.* Translated by Walter Lowrie. Princeton University Press; 1945.
Training	*Training in Christianity.* Translated by Walter Lowrie. Princeton University Press; 1944.
View	*The Point of View for My Work as an Author.* Translated by Walter Lowrie. New York: Harper Torchbooks; 1962.

NOTES

CHAPTER I – "THE STRANGE ONE . . . THE PECULIAR ONE"

page 4, line 4
"respect the police"   Letter from P. E. Lind to H. P. Barfod dated
Sept. 16, 1869, Archives, D, Pk. 5, Læg 32.

page 4, line 18
"the peculiar one"   Letter from Franz Welding to H. P. Barfod dated
Sept. 3, 1869, Archives, D, Pk. 5, Læg 55.

page 4, line 27
"mistaken for an old man"   Papers, X^1 A 234.

page 5, lines 4–18
Quotation from Welding to Barfod, Sept. 3, 1869.

page 5, line 21
Letter from Frederik Meidell to H. P. Barfod dated Nov. 7, 1869,
Archives, D, Pk. 5, Læg 36.

page 6, line 1
"in your pocket"   Sejer Kühle: *Søren Kierkegaards Barndom og
Ungdom* (Copenhagen: Achehoug Dansk Forlag; 1950), p. 42.

page 6, lines 4–19
Quotation from Welding to Barfod, Sept. 3, 1869.

pages 6–7, lines 33–4
Quotation from Papers, XI^1 A 277.

page 7, line 10
Danish critic   Rikard Magnussen: *Det særlige Kors* (Copenhagen: Ejnar Munksgaard; 1942), p. 21.

page 7, line 14
The certificate releasing Kierkegaard from service in the Guards can be found in Letters, I, 7. It states only that he was released from duty on the basis of a doctor's written statement. No information is given as to what medical condition made Kierkegaard "unfit for duty."

pages 7–8, lines 23–1
Quotations in this paragraph from Papers, VI A 103. X¹ A 78. VII¹ B 37. VI A 103. X¹ A 234. Among many entries on the theme of cripples, see Papers, X⁴ A 652 and X⁵ A 72.

page 8, lines 20–28
Quotations in this paragraph from Papers, V A 3 and XI² A 439. See also XI¹ A 219.

CHAPTER 2 – HOME

page 11, line 11
Value of town house   Frithiof Brandt and Else Rammel: *Søren Kierkegaard og Pengene* (Copenhagen: Levin & Munksgaard; 1935), p. 65ff.

page 12, lines 12–18
Reminiscence from Papers, I A 169.

page 12, lines 32–33
Quotation from I. Plenge: *Nogle Træk af Livet i København for en Menneskealder Siden* (Copenhagen: Gyldendal; 1873), p. 25.

page 13, line 5
This pageant is described by Henriette Lund in her *Erindringer fra Hjemmet* (Copenhagen: Gyldendalske Boghandel; 1909), p. 26.

page 13, line 17
Valdemar Ammundsen provides a complete genealogy of the Kierkegaard family, together with a list of birth and death dates, on pp. 132–3 of *Søren Kierkegaards Ungdom* (Copenhagen: G. E. C. Gads Forlag; 1912).

page 14, line 14
marriage contract   Kühle: *Søren Kierkegaards Barndom og Ungdom,*
pp. 12–14.

page 14, line 29
"her chicks"   Lund: *op. cit.,* p. 20.

page 15, line 8
papers of her sons   Kühle: *op. cit.,* p. 21.

page 15, lines 12–17
Quotation from Lund: *op. cit.,* pp. 18–19.

page 15, line 21
Boesen cautioned Michael   Koch: *op. cit.,* p. 12.

page 16, lines 12–13
Quotation from Peter Christian Kierkegaard's Journal 1826–1850,
section entitled "Ungdoms Minder" (Royal Library, *Ny kgl. Sml.,*
2656, 4°).

pages 16–17, lines 30–15
Quotations in this paragraph from Papers, IV B 1, p. 108; II A 205;
II A 238; V A 2.

pages 17–18, lines 20–13
Quotations in this paragraph from *View,* 82; *SV,* XIII, 568. Lund:
op. cit., p. 17. Georg Brandes: *Søren Kierkegaard* (Copenhagen:
Glydendal; 1967), p. 16. Letter from Meidell to Barfod dated Nov. 7,
1869. Lund: *op. cit.,* p. 24.

page 19, lines 16–17
Brandes: *op. cit.,* p. 16.

CHAPTER 3 – FATHER

page 20, line 1
This scene is built upon a remark of Frederik Hammerich that he once
saw Michael Kierkegaard trudging home with a fat goose slung over
his shoulder. See Hammerich: *Et Levnetsløb* (Copenhagen: Forlags-
bureauret; 1882), p. 59.

pages 20–21, lines 23–10
Quotations from Lund: *op. cit.*, p. 22.

page 22, lines 5–12
Christian Wolff: *Vernünfftige Gedanken von Gott der Welt und der Seele des Menschen, auch allen Dingen überhaupt* (Halle: Rengers Buchhandlung; 1725), p. 672. After running through the various works by Wolff available to Michael Kierkegaard, Ammundsen argues that he was most likely to have read this book (Ammundsen: *op. cit.*, p. 18).

page 22, line 19
fire   Henriette Lund describes the incident and Michael Kierkegaard's reaction to it, saying that "with an almost festive cheerfulness he went about doing what could be done" (Lund: *op. cit.*, p. 22).

page 23, line 12
cursed God   Søren Kierkegaard wrote in his journal in early 1846: "How terrible it is to think about the man who once, as a little boy herding sheep on the Jutland heath, suffering badly in hunger and want, stood up on a hill and cursed God—a man who was not able to forget it even when he was eighty-two years old." (Papers, VII[1] A 5.) When H. P. Barfod, the first editor of Kierkegaard's *Papirer*, found this note, he showed it to Peter Christian Kierkegaard, who replied: "That is my father's story and ours too."

page 23, line 33
release from serfdom   This document is preserved among Michael Pedersen Kierkegaard's papers in the Royal Library.

page 25, line 4
The gunboat carried two 18-pound cannons and four 4-pounders. It was damaged in action against the British near Lahals Aug. 30, 1811. See H. Degenkolv: *Oplysninger vedrørende den danske Flaades Skibe i Sidste Aarhundrede* (Copenhagen: Lehmann and Stages Boghandel; 1906), p. 186.

page 26, line 12
early death   Kühle cites a letter from F. C. Sibbern (Oct. 3, 1869) stating that Michael Kierkegaard "gave up his business because of a kind of hypochondria, believing that he too would not live much longer" (Kühle: *op. cit.*, p. 15).

page 27, lines 1–11
Marriage contract and will are described in Kühle: *Søren Kierkegaards Barndom og Ungdom*, p. 12, where the contract is excerpted; pp. 14, 16.

CHAPTER 4 – SON

page 30, line 7
Kierkegaard describes these imaginary walks in a long, unpublished essay called *Johannes Climacus eller De Omnibus Dubitandum Est.* There is little doubt that he is describing a customary event in the family home. In a letter written in 1844 to Henriette Glahn Kierkegaard he relates how as a child "I got permission from my father to go out to Frederiksberg, but with his hand in mine walked up and down the floor—to Frederiksberg." Archives, D, Pk. 1, Læg 3. Kierkegaard also told Hans Brøchner that these imaginary walks were a regular feature of his childhood; see Brandes: *op. cit.*, p. 214.

pages 30–31, lines 15–13
Quotations in this paragraph from Papers, IV B 1, pp. 106–7; *Climacus*, 105. Papers, IV B 1, pp. 107–8; *Climacus*, 105–70. Letter from Søren Kierkegaard to Peter Christian Kierkegaard dated May 19, 1847; Letters, 1, 167.

page 31, lines 18–33
Quotations in this paragraph from Papers, IV B 1, pp. 108–9; *Climacus*, 107–8. Ammundsen, *op. cit.*, p. 27.

page 32, lines 2–29
Quotations in this paragraph from SV, XII, 162–4; *Training*, 174–6 and Papers, X¹ A 272.

page 33, line 2
"charitable institution"   Papers, IV B 1, p. 111; *Climacus*, 110.

page 33, line 9
"melancholy men"   Papers, V A 33.

page 33, lines 17–23
Quotations in this paragraph from Papers, VIII¹ A 650 and X¹ A 8.

pages 33–34, lines 26–5
Quotation from *SV*, XIII, 566–7; *View*, 80–1.

page 34, lines 16–25
Quotation from Papers, IV A 60.

page 34, line 28
melancholy   Papers, VII¹ A 126.

page 35, line 21
"open one's heart"   Papers, II A 20.

page 35, line 25
"hand of God"   Papers, II A 805.

page 36, line 30
"ruled the world"   *SV*, XIII, 548–9; *View*, 52.

page 37, line 3
"strict in Christianity"   Papers, VIII¹ A 663.

page 37, line 5
"botched"   Papers, XI¹ A 299.

page 37, lines 7–12
Quotation from Papers, IX A 411.

page 37, line 21
"fear of God"   Papers, X² A 454.

pages 37–38, lines 24–1
Quotations in this paragraph from *SV*, XIII, 564; *View*, 76. Papers,
VIII¹ A 680. VIII¹ A 177. Reference to his father as playmate in
Papers, IX A 247.

page 38, lines 8–14
Quotation from II A 804. Kierkegaard did not know English, but jotted
down the lines in question from Ernst Ortlepp's *W. Shakespeares
dramatische Werke* (1838). This edition of Shakespeare was found
in Kierkegaard's library at his death; see H. P. Rohde: *Auktionspro-
tokol over Søren Kierkegaards Bogsammling* (Copenhagen: Det
kongelige Bibliotek; 1967), p. 99.

page 38, line 22
"stems from love"   Papers XI¹ A 299.

page 38, line 26
"divine father-love"   Papers III A 73.

pages 38–39, lines 31–4
Quotation from X¹ A 8.

page 39, lines 24–28
Quotations in this paragraph from Papers, X² A 61. X³ A 343. X³ A
77; see also *SV*, XIV, 355; *Attack*, 285–6.

CHAPTER 5 – GILLELEJE 1835

page 43, line 13
"eight children"   Letter from I. Rudelbach to Dr. A. G. Rudelbach
dated Feb. 20, 1835 (*Ny kgl. Sml.*, 1543, 2).

page 43, line 11
"told her the truth"   Hammerich: *op. cit.*, p. 59.

page 43, line 22
"too late"   Kühle: *op. cit.*, p 82.

page 44, line 11
"like two children"   Lund: *op. cit.*, p. 42.

page 44, lines 15–16
"silence of death"   Papers, II A 805.

pages 45–46, lines 27–4
Quotations in this paragraph from Papers, X² A 134. IX A 99. P. C.
Kierkegaard's Journal 1826–1850 (*Ny kgl. Sml.*, 2656, 4°).

page 46, line 14
university career   Valdemar Ammundsen (*op. cit.*, pp. 77–92) provides a superb summary of Kierkegaard's academic courses and
achievements. Reading notes from this time can be found among
Kierkegaard's Papers at I C 35.

page 47, line 11
"day of the week"   Papers, I A 72.

page 47, lines 27–28
Quotation in this paragraph from Papers, I A 63. Hertz's notebooks in
Hans Kyrre: *Henrik Hertz: Liv og Digtning med et Tillæg af*

Efterladte Papirer (Copenhagen: H. Hagerups Forlag; 1916), pp. 9, 10.

page 48, line 16
"life in many"   *SV*, XIII, 6.

page 48, lines 26–29
Quotations in this paragraph from H. L. Martensen: *Af mit Levnet, I–III* (Copenhagen: Gyldendal; 1882–3), Vol. I., p. 78. Hammerich: *op. cit.*, p. 59.

page 49, line 24
"King Valdemar's hunt"   Papers, I A 64.

pages 49–50, lines 29–6
Quotation from Papers, I A 68.

page 51, lines 6–35
With the five preceding quotations, Papers, I A 75.

page 52, line 32
"Sartre has suggested"   The following discussion was suggested by Sartre's analysis of dreaming in *The Psychology of Imagination* (New York: The Citadel Press; 1965), pp. 231–55.

pages 53–54, lines 30–8
Quotation from Papers, II A 125.

page 54, lines 12–20
Quotation from Papers, II A 487. At II A 415, Kierkegaard remarks: "I am so unhappy at the present time that in my dreams I am indescribably happy." For parallel statements from Kierkegaard's Papers where he seems to be fleeing the world in the direction of an experience of life transformed into dream, see I A 235, I A 327, I A 91, and II A 58.

CHAPTER 6 – A HOST OF SHADOWS

page 56, line 4
letter to Lund   Papers, I A 72.

page 56, lines 10–15
Quotation from Papers, I A 95–6.

pages 56–57, lines 19–10
Quotation from Papers, I A 99.

page 57, line 29
"life's dry nurse"   Papers, II A 59.

page 58, lines 4–13
Quotations in this paragraph from Papers, II A 207. VI A 125.

pages 58–59, lines 29–3
Quotations in this paragraph from Papers, I A 75, 68.

page 59, lines 5–16
Quotations in this paragraph from Papers, I A 72, 333 and from IV
A 21.

page 60, lines 7–21
Quotation from *SV*, XIII, 68–9.

page 60–61, lines 32–5
Quotation from Papers, II A 449.

page 61, lines 14–20
Quotations in this paragraph from Papers, III A 108 and I A 150.

page 61, lines 26–29
Comparisons of irony and humor from Papers, II A 672, 694 and from
III B 20.

page 62,, lines 4–5
represent a life view   Papers, II A 683.

page 62, lines 15–22
Quotation from Papers, I A 12.

page 62, lines 24–31
Quotation from Papers, I A 13–15.

page 63, lines 3–11
Quotation from Papers, I A 18.

page 63, lines 23–32
Quotations in this paragraph from Papers, II A 26 and I A 333.

page 63, lines 33–34
"a host of shadows"   *SV*, III, 194; *Repetition*, 43.

page 64, line 10
1838   Papers, II A 807.

CHAPTER 7 – SO I FARED FORTH INTO LIFE

pages 65–66, lines 5–5
Quotation from *SV*, XIII, 566–7; *View*, 79–80.

page 66, lines 9–13
Receipts for the amounts cited can be found in a rough paper notebook preserved in the Royal Library. On the outside cover is the single word "Søren" written in Michael Pedersen Kierkegaard's shaky hand. Archives, D, Pk. 8, Læg 2: *Faderens Regnskabbog for "Søren."* For Søren's signed note to "Herr Sager" and for the warning from the Student Union, see Archives, D, Pk. 8, Læg 1; for Reitzel's bill showing a payment of 50 rd. in cash to Søren, see Archives, D, Pk. 8, Læg 3.

page 67, line 10
"drank their wine"   Kühle: *op. cit.*, p. 137.

page 67, lines 19–25
Quotation from Papers, I A 166.

page 68, lines 1–14
Anecdote from Brøchner: *op. cit.*, p. 50.

pages 69–70, lines 28–7
Quotation and description of card game from Brøchner: *op. cit.*, pp. 16–18.

page 70, lines 16–32
Quotation from Brøchner, *op. cit.*, pp. 18–19.

page 71, line 2
Lund letter   Archives, *Ny kgl. Sml.*, 3621, 4°.

page 71, line 6
"wandering rheumatism"   Papers, II A 222.

page 71, line 17
The description of the Royal Theater's clientele is based upon J. H. Lorck's *Femoghalvfjerdsindstyve Aar* (Cophenhagen: Gyldendal; 1885), p. 107f. For a description of Kierkegaard's attempt to draft

the by-laws see Angul Hammerich: *Festskrift i Anledning af Musik-foreningens Hundredaarsdag, II. Musikforeningens Historie 1836–1886* (Copenhagen: Musikforeningen; 1886), p. 6. See also Lorck: *op. cit.*, p. 108.

page 72, lines 7–23
Quotations in this paragraph from Papers, II A 491. I C 125. I A 297.

page 72, line 26
Vilhelm Birkedal: *Personlige Oplevelser i et langt Liv,* Vol. II., p. 85.

page 72, line 32
Holger Frederik Rørdam: *En gammel Præsteslægts Historie, I–II* (Copenhagen: G. E. C. Gads Forlag; 1878), Vol. II, p. 64, note 1.

page 73, line 2
Letter from J. A. Ostermann to H. P. Barfod dated April 25, 1868, Archives, D, Pk. 5, Læg 41.

page 73, line 8
Text of speech in Papers, I A 2.

page 73, line 18
Letter from Ostermann to Barfod dated April 25, 1868.

page 74, line 1
Letter from Peter Rørdam to Hans Rørdam dated Feb. 23, 1836, printed in H. F. Rørdam (ed.): *Peter Rørdam* (Copenhagen: Karl Schønbergs Forlag; 1891), p. 79.

page 74, lines 28–33
Quotation from Papers, I A 161.

CHAPTER 8 – SOMETHING GHOSTLY ABOUT ME

pages 75–76, lines 19–11
Quotation from Archives, D, Pk. 5, Læg 31: *Hr. Cand. Israel Levins Udtalelser om S. Kierkegaard 1858 og 1869.*

page 76, lines 14–19
Quotation from Papers, X^2 A 3.

page 76, line 26
"outside myself"   Papers, X^1 A 8.

page 77, line 3
"a new body"   Papers, III A 603.

page 77, line 9
"what I lack"   Papers, VIII¹ A 177.

page 77, lines 16–32
Quotations in this paragraph from Papers, II A 662, 649. Levin: *Udtalelser*, Archives, D. Pk. 5, Læg 31. Papers, I A 123. *SV*, XIII, 560; *View*, 70. Papers, IX A 411.

page 78, lines 6–7
studied conversation   Brøchner: *op. cit.*, p. 35.

page 78, line 8
Meyer Goldschmidt: *Livs Erindringer og Resultater, I–II* (Copenhagen: Gyldendal; 1877), Vol. I., pp. 214–15.

page 78, line 28
Jean-Paul Sartre: *Baudelaire* (New York: New Directions; 1950), p. 22.

page 79, line 3
"cannot forget myself"   Papers, I A 162.

page 79, lines 9–13
Diary entries in Papers, III A 17 and 15.

page 79, line 13
Brøchner: *op. cit.*, pp. 28, 42.

pages 79–80, lines 32–15
Quotations in this paragraph from Papers, I A 335. VIII¹ A 246. II A 420.

pages 80–81, lines 30–6
Quotation from Papers, II A 609.

page 81, lines 11–12
"can't argue away"   Papers, II A 607.

page 81, lines 22–31
Quotation from Papers, III A 218.

page 82, line 2
"sickness"   *SV*, I, 278; *E/O*, I, 302.

page 82, lines 15–26
Quotations from I A 336, 156, 158.

page 82, line 29
"strange vibrations"   Papers, I A 175.

page 83, line 4
"terrible" suffering   See, for example, Papers, I A 123, 181, and 333 where his complaints seem so artful and literary.

page 83, lines 22–33
Quotations in this paragraph from Papers, II A 549. III A 224. II A 171, 637.

page 84, lines 7–16
Quotations from Papers, III A 225. II A 495, 435.

page 84, line 20
"is dead"   Papers, II A 690. About the same time he told Brøchner that he was "in reality a dead person" (Brøchner: *op. cit.*, p. 47).

page 84, line 19
"old man"   Papers, X^5 A 105.7.

page 84, lines 20–21
"ice flowers"   Papers, II A 641.

page 84, line 22
Ronald Laing: *The Divided Self* (Baltimore: Penguin Books; 1965), p. 75.

page 85, line 19
Rudolph Friedmann: *Kierkegaard* (New York: New Directions; 1949), p. 24.

page 86, lines 1–7
comments on melancholy   Papers, VIII[1] A 641 and IX A 65.

CHAPTER 9 – THE LONGEST PARENTHESIS

page 87, line 9
Letter from Peter Christian Kierkegaard to Frederik Pedersen dated Jan. 13–15, 1877; cited by Carl Weltzer: *Peter og Søren Kierkegaard* (Copenhagen: Gads; 1936), p. 99.

page 88, lines 2–7
Marie's death   *Ny Kgl. Sml.*, 2656, 4°: *Peter Christian Kierkegaards
Journal, 1826–1850.*

page 88, line 9
funeral   Weltzer: *op. cit.*, p. 116.

page 88, line 25
"repressed pain"   Letter from Fogtmann to F. C. Sibbern dated May
25, 1838; cited in C. L. N. Mynster (ed.): *Breve til og fra F. C.
Sibbern* (Copenhagen: Gyldendal; 1866), p. 187.

page 88, line 28
"so polemical"   Papers, XI¹ A 275, 276.

page 88, line 34
"my departed friend"   Papers, V B 46.

page 89, lines 3–7
Quotation from Papers, II A 209.

page 89, line 12
"still remember him"   Papers, II A 216.

page 89, lines 20–21
"burn brighter"   *SV*, XIII, 79.

page 89, line 32
publication of review   Letter from Emil Boesen to Martin Hammerich
dated July 20, 1838, cited by Carl Weltzer in *Kirkehistorisk Samlinger*, VII Række, Bd. 1 (1952), p. 413.

page 90, line 12
"eternal habitations"   Papers, II A 228.

page 90, line 14
Carl Jørgensen: *Søren Kierkegaard* (Copenhagen: Nyt Nordisk Forlag;
1964), Vol. I., p. 97.

page 90, line 18
the consumptive   Papers, I A 75.

page 91, lines 1–6
This description of Michael Pedersen Kierkegaard's final illness and
death is taken from *Peter Christian Kierkegaards Journal, 1826–1850*
(*Ny kgl. Sml.*, 2656, 4°).

page 91, lines 11–23
Quotation from Papers, II A 243.

page 92, lines 15–35
Quotation from Papers, II A 805.

page 93, line 25
SK's share of estate   Brandt and Rammel: *op. cit.*, p. 9.

page 93, line 30
"fob the old man off"   Letter from cand. polyt. J. C. Barth to H. P. Barfod (undated but most likely from 1869), Archives, D, Pk. 5, Læg 7.

page 93, line 31
Brøchner: *op. cit.*, pp. 21–2.

page 94, lines 19–20
"studied diligently"   Lund: *op. cit.*, pp. 106–7.

page 94, lines 22–31
Quotation from Papers, II A 414.

page 95, lines 1–2
"the Guadalquivir"   Papers, II A 497.

page 95, lines 6–13
Quotation from Papers, II A 576.

page 95, line 16
"longest parenthesis"   Papers, III A 335.

page 95, line 22
Records of the exam, from Universitets Arkiv, 1172, have been extensively excerpted in Weltzer: *op. cit.*, pp. 155–6.

page 96, line 9
examiners' judgment   Brøchner: *op. cit.*, p. 22.

page 96, lines 16–17
Sæding trip   Arthur Dahl's elegant little book, *Søren Kierkegaard's Pilgrimage to Jutland* (Copenhagen: The Danish Tourist Association; 1948) gives a full account.

page 97, line 4
"my body"   Brøchner: *op. cit.*, p. 30.

page 97, lines 9–12

This and all following quotations from Kierkegaard's travel notebook can be found in Papers, III A 15, 17, 67, 54, 73, 56, 75, 78, 77.

page 100, line 4

Brøchner: *op. cit.*, pp. 39–40.

CHAPTER 10 – SOVEREIGN OF MY HEART, REGINE

page 101, line 12

"a very strong impression"   Hjalmar Helweg: *Søren Kierkegaard* (Copenhagen: H. Hagerups Forlag; 1933), pp. 385–6. After her husband's death in 1896, Regine Olsen Schlegel (then a *grande dame* in her late 70's) took steps to make sure that her recollections of her engagement to Søren Kierkegaard would not die with her. She had long conversations with a writer and friend, Hanne Mourier, who wrote down the substance of their talks. Miss Mourier's notes were then read through and approved by Mrs. Schlegel. Subsequently these notes found their way into the hands of J. C. Koll, who delivered them to Dr. Helweg. They were printed for the first time as an appendix to Helweg's psychiatric study of Kierkegaard which appeared in 1933.

But this was not the only precaution Mrs. Schlegel took. In October 1898 she asked a young friend, Raphael Meyer, to listen to her recollections. In addition, she turned over to Meyer a collection of letters Kierkegaard had written to her during the engagement period (her own letters to Kierkegaard, she told Meyer, "I have fortunately burnt"). In 1904 Meyer published the letters together with a narrative drawn from his conversations with Mrs. Schlegel under the title, *Kierkegaardske Papirer: Forlovelsen* (Copenhagen: Gyldendalske Boghandel; 1904).

Miss Mourier's notes and Meyer's narrative form the basis of our knowledge of the affair from Regine's side.

page 101, line 17

"in standing alone"   Papers, II A 68.

page 102, lines 1–22

Quotation from *SV*, I, 389–90; *E/O*, I, 416–17.

page 102, line 32

Regine's route   All this is explained in a letter to Emil Boesen written from Berlin, Oct. 31, 1841. Kierkegaard asked Boesen to spy on Regine to determine if she was getting over their love affair, and then went on to give Boesen detailed instructions for spying. Letters, I, 72.

page 103, lines 3–28

Quotation from *SV*, VI, 192–3; *Stages*, 193–5.

page 104, line 1

Edvard Brandes: "Søren Kierkegaards *Papirer*," *Politiken* (Jan. 12, 1928).

page 104, line 13

"wrap itself around mine"   Papers, X^5 A 249.

pages 104–105, lines 16–6

Quotation from Papers, II A 347.

page 105, lines 14–24

Quotation from Papers, III A 64.

page 105, line 29

"to approach her"   Papers, X^5 A 149.5.

page 106, lines 3–32

Quotation from Papers, X^5 A 149.5.

page 107, line 7

"never really thought"   Papers, III A 166.

page 107, lines 24–25

"prolong eternity"   *SV*, II, 125–6; *E/O*, II, 141.

page 108, lines 3–9

Quotation from *SV*, II, 275; *E/O*, II, 312.

page 108, lines 16–23

Quotations in this paragraph from Papers, VII^1 A 169 and IX A 67.

page 109, lines 17–18

"the signal rang"   Papers, III A 168.

page 109, line 27

"a good man"   Papers, X^5 A 149.3.

page 110, line 7
judges' report   Letters, I, 14, 15.

page 110, line 19
A full discussion of Kierkegaard's dissertation and its reception can be
found in Carl Weltzer: "Omkring Søren Kierkegaards Disputats,"
Kirkehistorisk Samlinger, VII Række, Bd. 7 (1948–50), pp. 284–311.

page 110, line 29
ironic work on irony   See Lee M. Capel's interesting introduction to
his translation of "The Concept of Irony" (*Irony*, 13–38).

page 111, lines 9–10
"spiritually determined"   Ammundsen: *op. cit.*, p. 122. One can
search Kierkegaard's journal in vain for any description of a personal sexual encounter. The closest thing is a priggish reference to an
incident that may or may not have occurred in 1849—Kierkegaard's
36th year. The Swedish authoress Frederika Bremer visited Copenhagen that spring and made an effort to see him. He wrote that she
was having intercourse with many of Copenhagen's notables and that
"she also wanted to have sexual intercourse with me, but I was virtuous
[*dydig*]" (Papers, X¹ A 658). In fact, there is no evidence that
Kierkegaard ever had a sexual relationship with anyone; very likely
he remained "virtuous" to his death.

pages 111–112, lines 16–22
letter to Regine   Letters, I, 54–5.

page 112, line 30
Regine on SK   Meyer: *op. cit.*, p. III.

page 113, line 9
"too old"   Papers, IX A 108.

page 113, lines 12–18
Quotation from Papers, X² A 3.

page 113, line 22
"at a distance"   Papers, XI¹ A 424.

pages 113–114, lines 32–8
Quotation from Papers, X⁵ A 149.25.

page 114, line 10
Lund: *op. cit.*, pp. 112–13.

page 114, lines 27–34
note breaking engagement   Papers, X⁵ A 149.8; see also its use at
Stages, 304.

page 115, line 1
Regine's reaction   Meyer: *op. cit.*, p. IV; see also Papers, X⁵ A 149.1.

pages 115–116, lines 10–4
Quotation from Papers, X⁵ A 149.12.

page 116, lines 9–20
Lund: *op. cit.*, p. 114.

page 116, line 27
"I chose death"   Papers, VIII¹ A 100.

CHAPTER 11 – MY SORROW IS MY CASTLE

page 119, line 4
SK's complaints   See Papers, IX A 375; X² A 10; VIII¹ A 648. On
March 27, 1848, Kierkegaard wrote in his journal: "And so I sit here.
Outside everything is in movement . . . I sit here in a still room . . .
and know only one danger: religiosity's" (VIII¹ A 602).

page 119, line 8
Brøchner: *op. cit.*, p. 43.

page 119, line 14
"uproar and hubbub"   Papers, XI² A 203.

page 120, lines 3–10
Quotation from *SV*, XIII, 526; *View*, 18.

page 121, lines 5–9
This and subsequent comments from Levin in *Udtalelser*; Archives, D,
Pk. 5, Læg 31.

page 121, line 14
profits on books   Brandt and Rammel: *op. cit.*, p. 36.

page 121, line 18

master plan for books   For a discussion of why Kierkegaard's own interpretation of his pseudonymous authorship is not to be trusted, see Lars Bejerholm: *Meddelelsens Dialektik* (Copenhagen: Munksgaard; 1962), pp. 316–18, 322. See also Niels Thulstrup's Commentary to *Philosophical Fragments* (*Fragments*, 147).

page 121, lines 23–30

Quotation from Papers, X^5 A 146.

page 122, lines 25–26

"tanner's yard"   Papers, X^3 A 144.

page 122, line 27

"barking dog"   Papers, X^3 A 144; X^4 A 301.

page 123, lines 3–16

Quotations in this paragraph from Levin: *Udtalelser*; Archives, D, Pk. 5, Læg 31.

page 123, line 21

Many pieces of Kierkegaard's furniture have been preserved in Copenhagen's *Bymuseum*, where they may be viewed by the public. Policies found among Kierkegaard's papers at his death show that he insured the furnishings of his apartment at Nytorv 2 for 3,400 rd. ($23,800) during the period 1844–46 (Archives, D, Pk. 8, Læg 24).

page 123, line 26

Anders's recollections in letter from A. F. Schiødte to H. P. Barfod dated Sept. 12, 1869, Archives, D, Pk. 5, Læg 51.

page 124, line 4

food delivered   Archives, D, Pk. 8, Læg 9. It should be pointed out that Mrs. Andersen's account book does not include beverages. These are separately entered in Anders Westergaard's accounts for Jan. 2, 1847–April 30, 1848 (Archives, D, Pk. 8, Læg 10). For the period named in the text (April 6, 1847–March 28, 1848) the cost of beverages delivered to Kierkegaard's apartment was slightly over 157 rd. ($1,100). From another account book kept by Mrs. Andersen, we know that during the same period she was paid 40 rd. ($280) just for oil to keep lamps burning in the many rooms of Nytorv 2.

page 124, lines 15–31

Quotation from Levin: *op. cit.*; Archives, D, Pk. 5, Læg 31.

page 125, lines 20–21
"fictitious guests"   Otto Zinck: *Fra mit Studenter og Teaterliv*
(Copenhagen: 1906), pp. 25–6.

page 125, line 29
Brøchner: *op. cit.*, p. 29.

page 125, line 11
"feel my own languor"   Papers, II A 637.

page 125, line 18
SK's coach ride   The following description is based upon an account
by Levin, who accompanied Kierkegaard on several drives.

page 128, line 2
SK's money management   Brandt and Rammel: *op. cit.*, pp. 36, 78,
96, 85–7.

page 128, line 19
"30 bottles of wine"   Letter from Johann Christian Lund to Peter
Christian Kierkegaard dated March 21, 1856; excerpted in Weltzer:
Peter og Soren Kierkegaard, p. 288.

page 128, line 26
"how small everything is"   Letters, I, 81.

pages 128–129, lines 30–8
Quotation from *SV*, I, 26; *E/O*, I, 41.

page 129, line 10
"my extravagance"   Papers, X² A 511.

page 129, lines 27–28
"large reception room"   Lund: *op. cit.*, p. 119.

page 130, line 2
Brøchner: *op. cit.*, p. 25. According to Julie Sødring (*Erindringer fra
min Barndom og Ungdom* [Copenhagen: Gyldendal, 1894], Vol. I.,
p. 183), Kierkegaard used to "hump along with his short trouser legs,
swinging his little cane." Arthur Abrahams (*Minder fra min Barndom
og tidlige Ungdom* [Copenhagen: Det Schubotheske Forlag; 1895],
p. 55) speaks of Kierkegaard's "uneasy and somewhat hopping gait."

page 130, line 16
"a beer retailer"   Brøchner: *op. cit.*, p. 44.

page 130, lines 20–25
Quotation in letter from J. A. Ostermann to H. P. Barfod dated April
25, 1868; Archives, D, Pk. 5, Læg 41.

pages 130–131, lines 32–10
Quotation from Brøchner, *op. cit.*, p. 24.

page 131, lines 18–19
Martin Hammerich: *op. cit.*, Vol. II., p. 51.

page 131, line 23
"while walking about"   Papers, XI[1] A 214. The amount of walking
Kirkegaard did is reflected in his shoe bills; during 1850 he paid out
over 42 rd. ($294) for shoes and shoe repairs (Archives, D, Pk. 8,
Læg 26).

page 131, line 25
Brøchner, *op. cit.*, p. 28, 55.

page 132, line 4
"not lovable"   In fairness to Kierkegaard it should be pointed out
that he and Levin were never personally very close. Levin remained
principally Kierkegaard's servant, although he was well educated
and intellectually alert. It seems unlikely that Kierkegaard ever had
"disciples."

page 132, line 19
Lund, *op. cit.*, p. 116.

page 133, line 4
Spang Recollections; see Barfod (ed.): *Søren Kierkegaards Efterladte
Papirer*, Vol. III., p. 871.

page 133, lines 15–23
This and following quotation from Troels-Lund: *Et Liv: Barndom og
Ungdom* (Copenhagen: H. Hagerups Forlag; 1924), pp. 218–19.
In her *Erindringer* Julie Sødring tells a similar story about how her
father and Kierkegaard used to enjoy "experimenting." On at least
one occasion Kierkegaard "experimented" by giving a poor woman
a 5 rd. note (Sødring: *op. cit.*, p. 183).

pages 135–136, lines 26–2
Quotation from Papers, IX A 217.

page 136, lines 4–14
Quotations in this paragraph from Papers, VII^1 A 222; VIII^1 A 27. *SV*, XIII, 519; *View*, 7. Papers, IX A 411.

page 136, line 22
Stéphane Mallarmé: *Œuvres complètes* (Paris: Gallimard/Bibliothèque de la Pléiade; 1945), p. 262.

page 136, line 27
"trivialities"   Papers, VII^1 A 168. For additional journal entries on this theme see IV A 110, VIII^1 A 27, X^1 A 442, X^2 A 92, X^3 A 92, X^4 A 560, X^5 A 105.

page 137, lines 10–22
Quotation from Letters, I, 121.

page 137, lines 24–25
"to produce was my life"   Papers, X^2 A 442.

CHAPTER 12 – MASTER OF IRONY

page 138, line 5
"printshop"   Papers, VII^1 A 81.4.

pages 138–139, lines 16–4
Quotation from *SV*, VII, 545–6 unpaginated; *Postscript*, 551–2 un-paginated.

page 139, line 16
Stephen Crites: "The Author and the Authorship: Recent Kierkegaard Literature," *Journal of the American Academy of Religion*, Vol. XXXVIII (March 1970), p. 38.

page 140, line 32
"vegetative luxuriance"   Papers, VIII^1 A 120.

page 141, line 7
commission basis   Brandt and Rammel: *op. cit.*, pp. 11–34.

page 141, line 15
"impulse"   *SV*, XIII, 519; *View*, 7.

page 141, lines 15–16
"emptying-out"   *SV*, XIII, 562; *View*, 73.

page 142, line 22
"brain-figment-like"   Georg Brandes: *op. cit.*, p. 17.

page 145, lines 21–25
Quotation from *SV*, XIII, 570 note; *View*, 85–6 note.

page 148, line 32
"resignation"   Papers, VIII¹ A 650.

page 146, line 18
John Updike: "The Fork," *The New Yorker* (Feb. 26, 1966), p. 134.

page 146, line 22
Chinese puzzle boxes   Victor Eremita describes the structure of
Either/Or in these words at *SV*, I, x; *E/O*, I, 9.

page 146, line 28
"acoustic illusion"   This is the subtitle of an appendix to Chapter
III of *Philosophical Fragments*. See *SV*, IV, 215–19; *Fragments*, 61–7.

page 146, lines 28–29
"thought experiment"   The pseudonym Frater Taciturnus describes
Quidam's diary in these words in his closing "Epistle to the Reader."
See *SV*, VI, 371–450; *Stages*, 363–436.

page 146, line 9
Louis Mackey: *Kierkegaard: A Kind of Poet* (Philadelphia: University
of Pennsylvania Press; 1971), p. 274.

page 148, line 10
Brandes, cited by Lee M. Capel in the Historical Introduction to his
translation of *Irony*, 7–8. Capel's reference is to the 1877 edition of
Georg Brandes's pioneering work, *Søren Kierkegaard: En kritisk
Fremstilling i Grundrids*, p. 187.

page 149, lines 18–24
Quotation from *SV*, XIII, 354–5; *Irony*, 300. For quotations preceding
this, see *SV*, XIII, 323, 322, 297, 329, 321, 333, 351–3; *Irony*,
265 *et passim*, 240, 271, 263, 276, 296–8.

pages 149–150, lines 30–23
Quotation from *SV*, XIII, 354–6; *Irony*, 300–2.

pages 150–151, lines 29–2
Quotations in this paragraph from *SV*, VIII, 347–348, 362; *Irony*, 292,
308.

page 151, lines 11–18
Quotations in this paragraph from *SV*, XIII, 367, 335, 392; *Irony*, 313, 279, 341.

page 151, line 26
"my other self"   Papers, I A 333.

page 154, lines 13–19
Quotation from *SV*, I, 278; *E/O*, I, 302. For quotations preceding this, see SV, I, x, xv, 276–7; *E/O*, I, 9, 13, 300–1.

page 154, lines 27–28
"thought has hurried on"   *SV*, II, 175; *E/O*, II, 199.

pages 155–156, lines 27–3
This and quotations in preceding paragraph from *SV*, I, 197–200; *E/O* I, 220–4.

page 158, line 9
"It feeds dread"   *SV*, IV, 313–14; *Dread*, 38. For quotations preceding this, see *SV*, I, 384, 6, 10, 21, 58; *SV*, II, 143; *E/O* I, 412, 317, 400, 24, 25, 36, 75.

page 158, line 17
"homesickness for himself"   Kierkegaard applies this phrase to the fictitious Quidam in *Stages on Life's Way*, p. 303 (SV, VI, 307). It would appear to characterize vividly at least one aspect of dread. See also Papers, II A 127 and II A 191. In Papers, X² A 384 Kierkegaard remarks that "dread is really nothing but impatience."

page 158, lines 21–29
Quotation from *SV*, I, 62; *E/O*, I, 79.

page 159, line 12
"is this dread"   *SV*, I, 108; *E/O*, I, 128.

page 159, line 15
Albert Camus: *Carnets: Mai 1935–Février 1942* (Paris: Gallimard; 1962), p. 38.

page 160, lines 20–31
Quotation from *SV*, II, 225; *E/O*, II, 255–6; preceding quotations from *SV*, I, 266, 9, 278, 280; *E/O* I, 290, 23, 302, 304.

page 161, lines 18–19
"manifestly defined task"   *SV*, II, 231; *E/O*, II, 262. Preceding quotations from *SV*, II, 224, 231; *E/O*, II, 255, 263.

page 161, lines 30–31
"this natural order"   *SV*, II, 235; *E/O*, II, 267.

page 163, lines 13–20
Quotation from *SV*, II, 273–4; *E/O*, II, 310. Preceding quotations from *SV*, II, 226, 222, 61, 185, 275, 290; *E/O*, II, 256, 252, 67, 209–10, 312, 329.

page 164, line 27
"think of yourself"   *SV*, II, 304; *E/O*, II, 342. Preceding quotations from *SV*, II, 279, 310–11; *E/O*, II, 316, 347.

page 165, line 33
Victor Eremita   *SV*, XIII, 526; *View*, 18.

page 166, line 21
"no less false"   *SV*, I, 249; *E/O*, I, 275.

page 167, line 11
"renders actuality infinite"   *SV*, XIII, 367; *Irony*, 313.

page 169, lines 18–19
"readable by everyone" *SV*, III, 124; *Fear*, 86. Preceding quotations from *SV*, III, 57, 166, 112, 64–7, 82, 110, 122–3; *Fear*, 22, 129, 73, 27–9, 41, 70, 84.

page 170, line 29
"the right course"   *SV*, III, 128; *Fear*, 90. Preceding quotations from *SV*, III, 124, 126–8, 84, 74–5, 114; *Fear*, 86, 88–9, 43, 36, 75.

page 170, lines 30–31
Immanuel Kant: *Critique of Pure Reason* (New York: St. Martin's Press Inc.; 1961), p. 29.

page 171, line 5
Johannes Climacus was a monk from a monastery in Sinai who wrote a manuscript in Greek, *The Ladder of Heaven*. His surname is derived from the Greek word for "ladder." His book told in thirty chapters (or "steps") what virtues the monks ought to cultivate in order to achieve a more perfect existence. Kierkegaard first learned of Climacus while studying for his theological exam in 1839. In 1842–43 he wrote

(but never completed) a manuscript entitled *Johannes Climacus* or *De Omnibus Dubitandum Est*. In 1844 he used the pseudonym on the title page of *Philosophical Fragments*.

pages 171–172, lines 30–3
Quotation from *SV*, IV, 207; *Fragments*, 50. Preceding quotations from *SV*, IV, 207, 246, 245; *Fragments*, 102, 100.

page 172, lines 11–18
Quotation from Papers, IV B 1, p. 146; *Climacus*, 148.

page 172, lines 30–31
"when they collide"   This and preceding quotation from Papers, IV B 1, p. 148–9; *Climacus*, 151–3.

page 173, lines 6–25
Quotations in this paragraph from *SV*, IV, 250, 167 note, 250, 245; *Fragments*, 108, 179 note, 108, 101.

page 174, line 6
uncertainty of historical knowledge   See the discussion of this in the "Interlude" section of *Philosophical Fragments*, pp. 89–110.

page 174, line 10
satisfied with belief   See Chapter II of the *Postscript*, "The Subjective Truth, Inwardness; Truth is Subjectivity," pp. 169–224.

page 174, line 12
"whole of finiteness"   *SV*, III, 87; *Fear*, 47.

pages 174–175, lines 23–9
Quotations in this paragraph from *SV*, VII, 66, 271; *Postscript*, 78, 280.

page 175, lines 17–18
"face the worst"   *SV*, VII, 258; *Postscript*, 267.

page 175, line 32
existence   *SV*, VII, 100; *Postscript*, 111.

page 176, line 2
"phantasm"   *SV*, VII, 166; *Postscript*, 178. For similar statements see *SV*, VII, 157, 160; *Postscript*, 169, 172.

page 176, lines 17–27
Quotation from *SV*, VII, 298; *Postscript*, 308. Preceding quotations from *SV*, VII, 190, 260, 259; *Postscript*, 203, 269, 268.

page 176, lines 28–30
"becoming a phantom"   *SV*, VII, 265, 275; *Postscript*, 274, 284.

page 176, lines 30–31
"vanish from reality"   *SV*, I, 278; *E/O*, I, 302.

page 177, lines 1–33
Quotations in this paragraph from *SV*, VII, 140, 310, 57, 304, 306, 165, 307, 112; *Postscript*, 151, 320, 69, 314, 316, 176–7.

page 178, lines 2–3
"Concrete thinker" is used at *Postscript*, 296. For many uses of "subjective thinker" and "existential thinker" see Chapter III of the *Postscript*, "Real or Ethical Subjectivity—The Subjective Thinker," p. 267–322.

page 178, line 8
"infinite concentration"   *SV*, VII, 105; *Postscript*, 116.

page 178, line 10
"to will one thing"   This is the principal theme of a religious discourse published by Kierkegaard in 1847; see *Purity of Heart* (New York; Harper and Brothers, 1948).

page 178, line 15
subjective truth   *SV*, VII, 170; *Postscript*, 182.

page 178, lines 31–32
Absolute Paradox   See *Fragments*, Chapter III, "The Absolute Paradox: A Metaphysical Crotchet."

page 180, lines 2–3
"God is a concept"   *SV*, IV, 208; *Fragments*, 51.

page 180, line 7
"crucifixion of the understanding"   *SV*, VII, 523; see also *Postscript*, 496, 501, 531.

page 182, line 30
"penetrate one's existence"   *SV*, VII, 264; *Postscript*, 273. Preceding quotations from *SV*, VII, 256, 174–5, 181, 160, 194, 539, 542, 154, 203, 171, 231; *Postscript*, 265, 186–7, 193, 172, 207, 547, 550, 165, 216, 183.

page 183, line 27
"like seriousness"   This is a familiar refrain of Johannes Climacus
in the *Postscript*. See *SV*, VII, 152; *Postscript*, 163.

pages 183–184, lines 31–7
Quotation from *SV*, VII 545–6 unpaginated; *Postscript*, 551 unpaginated.

page 184, line 16
"marionette theater"   Martin Thust applied this term to Kierkegaard's pseudonyms in "Das Marionettentheater Søren Kierkegaards,"
Zeitwende, I, No. 1 (1925), pp. 18–38.

page 184, line 20
Stephen Crites: "Pseudonymous Authorship as Art and as Act," in
Josiah Thompson (ed.): *Kierkegaard: A Collection of Critical Essays*
(Garden City: Doubleday & Company, Inc.; 1972).

page 185, line 29
"He is not there"   *SV*, VII, 204; *Postscript*, 218.

page 185, line 33
"the Unknown"   See *Fragments*, Chapter III, "The Absolute Paradox: A Metaphysical Crotchet."

page 186, line 4
"reason cannot advance"   *SV*, IV, 211–12; *Fragments*, 55.

page 186, line 28
"the other side"   *SV*, VII, 79; *Postscript*, 91.

CHAPTER 13 – AN UNWILLING POET

page 190, line 31
Goldschmidt: *op. cit.*, Vol. I., pp. 428–9.

page 191, lines 8–20
Quotations in this paragraph from Papers, VII[1] A 98 and VIII[1] A 163.

page 191, line 23
"a costly present"   Papers, VII[1] A 120.

page 191, line 27
Brandes: *op. cit.*, p. 171.

page 192, line 2
Drafts may be found in Papers, VII¹ B 9–72.

page 192, line 9
"Be a man"   Papers, VII¹ A 103.

page 192, lines 20–27
Quotations in this paragraph from Papers, VII¹ A 147; X² A 413; X¹
A 653.

pages 192–193, lines 30–6
Quotation from Papers, X¹ A 247.

page 193, line 16
"to be offered up"   Papers, IX A 283.

page 193, line 27
"most polemical"   VII¹ A 222.

pages 193–194, lines 30–22
Quotations in this paragraph from Papers, VII¹ A 229. VI A 119. VII¹
A 120. VII¹ A 221. VII¹ A 418. VIII¹ A 43. VIII A 138.

pages 194–195, lines 26–7
Quotations in this paragraph from Papers, VIII¹ A 548 and X¹ A 78.

page 195, lines 29–33
task of Apostle   *SV*, XI, 97, 107; *Age*, 143, 160.

page 196, line 10
"making truth their own"   Papers, IV A 87.

page 196, lines 13–28
Quotation from Papers, IX A 187.

page 197, line 4
"put me to death"   Papers, X¹ A 424.

page 197, line 9
"martyr for Christianity"   Papers, IX A 302.

pages 197–198, lines 14–3
Quotations in this paragraph from Papers, X¹ A 510. IV A 217. *SV*,
XIII, 562 note, 526, 569, 606, 507; *View*, 74 note, 18, 84, 131, 155.

page 198, lines 21–30
Quotation from Papers, X¹ A 281. Preceding quotations from Papers, X² A 475. X¹ A 280.

page 199, line 6
"unthinkable" *SV*, VIII, 66; *Age*, 6. Only the second half of *A Literary Review* was translated under the title *The Present Age*. The first half, dealing more specifically with Fru Gyllemburg's novel, *To Tidsaldre*, remains untranslated.

page 199, line 19
John Updike: "The Fork," *The New Yorker* (Feb. 26, 1966), p. 134.

page 200, line 18
Christendom *SV*, XII, 34; *Training*, 39.

pages 200–201, lines 32–9
Quotations in this paragraph from *SV*, XII, 51; *Training*, 57. Papers, XI² A 426. *SV*, XII, 65; *Training*, 72.

pages 201–202, lines 14–2
Quotations in this paragraph from *SV*, XI, 126, 130, 136, 128; *Sickness*, 146, 148, 155, 147.

page 202, line 6
Hölderlin The words quoted are the concluding lines of the ode *An die Hoffnung*, which can be found in Friedrich Hölderlin: *Hölderlin: Sämtliche Werke* (Frankfurt am Main: Insel-Verlag; 1961), p. 271. The translation is by Sophie Wilkins except for a minor change made at the last moment by the author.

page 202, line 26
"simple Christian" Papers, X¹ A 510.

CHAPTER 14 – ONCE AND FOR ALL SOMETHING GHOSTLY

page 203, lines 14–15
"elderly and hardened" Papers, XI² A 86.

pages 203–204, lines 17–6
Quotation from Zahle: *op. cit.*, p. 9.

page 204, line 7
Spang Recollections; see Barfod (ed.): *Søren Kierkegaards Efterladte Papirer*, Vol. III. p. 871.

page 204, line 22
expected to die   Shortly after his thirty-fourth birthday Kierkegaard exclaimed in his journal: "Extraordinary that I should have become thirty-four! It's incomprehensible to me; I was so certain that I'd die either before or on that birthday." (Papers, VIII^1 A 100.) In a letter to Peter Christian dated May 19, 1847, he expresses the same surprise and tells Peter how both he and Michael Pedersen Kierkegaard believed that none of the family should survive their thirty-third year (Letters, I, 166–7). Hans Brøchner recalled how Kierkegaard's expectation of an early death was so strong that he actually checked the church birth register to make sure there had been no mistake about his birthdate (Brøchner: *op. cit.*, p. 48).

page 205, line 13
cows drinking   C. Købke's famous painting, *Parti af Østerbro i Morgenbelysning*, shows the house occupied by Kierkegaard on Østerbrogade. Cattle can be seen taking their ease at a pump across the street from Kierkegaard's residence. The original is in the National Gallery, Copenhagen.

page 206, line 8
"object of interest"   Papers, XI^2 A 11.

page 206, line 30
"my brother's smallness"   Papers, VIII^1 A 545; see also IX A 99.

page 207, lines 10–32
letter to Regine   Letters, I, 263.

page 208, lines 21–22
"dear little Regine"   Papers, X^5 A 150.4; preceding citations in this paragraph from Letters, I, 263; X^2 A 210; X^5 A 59.

page 208, lines 23–25
dedication   *SV*, XII, 265.

page 208, line 30
"excavation of concepts"   Papers, X^3 A 239.

page 209, line 1
1800 years   Papers, VIII^1 A 94.

page 209, lines 15–27
Quotations in this paragraph from Papers, X⁴ A 164. XI² A 2. X⁵ A 105. X⁵ A 146.

page 210, line 6
eternity's firmness   Papers, XI² A 201.

page 210, lines 11–22
Quotation from Papers, XI² A 154.

pages 210–211, lines 27–20
Quotations from Papers, XI² A 163–4 and XI¹ A 295.

page 211, lines 24–25
"woman is egoism"   Papers, XI¹ A 226. Kierkegaard's antipathy to the sexual and to the feminine was not purely subjective. While living outside the city's walls in the early 1850's he had employed the family of a tailor's apprentice named Strube to cook his meals and do the housework. The family had two young daughters, and, when it came time for the eldest to be confirmed, Kierkegaard gave her a pretty confirmation dress, a shawl, and some gold jewelry. Like any young girl unfamiliar with such finery, she wanted to show it off, and on the evening of her confirmation went for a stroll in Frederiksberg Park. Pastor Ferdinand Schiødte, who knew both Kierkegaard and the family, tells what happened: "In the evening he [SK] saw her strutting about in the park, resplendent with all that finery, and with visible delight showing it off. He was shocked, and (perhaps also fearing people's gossip) immediately decided that the tailor's apprentice should move out and rent rooms elsewhere at Kierkegaard's expense. That decision was put into force as soon as possible, but it brought Kierkegaard great resentment from the family." Pastor Schiødte's recollections are in a letter to H. P. Barfod dated Sept. 12, 1869; Archives, D, Pk. 5, Læg 51.

pages 211–212, lines 30–3
Quotations in this paragraph from Papers, XI¹ A 341 and XI² A 378.

page 212, lines 5–28
Quotations from Papers, XI¹ A 558 and XI² A 422.

page 213, lines 3–4
Quotation from Papers, X¹ A 654; preceding quotations from Papers, X¹ A 444, 199, 209.

page 213, line 8
cholera   Papers, XI¹ A 506; see also Jørgensen: *op. cit.*, Vol. IV, pp. 77–8.

page 213, lines 16–30
Quotation from Papers, XI² A 426; see also XI² A 172.

page 214, lines 3–17
Quotations from Papers, XI² A 163 and XI² A 289.

page 214, line 24
knight   *SV*, III, 100; *Fear*, 61. See also Papers, IX A 321, XI² A 11, and *SV*, II, 76–7; *E/O*, II, 85–6.

page 215, lines 1–25
Quotation from Papers, XI² A 439. This last sheet from Kierkegaard's hand is unlined, approximately 6 by 8 inches, with 2-inch margins. Folded in half, it has been written on both inside and outside—four pages in all. It is preserved in the Royal Library, Archives, A, Pk. 52.

page 216, lines 15–17
Papers, X⁵ A 13; preceding quotation from Papers, X⁴ A 373.

CHAPTER 15 – TWO FUNERALS

pages 217–218, lines 1–9
Mynster's funeral   This description is based upon reports of the event in *Berlingske Tidende*, Feb. 7, 1854.

page 218, lines 22–30
"coming collision"   Barfod (ed.): *Søren Kierkegaards Efterladte Papirer*, Vol. IX, p. 496–8.

page 219, lines 3–13
Martensen, cited in Jørgensen: *op. cit.*, Vol. IV, p. 91.

page 219, lines 19–22
"witnesses"   See *SV*, IX, 350; X 226f; XI 74ff; XII 83, 310, 312, 315.

pages 219–220, lines 32–8
Quotation from *SV*, XIV, 8; *Attack*, 7–8.

page 220, line 13
"playing Christianity"   *SV*, XIV, 8; *Attack*, 8.

page 221, lines 30–31
King had backed Clausen   For this and the preceding anecdote, see
Troels-Lund: *op. cit.*, pp. 222–5.

page 222, line 14
"waste of time"   Papers, XI¹ A 538.

page 222, line 26
Martensen's article has been reprinted in the second edition of *Søren
Kierkegaards Samlede Værker* (Copenhagen: Gyldendal: 1920–36),
Vol. IX, pp. 383–7.

page 224, lines 1–13
Quotation from *SV*, XIV, 27–28; *Attack*, 19; preceding quotations
from *SV*, XIV, 93–100; *Attack*, 67–72. The article was published in
Fatherland on May 26, 1855.

page 225, lines 5–11
Quotation from *SV*, XIV, 85–6; *Attack*, 59–60; preceding quotations
from *SV*, XIV, 66–7; *Attack*, 45.

pages 225–226, lines 25–30
Quotations from *SV*, XIV, 217, 164, 218; *Attack*, 181, 136, 147–8, 182.

page 227, lines 17–23
Quotation from *SV*, XIV, 106; *Attack*, 79.

page 228, lines 8–15
Regine   Helweg: *op. cit.*, p. 391.

page 228, lines 23–26
Quotation from Brøchner: *op. cit.*, pp. 64–5.

page 229, line 15
convention of clergymen   Hohlenberg: *Søren Kierkegaard* (Copenhagen: H. Hagerup; 1940), pp. 288–9.

page 230, line 1
"He was sitting"   Levin: *op. cit.*; Archives, D, Pk. 5, Læg 31.

page 230, lines 24–25
"cold seltzer water"   Letters, I, 21.

page 230, line 29
Walter Lowrie: *Kierkegaard*, 2 vols. (New York: Harper Torchbooks; 1962), II, 493.

page 230, line 33
staphylococcus   This discussion of Kierkegaard's final illness, and in particular the thesis that he died from a staphylococcus infection of the lungs, draws on the arguments developed by Dr. Carl Jørgensen in Volume V of his Kierkegaard biography. Dr. Jørgensen is a distinguished Danish neurologist in addition to being Kierkegaard's most recent biographer. See Jørgensen: *op. cit.,* Vol. V, pp. 147–50.

page 231, line 22
"wanted to die"   Letter from Emil Boesen to his wife dated Oct. 15, 1855; cited in Koch: *Søren Kierkegaard og Emil Boesen*, p. 36. Jørgensen cites the report of Nikolai Lange that when he asked Kierkegaard if there were anything he could do for him, the sick man replied that Lange might pray for him to die (Jørgensen: *Søren Kierkegaard*, Vol. V, p. 151).

page 231, lines 23–24
Henriette Lund: *op. cit.*, p. 174.

page 231, line 27
Troels-Lund: *op. cit.*, p. 237–8.

page 232, line 33
These notes are printed at the close of the ninth volume of Barfod's *Søren Kierkegaards Efterladte Papirer*, pp. 593–9.

pages 235–236, lines 3–2
Kierkegaard's service in the Frue Kirke   See Lund, *op. cit.*, pp. 175–6, and Troels-Lund: *op. cit.*, pp. 239–40.

page 236, lines 3–17
This description of Peter Christian Kierkegaard's speech is based upon the account of the funeral published in *Folkevennen*, No. 9 (Dec. 7, 1855). The article was not signed, but the editor prefaced it by saying it was written by "an acquaintance, a layman living in Copenhagen, who was present at the funeral." A corroborative account of Peter Christian's speech can be found in *Berlingske Tidende*, Nov. 19, 1855. Additional descriptions can be found in *Holbæk Amts Avis*, Nrs. 180

and 182 (Nov. 19 and 23, 1855); *Tillæg til Berlingske Tidende,* Monday morning, Nov. 19, 1855; and *Berlingske Tidende,* Nov. 21, 1855.

page 236, line 21
"rest of the multitude"   The crowd was substantial, numbering over 1,000 persons. A somewhat larger crowd had gathered the day before in the adjoining Nytorv to witness a public execution (*Berlingske Tidende,* Nov. 17, 1855).

pages 236–237, lines 33–12
grave site scene   This description of the scene and events at graveside is drawn from Troels-Lund: *op. cit.,* pp. 240–1, and from the account of the funeral published in *Folkevennen,* No. 9 (December 7, 1855).

pages 237–238, lines 13–4
Lund's speech   Henrik Lund's speech at graveside was subsequently published (with certain alterations) in *Fatherland,* No. 273 (November 22, 1855). The description of the speech offered here is based upon the published text as well as on the eyewitness account published in *Folkevennen,* No. 9 (December 7, 1855).

BIBLIOGRAPHY

KIERKEGAARD IN DANISH

Breve og Akstykker vedrørende Søren Kierkegaard. Udgivet ved Niels Thulstrup. Bind I–II. København: Ejnar Munksgaard; 1953–4.

Samlede Værker. Udgivet af A. B. Drachmann, J. L. Heiberg. Først Udgave. Bind I–XIV. København: Gyldendal; 1901–6. A second edition of the *Værker* was published in 1920–31 which included a fifteenth volume as index. This edition was reprinted by Gyldendal in 1962–4 in twenty volumes, supervised by Peter P. Rohde.

Søren Kierkegaards Papirer. Udgivet af P. A. Heiberg, V. Kuhr, E. Torsting. Bind I–XI i 18 afdelinger. København: Gyldendal; 1909–1948. This edition was reprinted in 1969–70 with three additional volumes of papers and indices under the supervision of Niels Thulstrup.

KIERKEGAARD IN ENGLISH

In the list below only the most recent editions are given. When a paperback reprint incorporates important revisions in the translation, that edition alone is listed.

Attack upon Christendom. Princeton University Press; 1946.

Christian Discourses. Princeton University Press; 1940.

The Concept of Dread. Second Edition. Princeton University Press; 1957.

The Concept of Irony. New York: Harper & Row; 1966.

Concluding Unscientific Postscript. Princeton University Press; 1944.

Crisis in the Life of an Actress and Other Essays on Drama. New York: Harper Torchbooks; 1967.

Edifying Discourses, Vols. I–IV. Minneapolis: Augsburg; 1943–6.

Either/Or, Vols. I–II. Garden City: Doubleday & Co., Inc.; 1959.

Fear and Trembling and *The Sickness unto Death.* Garden City: Doubleday & Co., Inc.; 1954.

For Self-Examination and *Judge for Yourselves!* Princeton University
Press; 1944.

For Self-Examination. Another translation. Minneapolis: Augsburg;
1940.

The Gospel of Suffering. Minneapolis: Augsburg; 1948.

Johannes Climacus or *De Omnibus Dubitandum Est.* Stanford University
Press; 1958.

Judge for Yourselves! See above, *For Self-Examination,* etc.

On Authority and Revelation. Princeton University Press; 1955.

Philosophical Fragments. Second Edition. Princeton University Press;
1962.

The Point of View for My Work as an Author. New York: Harper
Torchbooks; 1962.

The Present Age. London: Oxford University Press; 1940.

Purity of Heart. New York: Harper & Row; 1948.

Repetition. Princeton University Press; 1946.

The Sickness unto Death. See above, *Fear and Trembling,* etc.

Stages on Life's Way. Princeton University Press; 1945.

Thoughts on Crucial Situations in Human Life. Minneapolis: Augsburg;
1941.

Training in Christianity. Princeton University Press; 1947.

Works of Love. New York: Harper & Row; 1962.

The Diary of Søren Kierkegaard. Translated by Gerda Andersen. New
York: Philosophical Library; 1960.

The Journals of Søren Kierkegaard. Translated by Alexander Dru. London: Oxford University Press; 1938.

The Last Years: Journals 1853–1855. Edited and translated by Ronald
Gregor Smith. New York: Harper & Row; 1965.

Søren Kierkegaard's Journals and Papers, Volume I, A–E. Edited and
translated by Howard V. and Edna H. Hong. Bloomington: Indiana
University Press; 1967.

Søren Kierkegaard's Journals and Papers, Volume 2, F–K. Edited and
translated by Howard V. and Edna H. Hong. Bloomington: Indiana
University Press; 1970.

A Selected Bibliography
of Kierkegaard Criticism in English

Books

COLLINS, JAMES: *The Mind of Kierkegaard*. Chicago: Henry Regnery Company; 1965.

CROXALL, T. H.: *Glimpses and Impressions of Kierkegaard*. London: James Nisbet & Co.; 1959.

———: *Kierkegaard Commentary*. London: James Nisbet & Co.; 1956.

DEWEY, BRADLEY R.: *The New Obedience*. Washington: Corpus Instrumentorium, Inc.; 1968.

DIEM, HERMAN: *Kierkegaard's Dialectic of Existence*. Translated by H. Knight. London: Oliver and Boyd; 1959.

DUPRE, L. K.: *Kierkegaard as Theologian*. London: Sheed & Ward; 1963.

FRIEDMANN, RUDOLPH: *Kierkegaard*. New York: New Directions; 1949.

GARELICK, H. M.: *The Anti-Christianity of Kierkegaard*. New York: Humanities Press; 1966.

GATES, J. A.: *The Life and Thought of Kierkegaard for Everyman*. London: Westminster Press; 1960.

GEISMAR, EDUARD: *Lectures on the Religious Thought of Søren Kierkegaard*. Minneapolis: Augsburg; 1937.

HAMILTON, KENNETH: *The Promise of Kierkegaard*. Philadelphia: J. B. Lippincott Company; 1969.

JOHNSON, H. A., and THULSTRUP, NIELS, eds.: *A Kierkegaard Critique*. New York: Harper & Bros.; 1962.

LOWRIE, WALTER: *A Short Life of Kierkegaard*. Princeton University Press; 1942.

MACKEY, LOUIS: *Kierkegaard: A Kind of Poet*. Philadelphia: University of Pennsylvania Press; 1971.

MALANTSCHUK, GREGOR: *Kierkegaard's Thought*. Edited and translated by Howard V. and Edna H. Hong. Princeton University Press; 1971.

SWENSON, DAVID F.: *Something About Kierkegaard*. Minneapolis: Augsburg; 1948.

THOMPSON, JOSIAH, ed.: *Kierkegaard: A Collection of Critical Essays*. Garden City: Doubleday & Co., Inc.; 1972.

————: *The Lonely Labyrinth: Kierkegaard's Pseudonymous Works*. Carbondale: Southern Illinois University Press; 1967.
THOMTE, REIDAR: *Kierkegaard's Philosophy of Religion*. Princeton University Press; 1948.

Articles

*ALLISON, HENRY E.: "Christianity and Nonsense," *Review of Metaphysics*, XX (March 1965), pp. 432–60.
AUDEN, W. H.: "A Preface to Kierkegaard," *New Republic*, CX (1944), pp. 683–6.
BLACKHAM, H. J.: "Søren Kierkegaard," in his *Six Existentialist Thinkers*. New York: Harper Torchbooks; 1952. Pp. 1–22.
BERNSTEIN, RICHARD: "Kierkegaard and Sartre," in his *Praxis and Action*. Philadelphia: University of Pennsylvania Press; 1971. Pp. 84–164.
BROUDY, H. S.: "Kierkegaard's Doctrine of Indirect Communication," *Journal of Philosophy*, LVIII (Apr. 27, 1961), pp. 225–33.
*CAVELL, STANLEY: "Kierkegaard's *On Authority and Revelation*," in his *Must We Mean What We Say?* New York: Charles Scribner's Sons; 1969. Pp. 163–79.
*CRITES, STEPHEN: "Pseudonymous Authorship as Art and as Act," in *Kierkegaard: A Collection of Critical Essays*. Edited by Josiah Thompson. Garden City: Doubleday & Co., Inc.; 1972. Pp. 183–229.
DIAMOND, MALCOLM L.: "Faith and its Tensions: A Criticism of Religious Existentialism," *Judaism*, XIII (summer 1964), pp. 317–27.
DIETRICHSON, PAUL: "Kierkegaard's Concept of Self," *Inquiry*, VIII (spring 1965), pp. 1–32.
EARLE, WILLIAM: "Phenomenology and Existentialism," *Journal of Philosophy*, LVII (Jan. 21, 1960), pp. 75–84.
GARDINER, PATRICK: "Kierkegaard's Two Ways," *British Academy Proceedings*, LIV (1968), pp. 207–29.
HEINEMANN, F. H.: "Søren Kierkegaard and Existential Christianity," in his *Existentialism and the Modern Predicament*. New York: Harper Torchbooks; 1953. Pp. 30–46.
HENRICKSEN, AAGE: "Kierkegaard's Reviews of Literature," *Orbis Litterarum* (Copenhagen), X (1955), pp. 75–83.

*Denotes that article appeared in Josiah Thompson: *Kierkegaard: A Collection of Critical Essays*. Garden City: Doubleday & Co., Inc.; 1972.

HOLMER, PAUL L.: "Kierkegaard and Logic," *Kierkegaardiana*, II (1957), pp. 25–42.

———: "On Understanding Kierkegaard," *Orbis Litterarum* (Copenhagen), X (1955), pp. 93–106.

KAUFMANN, WALTER: "Kierkegaard," in his *From Shakespeare to Existentialism*. Garden City: Doubleday & Co., Inc.; 1960. Pp. 175–206.

KRONER, RICHARD: "Kierkegaard or Hegel?" *Revue Internationale de Philosophie*, VI (1952), pp. 79–96.

MACKEY, LOUIS: "The Analysis of the Good in Kierkegaard's 'Purity of Heart,'" in Irwin C. Lieb, ed.: *Experience, Existence, and the Good: Essays in Honor of Paul Weiss*. Carbondale: Southern Illinois University Press; 1961. Pp. 260–74.

———: "Kierkegaard and the Problem of Existential Philosophy," *Review of Metaphysics*, IX (March, June, 1956), pp. 404–19, 569–88.

*———: "Loss of the World in Kierkegaard's Ethics," *Review of Metaphysics*, LX (June 1962), pp. 602–20.

*———: "The Poetry of Inwardness," in George A. Schrader, ed.: *Existential Philosophers: Kierkegaard to Merleau-Ponty*. New York: McGraw-Hill; 1967. Pp. 45–107.

*———: "The View from Pisgah: A Reading of *Fear and Trembling*," in Josiah Thompson, ed.: *Kierkegaard: A Collection of Critical Essays*. Garden City: Doubleday & Co., Inc.; 1972. Pp. 407–22.

MCKINNON, ALASTAIR: "Kierkegaard: 'Paradox' and Irrationalism," *Journal of Existentialism*, VII (spring 1967), pp. 401–16.

———: "Kierkegaard's Pseudonyms: A New Hierarchy," *American Philosophical Quarterly*, VI (1969), pp. 116–26.

POOLE, ROGER C.: "Kierkegaard on Irony," *New Blackfriar's*, XLVIII (Feb. 1967), pp. 245–49.

*POPKIN, RICHARD H.: "Kierkegaard and Scepticism," *Algemeen Nederlands Tijdschrift voor Wijsbegeerte en Psychologie*, LI (1958–9), pp. 123–41.

ROUGEMONT, DENIS DE: "Kierkegaard and Hamlet: Two Danish Princes," *The Anchor Review*, No. 1 (1955), pp. 109–27.

*SARTRE, JEAN-PAUL: "The Singular Universal," in Josiah Thompson, ed.: *Kierkegaard: A Collection of Critical Essays*. Garden City: Doubleday & Co., Inc.; 1972. Pp. 230–65.

*SCHRADER, GEORGE A.: "Kant and Kierkegaard on Duty and Inclination," *Journal of Philosophy*, LXV (Nov. 7, 1968), pp. 688–701.

SONTAG, FREDERICH: "Kierkegaard and the Search for a Self," *Journal of Existentialism*, VII (summer 1967), pp. 443–57.

TILLICH, PAUL: "Existential Philosophy," *Journal of the History of Ideas*, V (1944), pp. 44–70.

*UPDIKE, JOHN: "The Fork," *The New Yorker*, Feb. 26, 1966, pp. 115–34.

WILD, JOHN: "Kierkegaard and Contemporary Existential Philosophy," *Anglican Theological Review*, XXXVIII (1956), pp. 15–32.

INDEX

A NOTE ON THE TYPE

The text of this book was set in Garamond No. 3, a modern rendering of the type first cut by Claude Garamond (1510–1561). Garamond was a pupil of Geoffrey Troy and is believed to have based his letters on the Venetian models, although he introduced a number of important differences, and it is to him we owe the letter which we know as Old Style. He gave to his letters a certain elegance and a feeling of movement which won for their creator an immediate reputation and the patronage of Francis I of France.

Composed, printed, and bound by
The Haddon Craftsmen, Scranton, Pennsylvania
Illustrations printed by
Philips Offset Company, Inc., New York, N.Y.
Typography and binding design by
Earl Tidwell